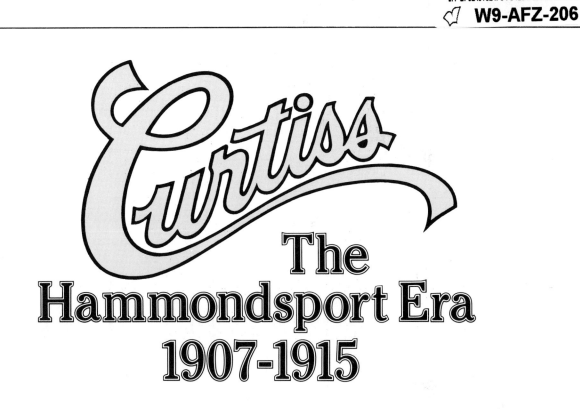

Curtiss
The Hammondsport Era
1907-1915

1254

The Curtiss *White Wing* on the shore of Keuka Lake, Hammondsport, New York.

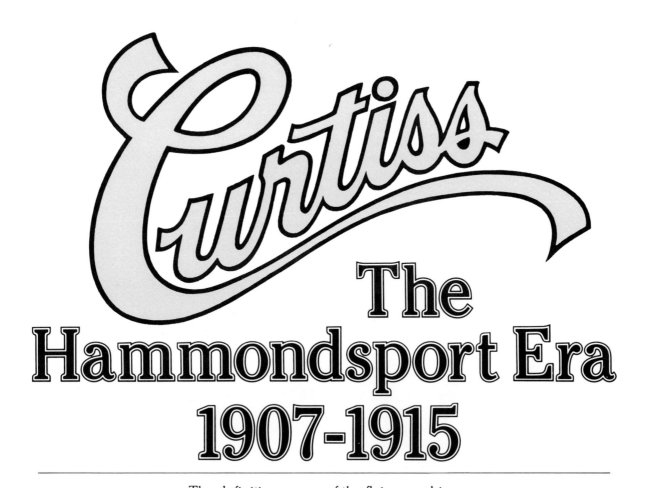

Curtiss

The Hammondsport Era 1907-1915

The definitive survey of the flying machines
produced by Glenn H. Curtiss, one of America's
pioneering aircraft designers and inventor of the flying boat

Louis S. Casey

Former Curator of Aircraft,
National Air and Space Museum, Smithsonian Institution

Crown Publishers, Inc.
New York

The author and the publisher wish to acknowledge their debt to Ray Tillman and Merrill Stickler of the Glenn H. Curtiss Museum of Local History, Hammondsport, New York, for their generous assistance in verifying much of the information in this book. While every effort has been made to make the book as accurate as possible, reconstructing events that took place more than sixty-five years ago was not easy, and the publisher would appreciate hearing from anyone who might set the record straight.

Inquiries should be addressed to Crown Publishers, Inc., One Park Avenue, New York, New York 10016

Printed in the United States of America

Published simultaneously in Canada by General Publishing Company Limited

Library of Congress Cataloging in Publication Data

Casey, Louis S.
    Curtiss, the Hammondsport Era, 1907–1915.

    Includes index.
    1. Curtiss aircraft—History.   I. Title.
TL686.C8C37   1981   629.133′343   81-3292
ISBN: 0-517-543265 (cloth)   AACR1
ISBN: 0-517-545659 (special edition)

10 9 8 7 6 5 4 3 2 1

First Edition

Design: Robert Aulicino

Contents

Acknowledgments

The preparation of a work of this type is not a one-person project. Many people have contributed generously of their time and talents to create this book. In the collecting phase, N. L. "Les" Mead and Ronald Gall of Curtiss-Wright assisted in transferring the archives of the company to the National Air and Space Museum (NASM); George A. Page, Jr. made available his collections; Kenneth M. Molson, formerly Curator of the Canadian National Aeronautical Collection, assisted, as did Robert W. Bradford, Curator of the Canadian Collection; J. M. "Jack" Bruce, Keeper of the Royal Air Force Museum at Hendon, was most helpful, as was Roland Rohlfs, former Curtiss test pilot, and Bruce C. Reynolds of the San Diego Aerospace Museum. The late Charles Forster Willard, who was the pilot of the first aircraft produced for the Aeronautic Society, *The Golden Flier,* was most helpful with original material and also in reading the manuscript. Other experts who read and checked the manuscript were George Page, Jr.; George E. A. Hallett, Maj., U.S. Army (Ret.) and my good friend, mentor and colleague, Paul E. Garber, who is also one of the best known lecturers on Glenn H. Curtiss and my predecessor as Curator of the National Aeronautical Collection of the United States, and who is responsible, more than anyone else, for the acquisition of this collection of the NASM.

Draftsmen who gave much time for very modest rewards in the preparation of the drawings were Warren A. Eberspacher, Donald Madison, William Koster and Charles J. Newcomb. Typing and retyping of the manuscript was done by Marion Davis, Shirley Ruggles, Corrine Morris and last but by no means least by my long-suffering wife, Rosanne, who by this time is a bit of an expert on this subject herself.

Preface

In the field of aeronautics no name is better known, or has had greater influence, than the name of Glenn H. Curtiss. The name brings visions of a pioneer, a giant industrial complex, an era in aviation and many other things to many people. Curtiss is all of these and second only to the Wright brothers in the annals of aviation.

Curtiss, the man and the company, moved with the vanguard of aviation. From the birth of the airplane at the turn of the century (it was spelled aeroplane at this time), to the midcentury, the Curtiss name was synonymous with aircraft of quality and quantity.

The pages of aeronautical journals abound in descriptions and records of Curtiss aircraft, though they also omit a goodly number of them. To bring these together into one compilation represents a project of some substance. The problem is compounded by the fact that much archival material relating to the aircraft production of the Curtiss-Wright Company was destroyed.

For my part, I look upon this loss with mixed feelings. It has made my task more difficult, but also more enjoyable. It has forced me to seek out the Curtiss "people," drawing from them many unrecorded details of the aircraft, and, at the same time, their reminiscences.

The documentation of these aircraft has been drawn from many sources: individuals, the aeronautical journals of five decades, bulletins of the Aerial Experiment Association and the research facilities of the National Air and Space Museum, the U.S. Navy, U.S. Air Force, the National Archives and the Library of Congress. During, and as a result of this research project, the bulk of the remaining aircraft-related company archives was presented to the National Air and Space Museum by the Curtiss-Wright Corporation.

Waldo Waterman, who was a witness and participant in the early Curtiss experiments at San Diego and the late A. V. "Fred" Verville, who was an apprentice engineer with Curtiss at Hammondsport, New York, also generously assisted me. George A. Page, Jr., who started where Charles Willard, a Curtiss pilot, left off, contributed generously of his time and archival treasures. Pete Janssen, the late Dr. T. P. Wright, Roland Rohlfs, Charles Kirkham, the late Glenn H. Curtiss, Jr., Ronald Gall, Bruce C. Reynolds, N. L. "Les" Mead and Kenneth M. Molson, to name only a few, were most helpful in assembling and recounting details of their experience with Curtiss and Curtiss airplanes.

The record of the development of the Curtiss airplane is, in fact, a tracing of the evolution of the airplane as we know it. On December 17, 1903, the Wright brothers, Orville and Wilbur, had succeeded in doing what man has dreamed of doing down through the centuries: they had successfully flown. More specifically, they had designed, constructed and flown the first heavier-than-air machine to carry a man in powered, controlled flight. Of related interest was the fact that they had patented the general configuration of this machine and, most important, their system of control.

From their eminent position the Wrights made it clear that if any flying was to be done, it would be done under license from them. The result was years of guerrilla warfare between the Wrights and other aircraft designers. This conflict continued until World War I, when military necessity demanded a solution to the multitude of legal skirmishes that were sapping the physical and financial resources of the embryonic aviation industry.

Many persons entered the legal arena with the Wright brothers, but none were as active and as ingenious in evading legal restrictions as Curtiss. The Wrights' excessive licensing fees, said to be over $1,000 per day, stimulated Curtiss and others to evade the patent laws and continually search for ways to accomplish controlled flight without infringing upon the Wright patents. Throughout the early development of Curtiss aircraft there is ample evidence that Curtiss had one eye on the air and the other on the Wright patents. Willard comments:

> Curtiss did not defy the law. We all defied a
> judge who refused to follow the law and

introduced his own law. Where there is a law, judges must follow it. Judges cannot legislate. This is Constitutional Law.

The federal judge refused to allow any aeroplane patent to be presented unless the aeroplane had flown. This is in direct *contrast* to patent law.

The question of law was not before his court and thus he had no jurisdiction, and when a judge is beyond his jurisdiction, his judgment is void, null. There was no claim in the Wright patent on the right to fly. Only one claim of the 21 claims was before the court: "Warping the rear marginal edges of the wing—one end up and one end down in conjunction with the use of the rudder." Now, the Curtiss planes were rigid and *could not be warped,* hence they could not infringe. But Curtiss was up against a sharp, well-informed patent attorney, a judgment rendered on hero worship, and a federal judge who admitted that he did not understand the case. I made four flights for Curtiss with my steering wheel locked with a sealed strip of paper, and moved my ailerons constantly up and down without the paper being broken. The trial judge disallowed the evidence. The judgment against Curtiss by Judge Hazel was very unpopular and no one stopped flying.

A number of the machines built and/or modified by Curtiss were intended specifically to demonstrate "prior use" of significant features. The appearance of these aircraft within the sequence of Curtiss designs emphasizes his constant efforts in defense of suits or to prove the impracticality of other devices.

The nearby presence of Lake Keuka at Hammondsport, New York, and San Diego Bay adjoining the Curtiss winter headquarters stimulated Curtiss to give early attention to waterborne aircraft. While it is correctly recorded that Henri Fabre of France made the first flight from water, it was Curtiss who produced the first continuously developed and successful hydro-aeroplane. By a process of evolution, quite traceable to his work, the hydro-aeroplane became a flying boat in 1911, and made its first successful flight in 1912. In this form of aircraft, Curtiss established the basic patents.

World War I intensified the development of the airplane. In the Curtiss camp many things were in process. The ubiquitous "Jenny" in its many variations, large and small flying boats, and a host of experimental designs of aircraft and engines poured out of the plants of the Curtiss Aeroplane and Motor Company.

The end of hostilities brought with it a sudden and devastating retrenchment in the aircraft industry. The availability of vast stocks of war-surplus aircraft and engines brought a halt to the incentive and financing of engineering developments that had only started to get off the ground. Instead of designing and producing new engines, the Liberty engine was worked and reworked. High compression versions, supercharged versions, inverted versions and geared versions were built. Civil aircraft fared even worse. The military surplus of Curtiss OX-5 engines glutted the market. There was one redeeming feature in that the large number of war-trained pilots operating war-surplus aircraft and engines brought aviation to the public-at-large through barnstorming from cow pasture airports. Barnstormers were a feature attraction at almost every county fair, where hundreds of persons lined up to take their first airplane ride.

During this postwar period, the Curtiss Aeroplane and Motor Company concentrated on development of limited numbers of high-performance aircraft and engines. Evidence of their eminence in this era is the comparatively large number of Curtiss aircraft purchased by the military services. Also, a review of the participation in, and records established at the various air races, further demonstrates the Curtiss prowess and application of engineering principles to aircraft design.

The Air Commerce Act of 1926 brought with it requirements for "proving" the design of aircraft to be used in air commerce. Certification under the Approved Type Certification (ATC) program brought greater public acceptance and, with it, tougher requirements for the engineers.

Aviation was spotlighted and stimulated by the transatlantic attempts, air races, exploration flights and the apparent prosperity of the country.

It was also during this period that financiers began to take an interest in the aircraft industry. The financial needs of this growth period resulted in mergers that paralleled the pattern of other industries of the time. The most interesting of these was the merger of the two antagonists of the pioneering era. The year 1929 brought together the Curtiss Aeroplane and Motor Company and the Wright Aeronautical Corporation into the Curtiss-Wright Company. The aftermath of the Depression of 1929 left all businesses in a shaky condition. Curtiss-Wright was no exception, but it did survive and continue the development work for which it was then the industry leader. The period of designing airplanes by "eyeball" and empirical methods was coming to a close. Replacing the "cut and try" system was the experimental laboratory and design team approach, using wind tunnels and materials-testing laboratories.* Coupled with this was the acceptability of aeronautical engineering as a field of academic discipline.

The nomenclature of the Curtiss aircraft has always been difficult to understand because a number of factors are involved. The main theme that follows through the early Curtiss aircraft designations is an alphabetical sequence, which is quite obscure for the first three letters of the alphabet. Coupled with this is the fact that the early aircraft were famous for specific events or records; and the title of the event, the trophy or the record overshadowed the use of the alphabetical identification. In addition, there is still great doubt as to the origin of the letter designation because Curtiss was initially an engine-oriented manufacturer, and his early contacts with flying were through his making of engines for Thomas S. Baldwin's airships and his participation as director of experiments for the Aerial Experiment Association (AEA). I have reason to believe that Curtiss began his alphabetical model series retrospectively, starting with the airplanes of the AEA. (Since Curtiss was director of experiments for the AEA and the planes were built in the Curtiss shops at Hammondsport, there is some rationale to this assumption by Curtiss.) These were followed by the Aeronautic Society machine, which was the first machine produced by Curtiss as an independent producer of aircraft. It is my contention that the Aeronautic Society machine was, in fact, the Model D, and subsequent variations and improvements resulted in designations such as D-II, D-III, D-IV, etc. The D series was characterized by a standard wingspan and chord with structural and control differences distinguishing the different models.

Since a number of variations developed during the evolution of the Model D, it is somewhat surprising that Curtiss identified his next variation as the Model E, which differed mainly in having a larger wingspan and chord.

Until the introduction of the F series aircraft, the wing construction of Curtiss aircraft was formed with a series of equal-sized panels joined together by wire-braced trussing between the plane's struts. For the most part, these equal-sized panels were interchangeable and, depending on the size of the center section (which included the engine, landing gear and a seat and controls for the pilot or pilots), added up to the wingspan of the aircraft.

Another factor that complicates this designation system is the fact that in the D, E and F series of aircraft, the same wings could be and were used interchangeably for either the landplane, the hydro-aeroplane and finally the flying boat.

Admittedly the D-type flying boats were the earliest and crudest forms of flying boat development; nevertheless, the D-type wings were used for the first flying boat. The E- and F-type wings were also used on flying boats.

As in the case of the wings, the power plants were usually interchangeable, so there was no way in which an airplane could be identified positively by a 4- or V-8-cylinder configuration of the engine.†

One of the early 4-cylinder, D-type "grass cutters" was used as a student training machine, while the same D-type airframe with a V-8, 60- or 75-horsepower engine was used by the early exhibition team pilots.

With all these variations, it is obvious that identification of the early Curtiss airplanes is difficult at best. However, a factor that has aided this writer in positive identification of a number of aircraft is a list, by number, of negatives in the early Curtiss photographic series. This list has made it possible to positively identify a number of aircraft, which otherwise would have been purely guesswork. It also explains why this writer feels a reasonably certain assurance in piecing together this chronology of Curtiss aircraft. Where there still remains an element of doubt, for any reason, such doubt will be made known

---

*As an example, the Curtiss T airplane, begun in 1915 under the direction of Charles F. Willard, used the RAF No. 6 airfoil curves and was stressed and checked by the pioneering aviation engineer Dr. Albert F. Zahm. The LWF aircraft of 1916 was designed in the MIT wind tunnel.

†Charles F. Willard comments: "All the engines I remember in early Ds were 4 × 4 four cylinder or 4 × 4 eight cylinder except for the *Golden Flier* and maybe one other, for the one I leased after the Domingues meet was a 4 × 4 four cylinder. The first army machine had a 4 × 4 eight cylinder engine."

to the reader with a request to all parties to provide this author with such information as may be available so that it can be considered for subsequent printings of this book.

As might be expected, changes and improvements took place in rapid succession during the early stages of the development of Curtiss aircraft, to the extent that hardly any two planes were alike.

There were D models produced from 1909 until 1913; the E models came in about the latter part of 1911, being carried forward until the beginning of World War I; and the F model came in about 1912, going on through 1914–1915.

Injected into this alphabetical sequence were a number of specialized aircraft, or variations, such as the *Albany Flier,* and the 1910 Monoplane; a number of variations in the flying boats, such as the McCormick Spoonbill; and a number of other variations in equipment and configuration. The net result is a rather confused picture, which I will now try to put into some form usable to aviation enthusiasts and technical historians. Where economics becomes a deciding factor in producing the illustrations for this series, a choice has been made in favor of reproducing the least known aircraft in order that it is not lost to future historians.

The Hammondsport Era
1907-1915

Glenn Hammond Curtiss

Glenn Hammond Curtiss was born at Hammondsport, New York. Hammondsport, a picturesque village on the south shore of Lake Keuka, is set in the midst of the vineyards of the New York wine-making industry, in the central Finger Lakes region.

While it was not realized at the time, the birth of Glenn Hammond Curtiss, on May 21, 1878, was destined to put the town on the map. His father was a harness-maker and maintained a small store in which he manufactured leather goods for the people of the neighboring countryside. When Glenn was four years old, his father died, leaving Glenn, his younger sister and their mother without much to keep them. When Glenn reached the age of twelve, his mother remarried—J. Charles Adams—and moved to Rochester to enable his sister to attend a special school for the deaf. Glenn attended public schools in Rochester and spent his free time as a Western Union messenger. When he grew older he was employed by Eastman Kodak, where he assembled cameras. He cared little for school, but was good in mathematics and liked anything to do with mechanics. During this time, he would spend his summer vacations with his grandmother in Hammondsport. He became interested in bicycles and soon began training as a bicycle racer. Riding up and down the hills around Hammondsport soon developed his muscles to the point where he was winning many of the races held in the area. He kept in training constantly, trying each time to better his previous record. Eventually he won the bicycle championship for western New York.

The local druggist, James H. Smellie, also owned a bicycle shop and salesroom. He had taken a liking to young Glenn, and when Glenn returned to Hammondsport to live with his grandmother, the druggist offered him a job in his bicycle shop. The skills that Curtiss had acquired in the Eastman shops now stood him in good stead. Within two more years he acquired his own bicycle business and opened two other shops, one in Bath and one in Corning. His fame as a bicycle racer spread rapidly. He attended all the meets in the area and won prizes wherever

he went. His quest for greater speed led him to attempt to mount a small engine on one of his cycles. *Scientific American* of the late 1890s carried an ad for castings that could be machined and assembled into an engine. Curtiss purchased a set of castings and had them machined at Neff's machine shop, after which Curtiss assembled the engine. The test of the powered cycle must have been quite an event, for, after a successful turn around the town park, he "opened it up" without any previous plans on how to stop the bike. Heading toward the lake and faced with the alternative of a ducking for the bike and himself, or a collision with a tree, he chose the latter. But from this time on, his only recreation was motorcycle races.

He had also found that he had competition in the manufacturing of cycles, and to make a success of his own business, he had to win races. To accomplish this, he had to build faster motorcycles. Since the bicycle frame was fairly simple in construction, and by this time quite standardized, opportunity for higher speed lay mostly in improving the engine and the drive system and perfecting his own skill.

He bought a second set of engine castings and had them machined by Kirkham's shop in Bath, New York. This engine had a bore of 3.5 inches and a stroke of 5 inches. Despite a weight of 190 pounds, the engine was capable of propelling the cycle at a speed of about 30 miles per hour, and enabled him to climb the steepest hills around Hammondsport.

A third engine became his production model and was the basis for a thriving manufacturing business.

The social life and gossip of Hammondsport revolved around the Curtiss Manufacturing Company. The success of his motorcycle and his skill as a rider extended his fame throughout the state and beyond and put Hammondsport on the map.

Eventually, his fame reached California. There, in 1904, "Capt." Thomas Scott Baldwin, a noted aeronaut of the day, heard a Curtiss motorcycle coming up the hill. After examining its engine, Baldwin decided that this was what he needed for his new airship, the *California Arrow*. He traveled east to meet Curtiss and arranged for the construction of a special air-cooled engine. With the Curtiss engine in his *California Arrow* airship, Baldwin, with Roy Knabenshue piloting the craft, won the airship event at the St. Louis Fair. Because of a fire in his California factory, and Curtiss's interest in airship construction, Baldwin decided to continue his airship construction at Hammondsport. Curtiss rigged up a special tricycle cart device for testing the thrust of the airship propellers. It was appropriately called the "Wind Wagon."

The high point of Curtiss's racing career occurred on January 23, 1907, when, at Ormond Beach, Florida, he achieved a speed of 136.3 miles per hour, a record for the time. The motorcycle used by Curtiss to set this record is preserved in the collections of the National Air and Space Museum (Catalog No. 1952–60).

The machine was less a motorcycle and more a performing engine test bed, reported George A. Page, Jr. He finished it in the winter and could not run it around Hammondsport. It was powered by a 40-horsepower V-8 air-cooled engine, for which he lacked an airplane to mount it in. Going with it to Ormond Beach, Florida, at the time of the motorcycle races was largely coincidence. The "motorcycle" didn't meet any recognized classification. It had no clutch and only primitive brakes. The "transmission" was a one-to-one coupling by shaft and gears of the crankshaft through the rear wheel. In order for the machine to start it had to be pushed, and, for the main test, used a five-mile stretch of beach—two miles to accelerate, one mile for the test and two miles to decelerate. The record was not an "official" motorcycle record, but the machine was in fact the fastest vehicle in world history up to that time and for several years more that ever carried a man.

The success of the Baldwin airships led in 1908 to a contract with the War Department to build an airship for the army. Specifications called for a speed of 20 miles per hour and a two-hour endurance for the engine. When the airship was tested that summer at Fort Myer, Virginia, for compliance with the contract, Baldwin was the pilot and Curtiss the engineer. This became the U.S. Army Signal Corps Dirigible No. 1. The power plant of this airship (Catalog No. NAM 02, 1928–12) is preserved in the National Aeronautical Collection. It can be said with accuracy that Curtiss advanced into aeronautics as a result of his motorcycle engine developments.

Through manufacturing engines for airships, Curtiss attracted the attention of Dr. Alexander Graham Bell, the noted inventor, who ordered an engine from Curtiss. The first engine did not perform as anticipated and when the second engine was ordered, Curtiss was asked to demonstrate it at Dr. Bell's laboratory at Baddeck, Nova Scotia. While there in mid-1907 Curtiss met two Canadians, F. W. "Casey" Baldwin and J.A.D. McCurdy and also Lt. Thomas E. Selfridge of the U.S. Army. At the suggestion of Mrs. Bell the Aerial Experiment Association (AEA) was formed to learn about the mechanics of flight. The experiments were funded by Mrs. Bell. The AEA produced a number of designs, each incorporating the ideas of a different member of the AEA. Curtiss was selected as director of experiments and the machines were constructed at the Curtiss plant at Hammondsport.

After the dissolution of the AEA in 1909, Curtiss continued building aircraft for himself and others. The first machine, the *Golden Flier*, was built on order for the Aeronautic Society of New York.

The success of Curtiss aircraft attracted much attention in the United States and abroad. In the United States Curtiss attracted the attention of the Wrights, who understandably contended that any aircraft infringed their basic patent. Litigation soon began, which kept the Wright brothers and Curtiss lawyers busy for several years until the beginning of World War I.

Curtiss attracted much attention in Europe with the winning of the Gordon Bennett Race, one of the events of the Rheims (France) meet of August 1909. This was the first real aviation meet.

During 1910 and 1911 Curtiss concentrated on the development of the hydro-aeroplane. In addition to its use in exhibition flying, the hydro-aeroplane was improved for naval aviation as well. After developing the hydro-aeroplane, the flying boat was the next logical step. In addition to the hydro-aeroplane and flying boat, Curtiss, in cooperation with the U.S. Navy, developed a system for takeoff and landing aboard a naval vessel. The pilot during these significant flights was Eugene Ely.

The next important step for Curtiss was the large twin-engined flying boat. John Wanamaker, proprietor of the famous New York department store, ordered such a flying boat for a transatlantic flight attempt. The result was the H-1 *America*. During the same time period, Curtiss engines were becoming known for their superior reliability and durability. When World War I began, the Curtiss OX-5 engine was ready and was produced in greater numbers than any other contemporary engine. Most of these found their way into the famed Curtiss JN-4 "Jenny" military trainer.

Production of aircraft for World War I made it necessary to increase the capitalization of the company as well as the management and production staff. Curtiss relinquished active management of the company at this time but remained as a major stockholder and director. He was retained as a technical adviser as well. In 1918 the Curtiss Company, in a collaborative role with the U.S. Navy, built the N-C (for Navy-Curtiss) flying boats. In 1919 a four-plane fleet attempted the first transatlantic flight. One of the aircraft, the N-C-4, succeeded in making the flight by stages from Rockaway to the European continent at Lisbon, Portugal.

Curtiss busied himself working on a host of special and experimental aircraft at Garden City, Long Island. During this period Curtiss took a vacation in Florida and there followed a period of land investment and development. He purchased large tracts of land near Miami, notably at Hialeah, where his luck and judgment resulted in very substantial profits. His inventive, mechanical mind continued to drive him to develop ingenious products like the first horse trailer and to build houses unlike anything then in production.

In July 1930 Curtiss was stricken with appendicitis and was operated on at the General Hospital in Buffalo, New York. Complications set in that caused his death on July 23, 1930, at the age of fifty-two.

The Aerial Experiment Association, 1907-1908

In 1905, the same year that he incorporated his business as the G. H. Curtiss Manufacturing Company, Curtiss met Dr. Alexander Graham Bell of telephone fame. Dr. Bell had been experimenting with an unusual tetrahedral kite, consisting of a number of cells in the form of triangular planes joined together to provide the lifting surface he hoped would lift a man into the air.

In 1907, Dr. Bell had ordered an engine from Curtiss and tried to persuade him to visit Baddeck, Nova Scotia, the site of his summer home and experimental laboratory. He was unsuccessful in enticing Curtiss at this time because of the business pressures at Hammondsport. Later, however, after having experienced difficulties with the first engine, Dr. Bell ordered a second, larger engine and this time he specified that Curtiss *must* come to Baddeck to demonstrate the engine. Curtiss personally delivered the engine in July 1907. During this visit he met the inventor's wife and an enthusiastic group of experimenters. Many interesting discussions took place at this time and, as a result, the group, financed by Mrs. Bell, formed the Aerial Experiment Association on October 1, 1907. The AEA group consisted of Dr. Bell, chairman; Curtiss; J.A.D. McCurdy; F. W. "Casey" Baldwin (no relation to the airship pioneer Thomas S. Baldwin) and Lt. Thomas E. Selfridge, U.S. Army, secretary.

This new group agreed to try to develop a powered aircraft by pooling their ideas and efforts. Curtiss was elected chief executive and director of experiments. (See Appendix for the group's agreement.)

One of the provisions of the AEA agreement was that the headquarters of the Association be moved to some place within the limits of the United States. In anticipation of this, Curtiss had written in his notes as follows:

Thursday, September 18, 1907
I believe that there will be experiments to make, and construction work to be carried out which can be done to the best advantage at Hammondsport. In fact I would suggest that Hammondsport be considered as a possible headquarters for the work after the Beinn Bhreagh Laboratory is closed for the season.

The entire power plant for the aerodrome,* and a car for launching it can readily be constructed there. When we have every facility, and if thought advisable, actual trials can be made.

Both hills and flat lands are available with plenty of water in close proximity to both. While a large aerodrome house (Baldwin's) is at the disposal of the Association.

Hammondsport is but a night's run from Washington, and excellent accommodations can be arranged.

G. H. Curtiss

Lieutenant Selfridge moved that the scene of the experiments be transferred to Hammondsport and that they begin by constructing a glider.

As a trained scientist, Dr. Bell realized the value of photographs and records. He therefore insisted that each member keep records of each day's activities. As he was far removed from the actual tests, he requested that telegrams be sent to him *every* night, or as often as something happened. These reports were dutifully typed in multiple copies under the title *Bulletin of the Aerial Experiment Association.*

Dr. Bell emphasized the importance of records in a letter of July 7, 1908:

Please ask each member to write to me a full account of what he is doing at Hammondsport. The information is to be incorporated in succeeding *Bulletins* to be issued

---

*During the early years of the aviation industry, the period covered in this book, the word "aerodrome," which has now come to mean an airport, landing field or aircraft hangar, was in general use as another term for the aircraft itself.

each week. In this way we can keep in touch with one another and, incidentally, secure written records of thoughts, ideas and work done. Trouble will be saved here by sending six copies of any drawings or photographs illustrating letters.

Scanning these *Bulletins* gives one an interesting insight into the state-of-the-art of that day. One item of particular interest in *Bulletin No. 2*, dated May 17, 1908, is a historical survey by Lieutenant Selfridge documenting the activities and results of the aeronautical experiments of their day (see Appendix).

Another paper of particular interest was presented by Curtiss in the *Bulletin* of May 17, 1908. It shows his preoccupation with the problems of propulsion. In this short paper Curtiss touches briefly on the possibility of a 7-cylinder radial engine weighing approximately 75 pounds, developing 35 horsepower. One can only wonder whether Curtiss was aware of the Langley-Manly-Balzer engine, which developed 52 horsepower using 5 cylinders and weighed 200 pounds.*

It is known that this paper was delivered at least six years after the Balzer engine and offers nothing new in this regard, but it does indicate the logical development of the engine as seen from the perspective of the Aerial Experiment Association in 1908.

Another Curtiss letter that was to bear fruit was dated August 19, 1908, Hammondsport, New York:

I have read the last two Bulletins with great interest. The scheme of starting a flying machine from and landing on the water has been in my mind for some time. It has many advantages, and I believe can be worked out. Even if a most suitable device for launching and landing on land is assured, a water craft will still be indispensable

for war purposes and if the exhibition field is to be considered, would, I believe, present greater possibilities in this line than a machine which works on land.

An arrangement of floats to support the flyer when at rest would be necessary. The small hydroplanes would carry it up out of the water and catch the shock of landing. I do not think the problem is difficult.

For work on land, I would submit the enclosed sketch of a new launching device. The one fixed wheel is used entirely for starting and alighting, the skids only acting as supports while standing. Balancing on the one wheel can be easily secured with the movable wing tips and the front horizontal rudder as when flying in the air. If we have the opportunity, would you advise trying this on the *June Bug?*

G. H. Curtiss

No claim is made that Curtiss made the first use of water as a takeoff and landing surface, since others, including Bleriot and Henri Fabre (March 28, 1910, Martigues, France), were successful in getting off and back onto a water surface before Curtiss. It is, however, an equally well-established fact that Curtiss carried on to the point where hydro-aeroplanes and flying boats (the latter patented by Curtiss) were commercially acceptable vehicles. Curtiss was seriously considering the subject and he had begun to think in terms of the single main float configuration with which he was to succeed later. No attempt will be made here to record in great detail the aircraft of the AEA, since this has been ably accomplished in J. H. Parkins's *Bell and Baldwin*, University of Toronto Press, 1964.

This writer intends to cover only the principal details of the aircraft of the AEA in order to show the root from which sprang the long line of Curtiss aircraft.

---

*See Robert B. Meyer, Jr., "Langley's Aero Engine of 1903," *Smithsonian Institution Annals of Flight*, no. 6 (Washington, D.C.: Smithsonian Institution Press, 1971).

The Aerial Experiment Association Glider, 1907

The Aerial Experiment Association had undertaken to fly the man-carrying tetrahedral kite designed by Dr. Bell and named the *Cygnet I*. This kite was launched from a barge towed behind a lake steamer and, with Lieutenant Selfridge aboard, attained a height of 168 feet. Upon landing, the *Cygnet I* was destroyed as a result of being dragged through the water. Lieutenant Selfridge was not impressed with the possibilities of this form of flight, since no control was permitted or was possible. That evening, during a business meeting of the members of the AEA, he made a strong plea for experiments with aircraft having greater maneuverability. After the meeting ended, Lieutenant Selfridge entered into the AEA *Bulletin* the following note:

Whereas for the training of the members of the Association as aviators, that they be in a position to successfully handle the flying machine the Association is to construct, Lt. Selfridge is anxious to make experiments with a gliding machine modeled after the machines that have been successfully flown in America and France, both as gliding machines and flying machines propelled by their own powers.

Resolved: That the Association aid in constructing such a machine in accordance with Curtiss' plan.

Moved and seconded that the gliding machine mentioned in the preceding resolution be constructed at Hammondsport under the direction of Mr. Curtiss.

The AEA Chanute-type hang glider being launched at Hammondsport, New York. Winter 1907–08.

Front view of the AEA 1907 glider showing construction details.

The glider was copied after the successful designs of Octave Chanute, who unselfishly provided data that he had compiled in his own experiments. The glider was a small biplane with a horizontal stabilizing plane in the rear. It is recorded that the glider would become airborne if a man were to run down a hillside into a 15-mile-an-hour breeze. Little else is known about this craft except what one can see in photographs of it in use by members of the AEA. At least one photograph shows the glider in the barn-hangar in company with the uncompleted Aerodrome No. 1, *Red Wing.*

In his résumé of the Aerial Experiment Association at Hammondsport, Curtiss begins by recording:

Before the Association headquarters were transferred to Hammondsport, word was received to build a glider, the object being to gain some experience before building a power driven machine.

This glider was built of bamboo and sheeting, and practiced with at various times for the first 60 days, many successful glides being made, some by each of the members. In the meantime, the power-driven machine was started, it being the majority of opinion that greater progress could be made by going at once to the power-drive and practice on the ice. This proved true, although considerable knowledge was gained with the gliders, which were tried with many different forms of tail and control.

The AEA glider of 1907 was not in itself important except that it gave the members of the AEA an opportunity to acquire some experience in the design and construction necessary to produce a successful aircraft. The glider lasted only a few weeks.

Dr. Bell persisted in trying to develop the tetrahedral design while the rest of the group, all younger than Dr. Bell, fixed their sights on less complex designs of biplane configuration. Their first glider flights were undertaken in the dead of winter of 1907–1908 and gave the younger members an opportunity to "try their wings" beginning about January 13, 1908. After acquiring a bit of experience and a number of bruises during the next two months and some fifty flights, the associates set to work to design their first powered aerodrome. Eventually the glider was smashed in a bad landing while being flown as a kite. It was not rebuilt.

Very little is known about the specifications of the AEA glider. J. H. Parkins, in his *Bell and Baldwin,* states that the chord was 5 feet, the gap 5 feet, and the overall length 25 feet. The structure was made of bamboo covered with cotton sheeting.

Transition from the Chanute-type glider (right) to the Aerodrome No. 1 *Red Wing* at left. The *Red Wing* is still under construction and lacks an engine. Note the airfoil contour strips on top of the wing surfaces, similar to Lilienthal's design.

Aerodrome No. 1
The *Red Wing*
(Curtiss Model B), 1908

The first motor-driven airplane built by the AEA was the *Red Wing,* named for the color of the silk fabric on its surfaces. The silk was left over from the construction of the *Cygnet I,* Bell's first man-carrying kite. It is recorded that the *Red Wing* was constructed in the short time of seven weeks, being ready for the first trials on March 9, 1908. On this date it was run over the ice on its runners, but no attempt was made to fly it. The *Red Wing* had been fitted with runners to enable it to be tested on the ice of Lake Keuka. The design is attributed to Lieutenant Selfridge, who, in company with the other members, built this machine. At this time of year, late spring, the condition of the ice caused much concern. By the time the group had completed the machine, the ice had already disappeared from the south end of Lake Keuka. It became necessary to transport the *Red Wing* three miles up the lake where the ice was still strong enough to bear the weight of the aircraft and AEA members. When the aerodrome was assembled, photographs were taken by Curtiss and two other AEA members. In addition, Harry M. Benner, a local photographer, made a number of photographs, which started him off on what almost became a career of photographing Curtiss's activities.

Benner's photographs have been outstanding in their recordings of the early Curtiss aircraft designs. On March 12, 1908, with the *Red Wing* fully assembled and ready for flight, the three AEA members present drew lots and F. W. "Casey" Baldwin won the honor of piloting Aerodrome No. 1. Upon taking off after a run of approximately 250 feet, the aircraft rose to an altitude of 10 or 20 feet before stalling and dropping back to the surface, 319 feet from the starting point. The aircraft was damaged upon landing. From the photographs taken during this flight, it was evident that the aircraft slid off on one wing, as the tail structure broke under the strain.

The *Red Wing* ended its short career soon afterward. It made one short flight of 120 feet on March 17, 1908, which was the second attempt, during which it crashed, demolishing the aircraft, but with no injury to the pilot or damage to the engine. This machine had no lateral controls.

Here is Selfridge's account of the first successful flight:

THE FIRST SUCCESSFUL TRIAL OF THE NEW AEROPLANE "RED WING" OF THE AERIAL EXPERIMENT ASSOCIATION, AT HAMMONDSPORT, N.Y.

The *Red Wing* on the ice of Lake Keuka.

By First Lieut. T. Selfridge, First Field Artillery, Secretary

The motor driven aeroplane *Red Wing* was completed and ready for trial March 9, 1908, in slightly less than seven weeks after she was started. This was the virgin attempt of the Aerial Experiment Association to construct a motor driven aeroplane of this type, and hence we were not over-sanguine of success at the first trials.

Completed, the dimensions of the apparatus are as follows: two superposed aero-curves of a mean depth of 5′3″ (6.3′ front to rear at the center and 4′ at the extremities) and the same mean distance apart. The front edge of the upper plane extends out 4′ beyond the last vertical connecting posts at each end and the silk surface tapers back from this point to the last verticals at each end of the rear edge. The total spread of the upper plane is 43 feet. The total spread of lower plane is 36′8″.

The total area of surfaces of the cell is 385.7 sq. ft.

The vertical struts are spindle-shaped, the greatest width of the cross-section being from a fourth to a third of the distance back from the front edge. The horizontal members are likewise spindle-shaped. The large center struts are 4″ from front to rear and 1″ greatest width. The next struts on either side are successively smaller down to those at the end, which are 1.5″ front to rear, with a thickness of .5″. The surfaces are of silk with transverse pockets in which are inclosed the bent laminated wood strips extending from the front to the rear edges of the surfaces to give the surfaces their curved form. Above each strut a T-shaped wood strip extends from front to rear and helps to strengthen the structure (and maintains the wing cambre in the same way that Lilienthal maintained his wing profile on his gliders). The spacing of the vertical struts decreases from the center toward the lateral ex-

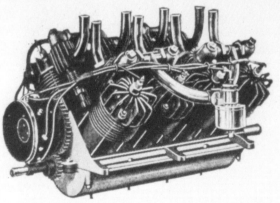
Advertisement for Curtiss Motors for 1908.

tremities. The two center struts at the front and rear edges are about 22″ apart; the first strut on either side of these two is 6.5′ distant, the next 5.5′ and then 5′ to the outer struts. The framework is still further strengthened by steel cable guys 1/32″ diameter.

The tail consists of a single surface 14′10″ by 3′, whose front edge is 10′ in the rear of the rear edge of the main surfaces.

In the center of the tail, and above, is placed a balanced vertical rudder 4′ by 4′. The tail is set at a fixed angle of 7.5 degrees with the front surfaces. A horizontal rudder 8′ by 2′ is supported at the end of a pointed bow of rectangular cross-section (22″ by 22″), which projects from the front of the middle panel. The rear edge of the rudder is 5′ in front of the front edge of the main planes, making the maximum longitudinal dimensions of the machine 26′3″.

The engine was mounted between the main aerodynamic surfaces and drove direct a 6′2″ propeller of two blades having approximately a 4′ pitch. The operator sat inside the bow, which was covered with silk, about 6″ in front of the front edge of the wings.

The total weight of the apparatus, without engine or operator, was 185 pounds. The operator weighed 185 pounds. The total weight complete with motor and operator was 570 pounds, the surfaces had effective area of 385.7 square feet.

On March 9 the machine, which was fitted with runners for the purpose, was put on the ice with a view of ascertaining the effect of the vertical rudder. The area of ice available was so restricted that it was out of the question to attempt a flight, and no runs of over 100 feet or so were made with the engine running. These trials were quite satisfactory and no alterations were made.

Owing to adverse weather conditions it was impossible to get the machine out on the large expanse of ice on the lower part of Keuka Lake, about five miles from the aerodrome shed, until the morning of the 12th. A steam barge was used to convey the apparatus to the starting point. The ice was found to be rather soft but in sufficiently good condition to warrant a trial. After assembling the machine, F. W. Baldwin, M.E., of Toronto, Can., mounted it and

AEA *Red Wing* being reassembled on the ice of Lake Keuka after a bad landing.

G. H. Curtiss, of Hammondsport, N.Y., its maker, started the engine.

It was hardly expected that the machine would rise at the first attempt. The motor was running with the spark retarded and no effort was made to have it develop its full power. The apparatus gathered momentum very quickly, and, much to the surprise of everyone, left the ice after travelling only 200 feet from the start. She arose to a height varying between 10′ and 20′, and had flown but a short distance when the right half of the tail buckled up, causing the right wing of the machine to lower and the apparatus to turn to the right, at the same time descending. The right auxilliary runner struck first, breaking the strut above it, while the machine pivoted about this runner and settled on the ice facing the starting point. The switch was then thrown out and the *Red Wing* came to a stop not far from where she left the ice, her momentum carrying her some distance after the power had been shut off.

Measured in a direct line from the point where the runners left the ice to the point where they first touched on descending, the distance was exactly 318′11″. The actual distance travelled was somewhat greater than this, as the machine described a curve while in the air. Twenty-five onlookers witnessed the flight.

As it was impossible to make the necessary repairs on the spot, the machine was brought back to her shed, thus terminating the trials for the day. The experiments will be resumed at the earliest opportunity, and upon the disappearance of the ice, the apparatus will be placed on wheels.

The actual thrust of the propeller was probably in the neighborhood of 130 pounds, but this was not definitely known, as it had not been measured, and the engine at the time of the flight was certainly not developing over 20 horsepower.

This engine has eight air-cooled cylinders, two sets of four set at an angle of 90 degrees on an aluminum crank case with two connecting rods attached to each throw of the cranks.

The cylinders are cast of air furnace iron and after being carefully bored, the flanges are turned on the outside. The cylinders are then ground on the inside to a perfectly true and smooth surface.

The pistons are made in the same manner and the rings, after being ground on the sides in a magnetic ring grinder, are slotted and carefully re-turned.

The crank shaft is made of vanadium steel, bored out hollow, especially treated, toughened and ground to size on all of the bearings. The bearing metal is Parson's "white brass," which makes a very light and durable bearing. All of the studs and bolts are vanadium or nickel steel. The exhaust valves are made with nickel steel heads electrically welded to soft steel stems. The exhaust valves all have a 30 degree seat and are operated from a single cam shaft. The intake valves are automatic.

The engine complete, with balance wheel, commutator and distributor, weighs 145 pounds, lubrication is effected by the splash system, the case being fed by two sight feed oilers, and the ignition is accomplished by six dry batteries and a single nonvibrating coil.

In a later report (May 17, 1908) to the AEA, F. W. Baldwin included some interesting descriptions of the machine:

Red Wing had double superposed surfaces and would come under the class generally known as the Chanute type.

The frame of the usual double decker, is the simple Pratt Truss.

In the *Red Wing* truss, the upper and lower chords were made converging toward their extremities . . . the structural advantage in having the chords bowed is obvious at a glance.

All the exposed members of the main planes, tail, and bow-control, which are substantially at right angles to the line of flight were made fish-shaped (streamlined) cross section giving a form of least resistance according to experiments made by Prof. Zahm and conforming fairly well to streamline theory.

F. W. Baldwin states:

The double curvature of the surfaces was obtained by the use of curved ribs made up of four laminations of wood each ⅛" thick. The two outside strips were of ash to give them the required stiffness and the inner ones of spruce. These strips were laid up on a form and after being carefully glued together, retained their shape admirably without any apparent warping.

It should be noted here that the stiffener boards of the T cross section were used also, as noted in F. W. Baldwin's description of Selfridge's *Red Wing* of the AEA *Bulletin,* May 17, 1908:

The fundamental idea in the design of the *Red Wing* was to produce an aeroplane with head resistance reduced to a minimum and power enough to ensure its getting into the air.

Specifications

Aerodrome No. 1, the *Red Wing*
(Curtiss Model B), 1908

Span	43 ft. 4 in.
Chord	6 ft. 3 in. (max.);
	4 ft. 0 in. (min.)
Gap	6 ft. 6 in. (max.);
	4 ft. 0 in. (min.)
Engine	8-cyl. V, air-cooled,
	40 hp @ 1,800 rpm
Weight	
net	385 lb.
gross	570 lb.

Aerodrome No. 2
The *White Wing*, 1908

Having succeeded in getting their first powered machine into the air, the members of the AEA were not discouraged by the crash of the *Red Wing* on March 17. On the contrary, no time was lost in getting started on their second machine. The new machine, *White Wing*, was named by its designer, F. W. Baldwin. With the exception of the empennage, which was covered with red silk, the aircraft was covered with nainsook. The white color of the material led appropriately to the name *White Wing*. Construction was begun on March 23, 1908, and the machine was ready on May 9.

While the *White Wing* was constructed to the same basic configuration as the *Red Wing*, there were many detail changes resulting from lessons learned in the construction and flight of the *Red Wing*. The most obvious change was the use of a wheel undercarriage in place of the runners. During the *Red Wing's* test, one of the problems was the softening of the ice on the lake. It was, in fact, the reason that the first flight of the *Red Wing* was made by Baldwin instead of Selfridge, the designer, the latter being absent on army business in Washington. With the arrival of springlike weather, the lake no longer provided

The *White Wing* takes off. Aerodrome No. 2 lifts off from a racetrack at Hammondsport on May 23, 1908, for its fifth flight. J.A.D. McCurdy was the pilot.

the wide-open vistas from which to launch the aircraft. Later, Curtiss was to relate that it was this situation that oriented his thinking toward the design of float-equipped hydro-aeroplanes. The flight operations were moved to the valley. In this valley was one field of adequate size, known as Stony Brook Farm, and the remainder of the AEA tests and many of the early Curtiss aircraft were tested here.

On May 17, the day before the first flight of the *White Wing,* Baldwin presented a paper to the AEA members that described in detail the principal differences between the *White Wing* and its predecessor.

AERODROME NO. 2, BALDWIN'S WHITE WING, SHOWING HOW IT DIFFERS FROM NO. 1:

By F. W. Baldwin

(A paper presented to the Aerial Experiment Association May 17, 1908, revised for this *Bulletin,* No. 6, August 17, 1908)

The second motor driven aeroplane which has just been completed is as nearly as possible a reproduction of the *Red Wing* in general design. It is built of heavier material throughout and with slightly larger surfaces. The improvements are nearly all in the details of its construction.

The AEA assembled. From left to right, F. W. "Casey" Baldwin, J.A.D. McCurdy, Glenn H. Curtiss, Dr. Alexander Graham Bell, Lt. Thomas E. Selfridge and Augustus Post.

In this machine, it was deemed advisable to get some positive method of controlling the lateral stability. The tips at the extremities of the wings are hinged about their fore edges and by a system of steering gear the angles of incidence can be changed by the operator. By this arrangement if the machine inclines to one side the man by leaning to the high side operates a tiller which is connected by steering ropes and increases the angle of incidence of the tips at the lower side and decreases the angle of incidence of the tips on the high side. This gives a righting couple, which should keep

Increased ground clearance and a third wheel at the front made the *White Wing* safer. This configuration is now considered normal for modern aircraft.

Close-up of the *White Wing* showing the engine before addition of the third wheel, probably on May 14, 1908, the date of the first trial flight. Lt. Thomas E. Selfridge, in a white shirt, is at the wheel. Augustus Post (with beard) is at the right.

the machine on an even keel, the idea being that the man will instinctively lean to the high side.*

The bow-control has been placed a foot farther in advance of the main plane, and is 9 feet across and 2.5 feet deep. This control is operated by a lever connected directly to the steering post, and not by yoke ropes as in the *Red Wing.*

Right and left steering is provided for by a triangular rudder which swings about a vertical axis behind the after central strut of the tail. The steering ropes from this rudder lead to the steering wheel in front of the operator

*This marked the beginning of the control system that was to be a characteristic of Curtiss airplanes for some time. It evolved into a yoke attached to the pilot's seat and attached to the ailerons in a manner to produce differential movement. Willard comments: "It was natural. This yoke system was an improvement over the Wright system of being prone and having to slide sidewise to maintain stability."

which works like the steering wheel of a motor car, turning to the right putting the rudder over to the right and turning to the left putting the rudder over to the left.

The tail is composed of two superposed surfaces giving about the same surface as in the *Red Wing* and is placed 10 feet (the same distance) behind the main plane. This was done to remedy the weakness shown by the faulty construction of the single surface tail first used on the *Red Wing.* The box which constitutes the tail is given a slight angle with the engine bed (1 in 27 or 2° 20'). In this it differs from the *Red Wing* in which the tail was parallel with the engine bed. The justification for this, by no means important, departure is that theoretically, it would seem that the machine when perfectly balanced should have all its surfaces, including controls, at the most efficient angle. That is, the angle at which the ratio of lift to drift is greatest.

In the new machine, all members of the truss outside of the center panel fit into sockets and are thus more easily repaired than in the old construction with its through members. The uprights are fitted with a setscrew in the socket so that they may be lengthened out or shortened, thus doing away with the necessity for turnbuckles on the diagonal wires.

The upper and lower chords of the *White Wing* are not true curves as was the case of the *Red Wing*, but the members are straight between each panel. Another change from the old design is in the joints of the center panel. Mr. Bedwin* devised a scheme for bolting the uprights through the upper and lower chords which is very much neater, stronger and lighter than the old way of straps and knees.

A wooden propeller is used on this machine with the same engine as before. The diameter is 6 feet, the pitch is slightly greater than the diameter. The weight of this propeller is only about 8 pounds and it should prove more efficient in every way.

The new machine is 43 feet 6 inches from tip to tip; the planes are 6 feet 6 inches deep at the center, and 4 feet deep at the outside panel, which gives a total supporting surface of 408.5 feet. The weight of the main planes with the engine bed is 133 lbs. as against 119 lbs. in the case of the *Red Wing*. The nose weighs 27 lbs., the tail including a light wheel weighs 30.5 lbs. The wheels and the spring frames which support them weigh 47 lbs. The engine, accessories and propeller weigh 192 lbs. So the total weight taking the man at 175 lbs. will be about 606 lbs. This gives a flying weight of about 1½ lbs. to the sq. ft. compared to 1¼ in the *Red Wing*.

The cloth used throughout (except for the tail which is silk) is of a quality of nainsook which weighs 70 grms. per square meter. Altogether the new machine is a great improvement over the old one in the matter of construction. While its struts are larger, more of its members are enclosed and it should not offer much more head resistance than the *Red Wing*.

On this same day, May 17, 1908, the *White Wing* was moved to the racetrack at Stony Brook Farm. No attempts were made to fly on this date. It had been thought that directional control, by use of the rudder, would be adequate, but it was found that some means of steering was required until sufficient airspeed was attained. In order to maintain control the forward wheel was provided with a tillerlike device to guide the craft on the ground.

A short flight was made on May 18 with Casey Baldwin, the designer, at the controls. During this short flight of about 95 yards, the air pressure on the trailing edge of the wing caused it to deflect into the propeller. In all, the *White Wing* made five flights as follows:

Date	Distance	Altitude	Pilot
May 18	95 yd.	10 ft.	Baldwin
May 19	100 ft.	3 ft.	Selfridge
	240 ft.	20 ft.	Selfridge

(Bad landing, nose wheel damaged.)

May 21	339 yd.	Unknown	Curtiss
May 23	183 yd.	20 ft.	McCurdy

(Bad landing, inverted and badly damaged; abandoned.)

This last flight of the *White Wing* resulted in extensive damage to the aircraft structure; so much so that members elected to proceed with the construction of the Aerodrome No. 3 under the direction of Curtiss. Neither the pilot nor the engine was damaged in the crash of the *White Wing*. The engine was the same as used in the *Red Wing*, an air-cooled V-8 with carburetors on each cylinder.

Specifications
Aerodrome No. 2, the *White Wing*, 1908

Span	42 ft. 3 in.
Length	26 ft. 3 in.
Chord	6 ft. 6 in. (max.); 4 ft. 0 in. (min.)
Gap	6 ft. 6 in. (max.); 4 ft. 0 in. (min.)
Engine	8-cyl. V, air-cooled, 40 hp @ 1,800 rpm
Weight	
net	430 lb.
gross	605 lb.

*William E. Bedwin, superintendent of Dr. Bell's laboratory and craftsman responsible for much of the actual construction of Aerial Experiment Association aircraft.

Aerodrome No. 3
The *June Bug,* 1908, Model C

The *June Bug,* so named by Dr. Bell because it was built and first flown in June, was destined to become the best known of all the Aerial Experiment Association aircraft.

The most notable and most widely reported of its accomplishments was the winning of the Scientific American Trophy for the first time. The trophy had been offered by *Scientific American* in the spring of 1908 for the first flight to exceed one kilometer (3,281 feet) flying in a straight line.

The month of June 1908 was indeed a most rewarding time for the AEA. The *June Bug* was completed on June 19 and given a ground test without its wings. On the twentieth the wings had been installed to the center section (an innovation in the aircraft construction by the AEA). Three attempts were made to get off the ground and each proved to be unsuccessful. It was found that the relatively open weave of the fabric allowed air to pass through, reducing lift. To remedy this condition, the fabric was treated with a "dope" consisting of paraffin dissolved in gasoline. This treatment improved the *June Bug's* performance to the extent that Curtiss was able to make three successful flights on June 21. Following the application of a second coat of

Preparing the *June Bug* for flight at Stony Brook Farm, Hammondsport.

"dope," the *June Bug,* piloted by Curtiss, made a spectacular flight of 725 yards on the twenty-fifth. On the twenty-seventh, Curtiss made three flights of 1,140, 400 and 540 yards and prompted the Association to telephone to the Aero Club of America that the AEA was now ready to try for the Scientific American Trophy.

In his report of July 4, 1908, the secretary, Lt. Thomas E. Selfridge, recorded the historic event as follows:

The Aerial Experiment Association's Aerodrome No. 3, Curtiss' *June Bug* today earned the right to have its name the first inscribed on the Scientific American Trophy, by making an official flight of one kilometer in a straight line measured from the point where it left the ground. After passing the flag marking the finish, the machine flew 600 yards further and landed at the extreme edge of the field near the railroad track, after crossing three fences

and describing a letter *S,* 2000 yards in all in 1 min. 42½ seconds at a speed of 39 miles per hour. This followed a 900 yard flight in 56 seconds.

The machine never behaved better and the long flight could have been continued at the will of the operator had he cared to rise over the trees which bounded the field. Though quite possible, it was not deemed wise to attempt it at the present stage of the aviator's development. There was hardly a breath of air stirring during either flight. This trial is really of the utmost importance as it is the first official test of an aeroplane ever made in America and there are only two other machines which have traveled further in public; Farman's and Delagrange's. The Wrights though have undoubtedly far outflown it in private, so that America is not so very far behind France as might be supposed. The last flight today was the 15th made by the machine, all having occurred

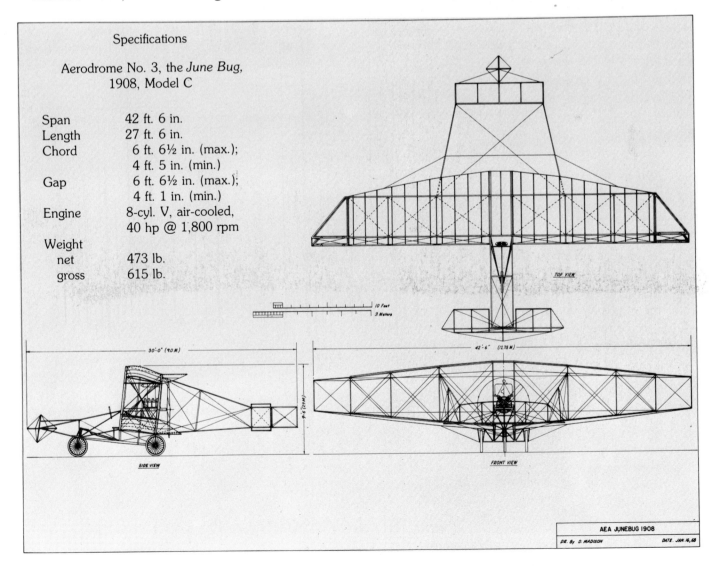

Specifications

Aerodrome No. 3, the *June Bug,*
1908, Model C

Span	42 ft. 6 in.
Length	27 ft. 6 in.
Chord	6 ft. 6½ in. (max.); 4 ft. 5 in. (min.)
Gap	6 ft. 6½ in. (max.); 4 ft. 1 in. (min.)
Engine	8-cyl. V, air-cooled, 40 hp @ 1,800 rpm
Weight net	473 lb.
gross	615 lb.

TOP VIEW

SIDE VIEW

FRONT VIEW

AEA JUNEBUG 1908

DR. By D. MADISON   DATE. JAN. 16, 68

under far more adverse conditions than those encountered by the French machines. It is hoped that there will be several other names on the cup before the new year. In order to possess it, this trophy must be won at least once in three separate years. The rules being changed and made more severe after each trial.

The Aero Club of America sent a number of witnesses for the July 4 flight. Among those present were Augustus Post, who always seemed to be present whenever photographs were taken; Charles M. Manly, who played an important part in the Langley experiments; Augustus M. Herring, close associate of Octave Chanute in his glider experiments and reputed to have developed a small compressed air engine, which he attached to one of the gliders; Ernest L. Jones, editor of *Aeronautics* magazine; and Capt. Thomas S. Baldwin of airship fame. The press was well represented in the crowd that gathered that day. In keeping with the festive atmosphere of the holiday, the town was flooded with crowds from the surrounding area, and picnic baskets were much in evidence. Judging from photographs of the event and recorded reports, the weather left something to be desired. Rain clouds threatened most of the day and dis-

charged some of their contents in an early afternoon shower. It wasn't until about six o'clock that Curtiss considered the conditions suitable for the trial flight. A little after six, Curtiss and his associates rolled the *June Bug* out of its tent, the course was measured and suitably marked, the engine was started and given a few minutes' warm-up and the flight began. Curtiss related his observations later:

When I gave the word to let go, the *June Bug* skimmed along over the old race track for perhaps two hundred feet, and then rose gracefully into the air. The crowd set up a hearty cheer, as I was told later, for I could hear nothing but the roar of the motor, and I saw nothing but the course and the flag marking a distance of one kilometer. The flag was quickly reached and passed, and still I kept the aeroplane up, flying as far as the open field would permit, and finally coming down safely in a meadow, fully a mile from the starting place. I had thus exceeded the requirements, and had won the Scientific American Trophy for the first time.*

---

*From unpublished manuscript by Fay Leone Faurote.

The *June Bug* in a tent hangar, partially assembled.

RECORD OF FLIGHTS OF THE AERIAL EXPERIMENT ASSOCIATION'S AERODROME NO. 3

"Curtiss' June Bug" G. H. Curtiss, Aviator

DATE	FLIGHT NO.	DISTANCE YDS.	TIME SEC.	CAUSE OF STOP	BREAKAGE
June 21	1	152	11	Aviator's lack of skill	None
June 21	2	139	9	Aviator's lack of skill	None
June 21	3	422	25½	Voluntary	None
June 24	4	40	3	Too much wind	None
June 24	5	100	6	Too much wind	None
June 25	6	725	41	Voluntary	None
June 27	7	1,140	60	Boundary of field reached	None
June 27	8	400	24	Voluntary	None
June 27	9	540	33	Voluntary	None
July 2	10	30	2½	Too much wind	None
July 2	11	150	14	Voluntary	None
July 3	12	30	2½	Voluntary	One wheel and one wing broken
July 3	13	1,300	68½	Boundary of field reached	None
July 4	14	900	56½	Wrong tail adjustment	None
July 4	15	2,000	102½	Stopped to avoid trees	None
July 5	16	1,500	75	Too short turn attempted	Front wheel and several struts broken
July 8	17	900	55		
July 10	18	Circled	90		

In a letter to Mrs. Bell, J.A.D. McCurdy recorded the following interesting experiments with the *June Bug:*

We have been having quite interesting flights with the old *June Bug* the last few days. We were anxious to try her without a tail so first we removed the top surface of the double decked tail and upon trying a flight no change in stability manifested itself.

We then removed the bottom surface (both removed now) and tried a flight under "bare poles" as it were. The difference in stability was very marked. The machine would answer the control so much more readily and quickly that the least possible movement in changing the angle of incidence of the control was necessary to preserve a flight in one horizontal plane.

Day before yesterday we removed the tail structure altogether, and simply built out a support for the rudder as follows: The center of the rudder came just opposite, or in continuation of the propeller shaft. We tried this day before yesterday afternoon Friday and found that the instability had disappeared and she could be handled with perfect ease.

This may have been due to several causes, more skill in management, or lack of drag of the tail structure.

The old ribs have all been removed, and ribs such as we are to use on the *Silver Dart* substituted. These ribs have just the single curve and are made of four plies instead of the three to obtain greater strength. Now upon trying the machine night before last (Friday) under these conditions new ribs of single curvature, and without a tail, (the man moving back seven inches to make up for load removed from rear by removing the tail) I found that the machine would glide!

Approaching the place I wanted to land on I shut off the motor as in former cases and expected to land just as I had planned but the machine kept on gliding for a distance of 200 feet and I was about 15 feet in the air when I shut off . . . Mr. Curtiss tried a short flight next, and he went through the same thing although from the knowledge gained from the flight he shut the motor off and allowed for a glide of about 200 feet. She lands beautifully and without any jar whatever.

Last evening (Saturday) we went up to the track about five o'clock and I attempted a flight. Everything worked beautifully and much to the pleasure of everybody I was enabled to describe the figure eight after covering a distance of two miles.

In a letter to Dr. Bell, Curtiss described how the *June Bug* differed from Aerodrome No. 2:

Hammondsport, N.Y., July 13, 1908: the following is an enumeration of the difference between Aerodromes No. 2 & No. 3:

In No. 3 the wing tips were so set that when not in use, they were at a neutral angle while those in No. 2 when not working as controls were parallel to the surfaces. The gearing of the wing tips was simplified by the new arrangement of wiring necessitated by the operator's seat being moved farther to the front.

The main weights are separated by a greater distance in No. 3 than in No. 2. The engine was set five inches farther back and the man two feet farther to the front. The front control was also moved farther out and the front edge of it now 10 feet 10⅛ inches in front of the front edge of the main planes thus making the machine 27½ feet long. Five square feet have been added to the area of the front control, its total spread being now 13 feet 10 inches as compared with 11 feet 8 inches of No. 2. The nose is now wedge shaped instead of pointed and has been left uncovered.

The running gear consists of three wheels as before, but the wheel base has been extended two feet. It has also been greatly strengthened by two large wooden members running fore and aft which are to be used as skids in case the wheels break down.

The wings have been made so that they can be easily removed from the engine bed section and their surfaces have been varnished with a mixture of gasoline, yellow ochre, parrafin and turpentine in order to make them air-tight. The yellow ochre was used for photographic purposes. The working surfaces of the machine have been reduced from 408 to 370 square feet. Switch and spark controls have been placed on the front steering wheel.

The lower plane has been greatly

strengthened by eight guy wires fastening it to the hubs of the wheels and bottom of the skids.

The engine section has been made up of lighter material, the struts being only ¾ of an inch thick at their widest part and 2¼ inches long instead of one inch thick at their widest part and 4 inches long as was used in No. 2. Additional guy wires have been added to this section and it is now more rigid than before.

The propeller has been cut down from 6 feet 2 inches to 5 feet 11 inches, and is now turning up to about 1200 rpm. instead of 1050.

The tail has been made spar-shaped from side to side so as to conform to the general shape of the main surface. The vertical surfaces of the tail have been removed and the area of the vertical rudder increased from 27 inches square to 36 inches square.

It has also been decided to do away with the screw sockets for the vertical posts and to cut turn-buckles on each socket. We are also to use balloon rubber silk for the surfaces. These last changes have not yet been made however. The distance between the center of gravity of the operator and the center of gravity of the engine is now 6 feet.

From a letter to Dr. Bell, dated September 11, 1908, we find an interesting report by Curtiss:

. . . as the weather was favorable and a number of out-of-town people were desir-

ous of seeing a flight of the *June Bug,* I went to the track at six o'clock in the evening, took the machine out, and flew for the first time with the new rudder and front controls . . .

The interesting feature of the flight was the fact that I had no sooner gotten in the air than four cylinders ceased running; caused by the breaking off of the gasoline pipe which feeds the four cylinders on one side. This pipe had been recently put in by the boys as they thought the old one might be too small. The big one did not stand the vibration. I knew immediately what had happened, and thought it would be a good opportunity to see how near I could come to flying with only four cylinders running. To my surprise, I kept on going and I made a good half mile, including quite a turn, with four of the eight cylinders working, which means that less than half the power was being developed. The number of revolutions did not decrease to the same extent, as the speed was over thirty miles an hour, and the propellers turned much more easily than when standing.

One final note on the *June Bug. Aviation Magazine,* March 1911, carried a news note to the effect that the *June Bug* was shipped to the Smithsonian Institution. Determined effort by the museum's first curator, Paul Edward Garber, failed to find any factual basis for this report, although he did locate the *June Bug's* propeller among the flight relics added to this collection.

A photograph by H. M. Benner showing the *June Bug* in flight.

A. G. BELL, F. W. BALDWIN, J. A. D. McCURDY, G. H. CURTISS & T. E. SELFRIDGE.

E. A. SELFRIDGE, ADMINISTRATOR OF T. E. SELFRIDGE, DEC'D.

FLYING MACHINE.

APPLICATION FILED APR. 8, 1909.

1,011,106.

Patented Dec. 5, 1911.

5 SHEETS—SHEET 1.

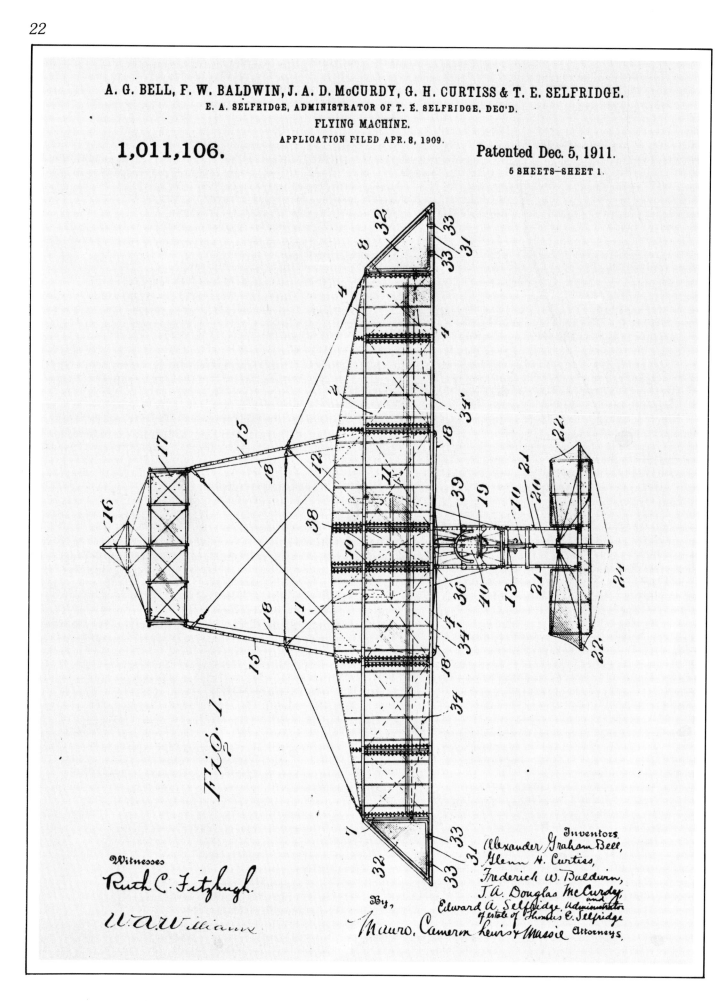

Fig. 1.

Witnesses

Ruth C. Fitzhugh.

W. A. Williams.

Inventors
Alexander Graham Bell,
Glenn H. Curtiss,
Frederick W. Baldwin,
J. A. Douglas McCurdy,
and
Edward A. Selfridge, Administrator
of estate of Thomas E. Selfridge

By,
Mauro, Cameron, Lewis & Massie Attorneys,

A. G. BELL, F. W. BALDWIN, J. A. D. McCURDY, G. H. CURTISS & T. E. SELFRIDGE.
E. A. SELFRIDGE, ADMINISTRATOR OF T. E. SELFRIDGE, DEC'D.
FLYING MACHINE.
APPLICATION FILED APR. 8, 1909.

1,011,106.

Patented Dec. 5, 1911.
5 SHEETS—SHEET 5.

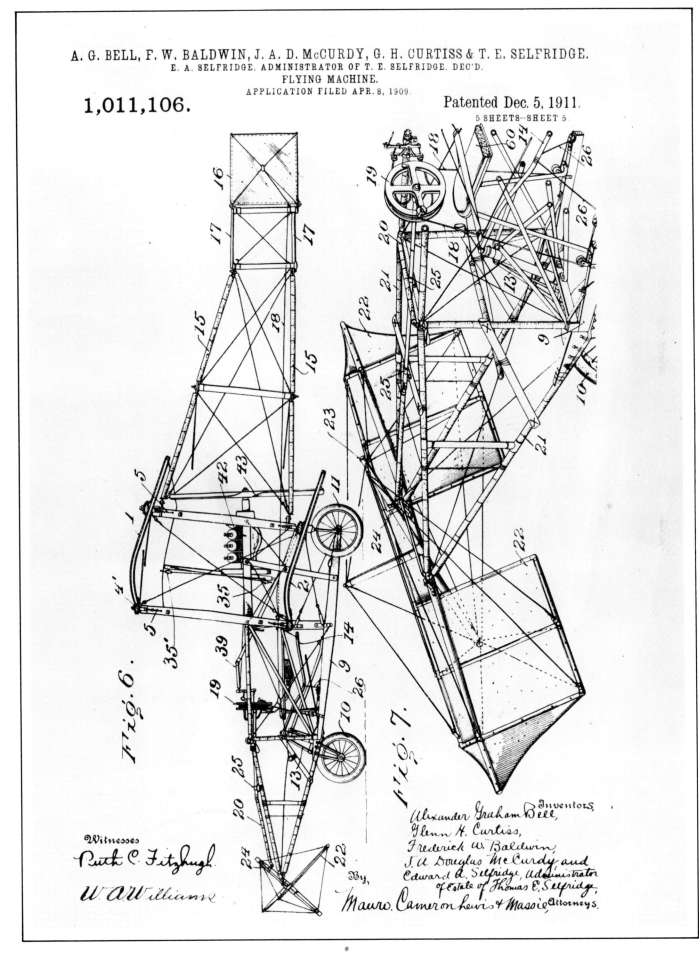

Fig. 6.

Fig. 7.

Inventors,
Alexander Graham Bell,
Glenn H. Curtiss,
Frederick W. Baldwin,
J. A. Douglas McCurdy, and
Edward A. Selfridge, Administrator
of Estate of Thomas E. Selfridge,
By,
Mauro, Cameron, Lewis & Massie, Attorneys.

Witnesses
Ruth C. Fitzhugh.
W. A. Williams

Aerodrome No. 3A
The *Loon*

For purposes of classification, I have called this machine Aerodrome No. 3A, for it is a hybrid using the modified airframe of the *June Bug,* the engine from the Aerodrome No. 4 *Silver Dart* then under construction, and the addition of twin floats. One document that casts some doubts on the derivation of the *Loon* was found in the Transcript of Record, *Curtiss* v. *Janin,* Glenn H. Curtiss For Plaintiffs-Direct, page 31:

Q. Will you please state to the Court in your own way how you came to conceive of that invention, giving the date and circumstances that led up to it?

CURTISS. I was a member of an association called the Aerial Experiment Association, which was headed by Dr. Alexander Graham Bell. The purpose of the Association was to develop a successful flying

AEA *Loon* en route to launching in Lake Keuka. *Wm. J. Hammer Collection*

machine. After the first successful flights from land were made, we turned our attention to the possibility of flying from the water. One of the land machines that we had built was equipped with two floats, catamaran style. This machine was attributed to Mr. McCurdy, another member of the Association. It was Dr. Bell's idea that each member should have an opportunity to express his own ideas in a machine. This being Mr. McCurdy's machine, he had the say as to the float system, and preferred these twin floats. At that time, which was in the fall of 1908, I conceived the idea of a single main supporting pontoon with small end balancing pontoons at the wing tips. I disclosed this idea to Mr. McCurdy at the time and resolved to try the plan of construction at the first opportunity.

Historians generally agree, however, that the *Loon* was, in fact, a modification of the *June Bug*.

We have seen from a letter, dated August 19, 1908, that Curtiss continued to think in terms of a waterborne aircraft. The *Loon* was the first attempt to try this new idea. In view of this letter expressing a preference for the single central float, there is reason to believe that McCurdy did, in fact, make the decision for the catamaran float system used on the *Loon*. In any event, two floats were constructed having a triangular cross section, with one of the flat sides as the bottom. With present-day knowledge of hydrodynamics, one can understand the difficulties they were to encounter. The rather marginal power available coupled with the unstepped flat bottom of the floats predoomed this experiment. The *Loon* was a crude machine but it was the beginning of

The *Loon* between work docks on the "runway" of Lake Keuka. *Curtiss Collection*

experiments with this type of aircraft in the United States.

During the experiments it was soon discovered that the engine with which the *June Bug* had originally been equipped was not adequate to attain the necessary speed for taking off. At one time the *Loon* was fitted with the more powerful engine that was intended for the Aerodrome No. 4 *Silver Dart,* and also with hydrofoils. Neither of these, however, because of other deficiencies, served to make the *Loon* airworthy.*

In a letter to Mrs. Bell, dated December 14, 1908, J.A.D. McCurdy mentions that the *Loon* was fitted with two small hydrofoils 9 feet long by 7 inches wide with a curve of 1 in 15 that were placed at an angle of incidence of 5 degrees and located 6 inches below the floats. One was placed forward and one aft.

In *Bulletin* No. 24 of the Aerial Experiment Association is the following item:

A SHORT ACCOUNT OF OUR EXPERIMENT WITH THE *LOON*
By J.A.D. McCurdy

Hammondsport, N.Y., Dec. 9, 1908: As the Hammondsport members of the Aerial Experiment Association were only waiting for the completion of the new motor to be installed in the *Silver Dart,* there was practically nothing to do in the flying game. The idea occurred to us on October 23rd to fill our time by trying some experiments along the line taken up by the Baddeck members. It seemed that [if] the boats, or floats, should rise out of the water while under way, the aeroplane would produce the lift and that perhaps the additional use of hydroplanes was unnecessary. As we had the old *June Bug* lying idle, just waiting to be used, it was decided to build two small floats large enough to support the total weight of machine and man, and place these boats under the *June Bug* in place of the running gear which was attached at that time for rising off the land. The expense of building these boats would be comparatively small, so designs were immediately gotten out to support a total weight of 850 pounds. We finally decided upon the following dimen-

sions: 20 ft. over all, 18 in. beam, and six inches of free board. These boats were constructed skeleton-like, of California Red Wood, and covered completely over with rubber oilcloth. Completed, they weigh 60 pounds each. They are spaced 7 feet apart, catamaran-like, and connected by fish-shaped trussing to the lateral chords and central panel of the *June Bug.* The vertical rudder, similar to that used in the *June Bug,* was mounted directly at the stern of the catamaran, while the single surface front control was mounted directly from the bow, thus doing away with the usual cantilever trussing employed in our former machines. This gave a great saving in head resistance and also made the whole thing when finished look very compact and neat.

The engine used was the one originally designed for the *Silver Dart.* It is a Curtiss, 8 cylinder, 3¾ bore × 4 in. stroke, water-cooled motor, and is mounted midway between the planes, driving direct an eight foot propeller of 6¼ ft. pitch. The machine thus constructed was named the *Loon.*

To transport the *Loon* from the aerodrome shed to the head of Lake Keuka, where two parallel wharves were built to serve as launching ways, a two wheeled cart was constructed upon which the *Loon* would balance, and by attaching a rope to the front end of the cart, the machine was easily hauled along the road.

On Saturday evening, November 28th, the first experiment was tried. The engine being started by Mr. Curtiss and the seat being taken by Mr. McCurdy, the machine started on its maiden flight. The exact push of the propeller at the time was not known, although it was probably in the neighborhood of 250 pounds. Hardly had the machine, however, covered 400 yards when the propeller shaft was twisted off, the propeller being thrown violently into the water. This concluded experiments for the day. The speed attained was calculated to be 20 miles an hour. The experiment was of such short duration that data as to the lift of the aeroplane was not obtained. A new propeller shaft was soon constructed of solid material, instead of the steel tubing formerly used, and on Sunday afternoon, November 29th, the second trial was made. The wind was blowing directly down the

---

*See *Bell and Baldwin,* by J. H. Parkins, University of Toronto Press, for a detailed description of the *Loon.* See also relevant issues of the AEA *Bulletin.*

The float for the *Loon*. Note the relatively flat bottom with no step.

Lake with a velocity of five or six miles an hour. The auxiliary ports in the engine which were closed on the former trial, were now opened up, and it was anticipated that the speed of the engine would be greatly increased. As before, Mr. Curtiss tuned up the motor and Mr. McCurdy operated. We had agreed to try running down the Lake with the wind and back again against the wind, to ascertain whether there was any difference in lift due to the wind. It seemed that after running about 100 yards the *Loon* obtained her maximum lift. By "shooting" her, (by suddenly elevating the bow control), the bows would entirely lift out of the water without any depression at the stern which would be the result in the case of an ordinary motor boat. We took a course a mile down the Lake, turning in coming back against the wind, thus covering a distance of two miles in 4 minutes and 26 seconds. This gives a speed of over 27 miles an hour. It was calculated by Mr. Selfridge that the speed required to lift the *June Bug* off the ground was about 23 miles an hour, and although the weight of the *Loon* was very little more than the *June Bug,* still an increase of speed of four miles on 23 was

insufficient to cause her to take the air. This seems to indicate that the suction of the water in holding down the boat is much greater than was anticipated.

As we unfortunately could not allow the experiments with the *Loon* to interrupt trials with the *Silver Dart,* it was decided to take the motor up the valley to the tent and start flying there as soon as possible. We hope, however, after we have gotten through with the *Silver Dart* for this year, we may go back to the *Loon* and have another trial with an experiment that promises so much.

J.A.D. McCurdy
Sec., Aerial Experiment Association

Specifications	
Aerodrome No. 3A, the *Loon*	
Span	42 ft. 6 in.
Chord	6 ft. 6½ in.
Gap	6 ft. 6½ in.
Power plant	8-cyl. V, water-cooled, 40 @ 1,800 rmp; 25 @ 1,200 rpm
Weight	615 lb.

Aerodrome No. 4
The *Silver Dart*, Model C

With the possible exception of the *June Bug*, the *Silver Dart* is the most important aircraft constructed by the Aerial Experiment Association. In addition to being the most advanced aircraft of the series built by the AEA, the *Silver Dart* carries the special distinction of having been the first heavier-than-air craft to make a flight in Canada. All of the construction details of the *Silver Dart* were much more refined than in the case of any of the preceding aircraft of the Association. In addition, it embodied all of the lessons learned from these earlier machines and was to be powered with a water-cooled engine of 50 horsepower instead of the earlier air-cooled engine used in the first three experimental aircraft. This new Curtiss engine had 8 cylinders in sets of four at an angle of 90 degrees. The cylinders were cast iron with copper water jackets, had a bore of 3¾ inches and a stroke of 4 inches. The valves were nickel steel, concentric; intake valve was automatic. The connecting rods were special forgings, with Parson's White Brass bearings, liberal dimensions. The shaft was 1⅜-inch chrome nickel steel specially treated and bored hollow. All bearings were ground to size. The lubrication was by splash system, pump feed. The ignition was effected by jump spark with single coil and distributor. The engine weighed 165 pounds.*

In a letter dated July 6, 1908, Dr. Bell wrote that if McCurdy wished to follow in the same line as the *June Bug*, he recommended that the airplane (the *Silver Dart*) be built in Hammondsport.

Construction details of the *Silver Dart* were contained in an article in *Bulletin* No. 21, November 30, 1908, and reproduced in *Aeronautics* magazine of December 1908, as follows:

Experiments with the *June Bug* seemed to indicate that more powerful tip controls would be an advantage, especially in attempting to complete a turn and possibly describing a circle. To accomplish this end we gave the machine greater lateral extension than in the case of either of the former machines, (49 ft.) and also increased the area of the tip controls themselves, (40 sq. ft. total area). Although it was conceded that a plane having the form of the letter S (roughly) in cross section was the form having the greatest efficiency, as demonstrated by W. R. Turnbull of New Brunswick, we came to the conclusion that

---

*This engine is exhibited at the National Science Museum, Ottawa, Canada.

The *Silver Dart* in a test flight in 1908. It was the first airplane to fly in Canada. *Curtiss Collection*

if a rib was formed-up being of single curvature, it would take the form of the Turnbull curve when acted upon by the air pressure as the machine glided through the air, if the rear was unrestricted and flexible, but if the rib were moulded with the double curve form the air pressure would bend it up abnormally at the rear and hence produce a detrimental effect.

We, therefore, decided to make up our ribs for the *Silver Dart* (as A.E.A. No. 4 was afterwards named), having the single curvature form. The depth of the planes was reduced at the center from 6 ft. 6 inches to 6 ft., and the distance between the planes consequently reduced in the same ratio, (6 ft. 6 in. to 6 ft.).

We designed the ends of the supporting planes to have a depth of 4 ft. as in former cases, and also to be 4 ft. apart. This reproportioning gave the lateral curve of the back edges an evener form and the machine as a whole finer lines.

The fish-shaped material used all through is of heavier stock and hence capable of greater rigidity of structure.

Turnbuckles are used on each individual wire, so that they can be separately adjusted to receive their proper strain. Two special instruments were devised; one as a tool for constructing the turnbuckle and the other a wrench to facilitate the screwing up of these turnbuckles.

The sockets used to connect the struts to the lateral chords are in their simplest form, doing away with the jack joint used on the *June Bug*. The projecting spike at the end of the socket passes through the straps to which the guy wires are secured and then into the hole prepared in the socket connecting the sections of the lateral chords.

The tightening up of the turnbuckles of the guy wires prevents these spikes from coming out. A single wire passing through the middle of the struts and connected by a V wire to both the top and bottom chord at

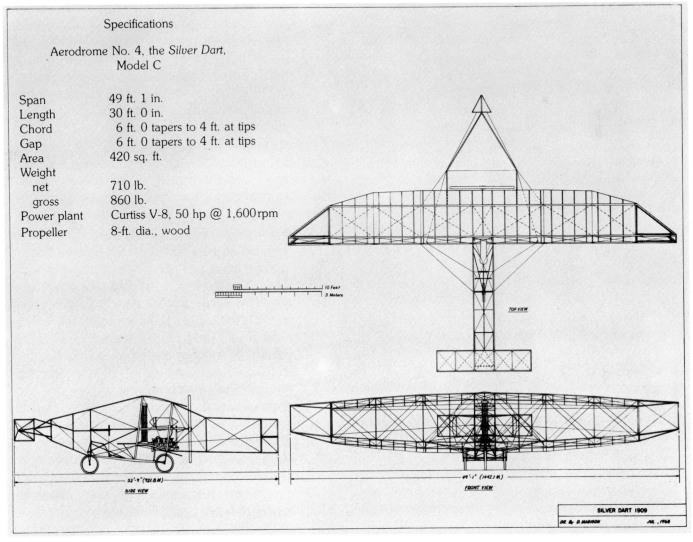

Specifications

Aerodrome No. 4, the *Silver Dart*,
            Model C

Span	49 ft. 1 in.
Length	30 ft. 0 in.
Chord	6 ft. 0 tapers to 4 ft. at tips
Gap	6 ft. 0 tapers to 4 ft. at tips
Area	420 sq. ft.
Weight	
net	710 lb.
gross	860 lb.
Power plant	Curtiss V-8, 50 hp @ 1,600 rpm
Propeller	8-ft. dia., wood

TOP VIEW

10 Feet
3 Meters

SIDE VIEW

FRONT VIEW

SILVER DART 1909

A close-up of the *Silver Dart* and J.A.D. McCurdy, pilot. *Wm. J. Hammer Collection*

This photo shows the low-mounted engine and the chain drive for the propeller. *Curtiss Collection*

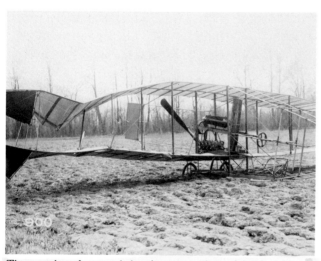

The results of a rough landing in a plowed field at Hammondsport. The frail landing gear suffered badly on this runway. *Curtiss Collection*

the lateral extremities of the machine seems to answer the purpose of steadying the struts better than two wires, as in former cases, and it also offers less head resistance.

The cloth used to cover the ribs, etc., forming the supporting surface is similar to that used by Capt. T. S. Baldwin for his Government balloons, although lighter in weight, (2 ounces per sq. yard) and having silk on only one side of the rubber coating. It forms a beautiful surface, rubber side down, and is easy to handle, and capable of being cemented, as ordinary rubber. The tip controls were covered by making the silk in the form of a triangular bag and drawing it on tightly over the frames thus making an equally clean surface on the top and bottom. As in the case of the *June Bug*, a steel tube rib is placed at the junction of each section and acts as a spreader for the lateral chords.

The central panel is made exceptionally strong for various reasons. The bending moments are greatest there and also as the dead load is located at that point the racking strains tell more there than elsewhere. This panel is made up first and is complete in itself. The four wings when placed in position fit into projecting sockets from each side of this panel, and are secured in place by the same method employed throughout the structure, viz. of attaching and tightening up the turnbuckles. Thus the four wings can be readily removed without disturbing the central panel, engine-bed, propeller or running gear.

The silk of the *Silver Dart* is made in sections corresponding to the panel where it is to be used, and laces to a steel rib at each end. Thus the whole machine, silk and all, is made in sections so as to facilitate repair work, should we be unfortunate enough to have an accident. The advantage of having the silk in sections in "knocking down" the machine is also apparent. The ribs slide into pockets prepared on the silk, from the rear passing under the back lateral chord and butting neatly against the back edge of the front chord and are secured in place by square tin caps, which slip over the rear end. These caps, one for each rib, are strung on a wire which passes through a seam in the rear of the silk and is secured at its ends to the lateral margin of the aeroplane, and to the central panel, being drawn taut by means of a turnbuckle. There are two of these wires to a plane, one for the port wing and one for the starboard.

The rudder used on the *Silver Dart* is of quite small dimensions (4 ft. high by 2 ft. deep) and is constructed, as far as the silk is concerned, similarly to the tip controls, i.e. covering made as a bag and drawn on over the framework and laced at the top. As both sides of the rudder act at different times, this method gives them even resistances. The rudder is placed 11 feet back from the rear lateral chord, and is supported simply by four hinged bamboos so constructed that by releasing two lateral guy wires the whole thing folds up flat against the rear of the planes. The rudder is operated by a small wire cable connected to the tiller of the front wheel. The bow control is double-decked, rigidly constructed throughout and placed 15 feet forward of the front lateral chord. It is operated similarly to that used in the *June Bug*, by a direct bamboo rod at the rear end of which is the steering wheel. Push the wheel forward, it depresses the machine; pull it back and the machine rises; turn it to port or starboard, and the machine obeys respectively, whether on the ground or in the air.

The front control measures 12 feet long by 28 inches wide and 30 inches between the planes. It is supported five inches back from its front edge by a bamboo cantilever truss.

The *Silver Dart* Curtiss engine as currently exhibited in the Museum of Science and Technology, Ottawa, Canada. *National Museums of Canada Aeronautical Collection*

It was our original intention to carry two persons in the *Silver Dart*, one sitting directly behind the other; hence a seat was designed for the purpose and made adjustable so that it could be slipped forward and backward readily in balancing up the machine. The second man would sit directly over the theoretical center of pressure at our traveling speed, so that the carrying of the passenger or leaving him behind would not affect the balance. The tips are controlled by a device which does not interfere with the man sitting behind the operator, and the device is also adjustable with the seat.

The pole connecting the steering wheel to the front control can be lengthened out or shortened in determining where the operator shall sit, by means of a telescopic tube which can be secured at any desired point.

The running gear or truck is almost the same as that used in the *June Bug*. There are improvements of construction and the material is heavier.

The engine used was especially built for the *Silver Dart* and is almost the same as that used in the *June Bug*. There are improvements of construction and the material is heavier.

The engine used was especially built for the *Silver Dart* and is a Curtiss eight cylinder water-cooled 50 H.P. motor, which weighs without water or oil, but including all water connections and counter-shaft 202 lbs. It is placed into its bed immediately on top of the lower rear lateral chord, and braced directly from the stringers of the truck. Its being placed so low will produce less strain of the structure in landing and will bring the center of gravity of the machine, as a whole, a little lower than in the case of the *June Bug*.

The radiator is designed somewhat after that used by the Wright Brothers, and the gasoline and oil tank (one tank having a partition) holds 10 and 2 gallons, respectively.

The propellers used are of different designs and are driven by a chain drive in the ratio of 1½ to 1 (engine turning 1500 revolutions and the propeller turning 1000). One propeller is used, and the thrust comes about through the line of resistance of the machine, but inclined above the horizontal 3¼ degrees. These are made of laminated wood and weigh, including the two clamps, 8¼ lbs; of 8 ft. diameter and 17 to 18 degrees pitch at the tip.

The supporting surfaces of the machine are given an angle of attack of 9¼ degrees at their lateral margins. This angle is excessive for economical flights, but it facilitates rising from the ground. After the machine is in the air, the angle will be reduced to perhaps 6 degrees.

It is for this reason that the propeller thrust is a little above the horizontal when the machine is on the ground. The proper angle at which to place the counter-shaft for propeller can only be determined by actual experiment.

The actual work of construction of the *Silver Dart* was under the supervision of our foreman, Mr. Kenneth Ingraham and too much cannot be said in his praise for the care taken by him in the detail work and in generally rushing the assembling to a successful finish.

All the structural members of the *Silver Dart*, fish struts, wires, tubing, bamboo, etc., were carefully measured and in accordance with the method and co-efficients used by Mr. Octave Chanute. The head resistance of the machine was computed and reduced to its equivalent flat surface in square feet. All figures in square inches.

Hence the total head resistance, 2188.47 sq. inches, or 15.19 sq. ft.

DATA

Total area of supporting
  surfaces . . . . .420 sq. ft.
Weight of machine, exclusive
  of engine and accessories . .345 lb.
Weight of engine, propeller
  and countershaft, etc. . . . . .210 lb.
Weight of radiator . . . . 15 lb.
Weight of water . . . . 30 lb.
Weight of gasoline, oil and tank,
  full .110 lb.
Weight of man, say . . . . .150 lb.
      TOTAL . . . . .860 lb.

The name *Silver Dart* was relatively simple and explained to Mrs. Bell by McCurdy in the following manner:

. . . the surfaces are silvered on one side, that suggested the ''Silver,'' and the word ''Dart'' will explain itself.

The *Silver Dart* was the best engineered and the best constructed of all the aircraft built during the existence of the Aerial Experiment Association. After its completion at Hammondsport it was flown briefly on December 6, 1908. The flight was terminated as a result of water in the gas tank. Three days later, on December 9, another flight was made; this time a combination of circumstances resulted in the destruction of the landing gear. On December 14, McCurdy made four short flights, during which time it was possible for him to determine that the balance of the aircraft and the control responses were what he had expected.

Dr. Bell stopped off at Hammondsport on his way from Washington, D.C. to Baddeck on December 20 and 21 to see the *Silver Dart* and the *Loon*. While he was there, McCurdy attempted to demonstrate the capabilities of the *Silver Dart* several times, but his efforts were thwarted due to the unpredictable weather at that time of the year. After Dr. Bell departed, the *Silver Dart* was crated and shipped, on January 6, to Baddeck, where further tests were to be undertaken. The crated aircraft arrived at Beinn Bhreagh on February 6, and the engine arrived five days later. As the new engine, the Curtiss No. 3, had been built primarily for the propulsion of the *Cygnet II*, the second of Dr. Bell's tetrahedrals, it was initially put in that machine, but, following a series of experiments and an accident on February 20, the engine was transferred to the *Silver Dart*.

In AEA *Bulletin* No. 34, dated February 23, 1909, there is an article describing the first trial of the *Silver Dart*:

The Curtiss engine was transferred from the *Cygnet II* yesterday to the *Silver Dart*, and this morning propeller experiments were made on the ice-boat machine to test which of the propellers we have would be most suitable for the experiment. The propeller 7 feet 8 inches in diameter was chosen which had been used upon the *Silver Dart* in Hammondsport.

In the afternoon the *Silver Dart* was taken out on the ice of Baddeck Bay; and a large concourse of people from Baddeck were present.

The congregation of people and teams upon the ice yesterday near the *Cygnet II* had shown the advisability of policing the crowd and keeping them scattered, and at a distance from the machine. Mr. Charles R. Cox, Mr. P. L. McFarlan, Fred McLennan, and Mr. John Arsenault were provided with the following notice, which they displayed to visitors wherever necessary.

NOTICE

In order to avoid the possibility of any accident visitors are requested to keep at a distance from the flying-machine *Silver Dart*, and not congregate together on the ice. They should remain behind the machine, or well off to one side, and leave a clear field for the Laboratory Assistants. They should not on any account place themselves in the path of the machine in front. It would be dangerous to be struck by it.

Alexander Graham Bell
Chairman, Aerial Experiment Assoc.

This served its purpose, and the visitors kept well scattered. McCurdy's account of the flight is as follows:

The morning of to-day (Feb. 23) was spent getting the *Silver Dart* ready for a trial flight. The transmission was changed from the four V-belt drive to a single chain drive which, it was anticipated, would not only give greater efficiency but would be of less weight. The gearing used was 18–24 (or 3–4), the engine turning over 24 revolutions to the propeller's 18 revolutions.

We had three propellers; and to decide which one was to be used a series of tests was made on the ice-boat, although the ice-boat was not allowed to advance during any of the tests.

The propeller finally decided upon was one having a diameter of seven feet 6 inches, and a pitch at the tip of 20°–22°. This propeller was *not* one of constant pitch speed.

The *Silver Dart* was finally taken across the Bay on the ice, and a start made at a spot just off Fraser's Pond.

In the first trial a gasoline pump broke after the machine had traveled about 100 ft.

Upon fixing this a second start was made which was very successful. The machine rose from the ice after traveling about 100 ft.; and flew at an elevation of about ten–thirty feet directly east for a distance of about half a mile. Landed without any jar whatsoever. The speed I should judge to be about 40+ miles per hour. The machine was operated by J.A.D. McCurdy.

McC.

Of the second flight of the *Silver Dart*, February 24, 1909, McCurdy had this to say:

The second flight of a flying-machine in Canada took place this morning (Feb. 24) at Baddeck, when the A.E.A. Drome No. 4, McCurdy's *Silver Dart*, flew a distance of 4½ miles.

Started off Fraser's Pond, and headed up the Bay towards the Log Cabin. The turn to port was started there, making the circle as large as possible. Ran down Beinn Bhreagh shore crossed the sand beach at the plaster dump, and attempted to turn again to port just off William Taylors. The space was however found to be too small in which to completely negotiate the turn, and so a landing was attempted.

The machine, however, struck her starboard wing on the ice, and spinning round smashed a few struts and chords. One wheel also was broken.

Curtiss No. 3 engine worked beautifully, not a skip all through the flight. The balance was about perfect, all the controls worked well.

The power developed was sufficient not only to drive the machine against a 5–6 mile wind, but also with it. The feel of the machine was the same both with and against the wind.

McC.

In these two straightforward statements we have, in the words of the designer-pilot, the description of the first successful flights of a heavier-than-air craft in Canada.

Aerodrome No. 5
Dr. Bell's *Cygnet II*

This aircraft never did attain the success that the aging scientist had hoped for. To be rather charitable in description, it was a very ungainly aircraft. The mass of small triangular surfaces that composed the tetrahedral design makes one wonder why anyone should have hoped to get it airborne. To put it in very common terms, the Aerodrome No. 5, *Cygnet II*, had a built-in headwind. Even the best engine of that time could not possibly have coaxed the machine into the air.

Dr. Bell's *Cygnet II* was tested on at least two occasions, February 22 and 24, 1909. In an account of the first test, given in *Bulletin* No. 34, March 1, 1909, Dr. Bell relates the following:

We have waited long for the arrival of the new Curtiss engine to try an experiment

with the Drome #5, Bell's *Cygnet II*. At last it came and was duly installed last Friday (February 19); but the smooth slippery ice upon which we depended had disappeared under about a foot of snow, so that the outlook for the successful experiment was disappointing.

We were considering plans for clearing off a track when a rain-storm on Saturday (Feb. 20) saved us the trouble. Heavy rain and comparatively high temperature began to melt the snow. On Sunday evening (Feb. 21) the rain was succeeded by frost; so that to-day (Feb. 22) ideal conditions were present for an experiment: Glassy ice, no wind, and a beautiful sunshiny day.

We therefore determined to make an experiment without waiting to test the ten-foot

A close-up of Dr. Bell's *Cygnet II*, Aerodrome No. 5, showing the tetrahedral design.

propeller that had been prepared, and ascertain the proper propeller gearing for the engine. The inevitable fussing over minor details that always occurs at the last moment took up the whole forenoon, so that it was afternoon before all was ready. The results are recorded among the experiments noted in this *Bulletin*.

It was hardly expected, on account of the great weight of the machine (over 900 lbs), that it would rise from the ice, and in this we were not disappointed! It was obvious however that the engine was overloaded with the ten-foot propeller at a gear ratio of 1–2 so that it did not give us its full power.

A.G.B.

The second trial of the *Cygnet II* was recorded on February 24, 1909, as follows:

Unwilling to lose the opportunity of the ideal weather conditions prevailing to-day we transferred the engine and propeller from the damaged *Silver Dart* to *Cygnet II* without awaiting the completion of the new nine-foot propeller being made for her. Tried her on the ice just at dusk.

It was quite evident that the Aerodrome No. 5, the *Cygnet II*, was never destined to fly. It is certain that the aged Dr. Bell was very disappointed with the inability of the aircraft. Perhaps in deference to him, the younger members, particularly J.A.D. McCurdy, continued with the experiments that were so dear to Dr. Bell's heart. It was not until well after the dissolution of the AEA that a short item in *Aeronautics* of April 1912 appeared:

Dr. A. Graham Bell has now the satisfaction of proving his statements in regard to his tetrahedral kite, ''Cygnet'' III and ''showing'' the skeptics. J.A.D. McCurdy made a number of straightaway flights with it over the ice of Lake Bras d'Or in Nova Scotia, on March 1st to 17th [1912].

The kite consists of 360 cells and weighs 540 lbs., with 70 h.p. Gnome engine, without operator. It flew at about 43 miles an hour with an 8 by 8 foot propeller turning 1200, giving a thrust on the ground of 500 lbs. Another trial was made of adding 262 cells, which, however, did not make it fly so well. The kite spreads 8 m. at the top and 6 m. at the bottom. The kite is triangu-

A front quarter view of the *Cygnet II*. The dated signboard shows Feb. 22, 1909. Note the vest-pocket camera in the right foreground, probably belonging to H. M. Benner, the ''official'' photographer of Curtiss aircraft.

The *Cygnet III* showing the much modified final form in which J.A.D. McCurdy succeeded in getting the tetrahedral configuration airborne ''to show the skeptics.'' Several straightaway flights were made between March 1 and 17, 1912, at Lake Bras d'Or, Nova Scotia. Powered by a 70-horsepower Gnome rotary engine, it attained a speed of 43 miles per hour. The aircraft was reduced to 360 triangular cells, which measured 8 meters in span, with a 2-meter chord. (Adapted from an item in *Aeronautics*, April 1912.)

lar in fore and aft cross-section by 2 m. fore and aft. Mr. McCurdy's weight is 160 lbs.

From examination of the photograph it is evident that much has been done to modify the structure, though the tetrahedral principle is still the basis of the design.

Specifications	
Aerodrome No. 5, Dr. Bell's *Cygnet II*	
Span	8 m upper; 6 m lower
Length	unknown
Chord	2 m
Gap	unknown
Engine	4 cyl.
Weight	
net	800 lb. est
gross	950 lb. est

End of the AEA

As the end of 1908 approached, it became more imperative that some decisions be made regarding the future of the Association. It is evident, from the substantial records compiled in the *Bulletins* of this period, that Dr. Bell wished to lay before the group the alternatives available to the Association. It is also evident that the approach of the end of the year had not brought the tetrahedral aircraft to a successful maturity. Dr. Bell was desirous of extending the term of the Association in the hope that by some means the *Cygnet II* would be demonstrated as an equally successful aircraft.

In his communiqués in the AEA *Bulletins*, Dr. Bell speculated at length about the means by which the Association might be continued or its format altered to include a larger number of persons. One of the foremost requirements for the Association under either circumstance was additional financing. It will be recalled that all operations to date had been financed through the generosity of Mrs. Bell. The tenor of the discussions was further depressed by the tragic death of Lt. Thomas E. Selfridge while flying with Orville Wright in the Wright machine at Fort Myer on September 17, 1908, when he became the first man to die as a result of an airplane crash. When the formal meeting was held at Beinn Bhreagh on September 26, 1908, Edward R. Selfridge, father of Lieutenant Selfridge, attended the meeting in his son's stead. Because unanimous consent was required in the actions of the Association, Dr. Bell presented a very comprehensive history of the Aerial Experiment Association for Mr. Selfridge; the content of this presentation is recorded in the *Bulletins* of the Association.

Dr. Bell, with his prior knowledge of the intricacies of patent work, proceeded, at his own expense, to apply for any patents that the Association might expect as a result of their work at Hammondsport. In his presentation for the patent attorney's examination, Dr. Bell prepared a very learned discussion, the conclusion of which indicated his own feeling that the AEA inventions did not in any way conflict with the Wright brothers' patent.

On January 29, 1909, all the associates arrived at Beinn Bhreagh during which time they held a detailed discussion of the patent application. Following this meeting an amended draft was agreed upon and the papers were prepared by attorneys.

During the discussions held at this time, perhaps the foremost subject was that of additional funding. Curtiss expressed his view that if properly handled the business of exhibitions might be a profitable means, since several substantial prizes had been offered in America and abroad. These prizes seemed within the realm of possibility, though the odds were quite high against winning. It was also during this meeting that Mrs. Bell undertook to provide additional funds up to the amount of $10,000 to extend the term of the Association to March 31, 1909.

With the death of Lieutenant Selfridge, McCurdy was elected secretary, and Charles J. Bell—a cousin of Dr. Bell, and president of the American Security and Trust Company—was appointed trustee of the Association.

At the end of February 1909, Curtiss went to New York, where he discussed a number of interesting facets of the aviation business. Among these was the entry of the AEA for the 1909 Scientific American Trophy. He found that their entry had been accepted, but learned also that the club had changed the rules of the contest and he was unable to learn what the new rules were. Perhaps carried away by the enthusiasm shown by the Aero Club, and possibly due to the dying pains of the AEA, Curtiss undertook to build for the Aeronautic Society of New York a machine that would fly and for which they were prepared to pay $5,000, which also included the instruction of two members selected by the Club. In reading through the *Bulletins*, one is brought up short by Curtiss's occasional mention of a friend in Rochester, who, it turns out, was Augustus M. Herring. Whatever the motivation or the circumstances, it is a matter of record that Curtiss and Herring formed a partnership, signing the papers on March 27, 1909, creating the Herring-Curtiss Company of Hammondsport.*

The company assets consisted of Herring patents. Herring had worked with Octave Chanute and claimed that he held patents predating the Wrights'. If these patents were granted, it would be most impressive in view of the Wright preeminence in the patent field at that time.

For his part, Curtiss put his entire company into this consolidation, and the financial interests were handled by Cortlandt Field Bishop, then president of the Aero Club of America.

There followed a period of very hazy, possibly strained relationships between Curtiss and the AEA regarding this company formation and its effect upon AEA and, finally, the disposition of whatever AEA assets existed.

On November 10, Baldwin and McCurdy executed assignments of their patent applications to C. J. Bell, as trustee of the Aerial Experiment Association, with the understanding that Dr. Alexander Graham Bell be reimbursed for his expenses in obtaining the patents upon the sale of the patent. With the defection of Curtiss from the ranks of the AEA, any thoughts of continuing the projects, past or future, came to an end. The Association, by virtue of its time limitation, terminated its affairs on March 31, 1909.

The Herring-Curtiss difficulties came to a head in 1910 and the company went into bankruptcy. On April 6, 1910, it was placed in the hands of receivers.

On December 19, 1911, Curtiss reorganized under the name of the Curtiss Motor Company. The Curtiss Motor Company controlled the Curtiss Aeroplane Company, manufacturer of aircraft and engines, and the Curtiss Exhibition Company, under the direction of Jerome Fanciulli, which managed a number of the most prominent aviators; and was also the sales agent and foreign representative for the aeroplane company.

---

*The certificate of incorporation of the Herring-Curtiss Company is dated February 19, 1909, at Hammondsport. The company was dissolved by proclamation of the governor, March 10, 1926.

The Curtiss No. 1
(Herring-Curtiss No. 1)
Aeronautic Society of New York Machine, the *Golden Flier* (Model D)

The Aeronautic Society had been founded in the city of New York in July 1908 by a group of gentlemen who were interested in aviation, many of them aspiring to become pilots. They were, for the most part, the younger, more dynamic group who split off from the Aero Club of New York. The Aeronautic Society members were primarily interested in heavier-than-air craft and flights. The Aero Club members preferred balloons and airships.

The principal activities of the Aeronautic Society had been to provide construction facilities and to purchase a few (possibly two) engines, which were made available on a rotation basis to the members for use in testing their own designs of aircraft. These aircraft were built at the Morris Park racetrack and most fell short of the expectations of their builders. At one of their regular meetings it was finally proposed by one of their members that they purchase a machine for the club and arrange for flight instruction. It was not long after this that Curtiss was approached and, following several conversations on the subject, an order was placed for the construction of an aeroplane by Curtiss for the use of the Society.

With receipt of the order from the Aeronautic Society, Curtiss began the manufacture of a machine and, in accordance with the terms of the contract, the aircraft was delivered at the Morris Park racetrack in the Bronx, New York City, on May 29, 1909, one week late. Under the auspices of the Society, he made the first airplane flight in New York City. The Morris Park racetrack was too small for the instruction of students, so Hempstead Plains, a large, level piece of land near Mineola, Long Island, was finally chosen as headquarters for the Society. Those interested in aeronautics met there frequently. The new field proved to be an ideal one, with an almost complete absence of trees. It was level, well-drained, lacked smokestacks and other obstacles, and provided a long open sweep with plenty of room for maneuvering.

The delivery date of the machine had been scheduled to coincide with a planned exhibition sponsored by the Aeronautic Society. Delays in completing the aircraft made it necessary to postpone the delivery date and caused considerable speculation as to whether or not it would be delivered at all. The delivery had originally been scheduled for May 22, 1909, but it was necessary to grant an extension of another week, to

A rear quarter view of the Aeronautic Society *Golden Flier*, the Curtiss No. 1 machine. First airplane contracted for and sold by Curtiss. Note the fixed rear horizontal stabilizer, notched ailerons hinged to the forward interplane struts and wing extensions beyond the outboard interplane struts. *Curtiss photo*

May 29. When Curtiss did arrive he brought a beautiful and perfect machine, but he did no flying at the meet. The machine created a sensation among the inexpert, and the knowledgeable experts congratulated the Society and acclaimed the machine to be the finest one that had ever been produced. Although the delay meant a great loss to the Society, its primary desire was to do anything it could to help Curtiss, as he was entirely dependent upon the machine for any practice he could get to enable him to take part in the forthcoming contest at Rheims. The Rheims meet was the first international aviation meet. It was held from August 22 to 29, 1909, at Rheims, France. Curtiss was selected by the Aero Club of America to be the sole American participant. By this means, and through the courtesy of the Society, he was able to continue his practicing at Mineola the very morning he sailed for Europe. Until he had obtained the order to build the machine for the Society, Curtiss had never been able to stay in the air for any length of time because the air-cooled engines he had previously used would not maintain their power. It was at Mineola, in the *Golden Flier*, that Curtiss really learned to fly for extended periods. During this time he acquired the skill that allowed him to compete with the foremost aviators of Europe and win one of the greatest trophies. This made America the host country for the next international meet.

The often quoted comment about the "power of the press" is nowhere better illustrated than in the case of the Curtiss No. 1 machine of 1909. This machine is variously recorded as the Aeronautic Society (of New York) machine, the *Golden Flier* or the *Gold Bug*.

Of the three names, the first two could be considered correct. The term "Gold Bug" was recorded briefly in the press and has forevermore been repeated by subsequent writers and historians. It is the result of a reporter coupling the "Golden" part of *Golden Flier* with a reference to the *June Bug* of Scientific American Trophy fame, resulting in a much repeated but erroneous name for this machine.

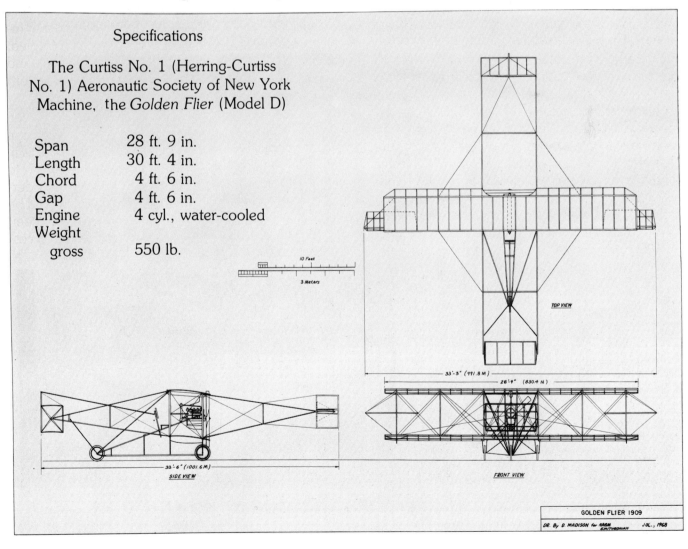

Specifications

The Curtiss No. 1 (Herring-Curtiss No. 1) Aeronautic Society of New York Machine, the *Golden Flier* (Model D)

Span	28 ft. 9 in.
Length	30 ft. 4 in.
Chord	4 ft. 6 in.
Gap	4 ft. 6 in.
Engine	4 cyl., water-cooled
Weight gross	550 lb.

TOP VIEW

SIDE VIEW

FRONT VIEW

GOLDEN FLIER 1909

In a telegram to Curtiss from Baddeck, Nova Scotia, dated March 6, 1909, Bell requests:

Please write fully concerning your arrangement with Herring and how it affects your relations with the Aerial Experiment Association.

Curtiss replied to Bell on March 6:

Proposed Herring arrangement will not affect Association's plans. Letter to you today.

The first hint of the details of the Aeronautical Society machine appeared in a letter dated March 5, 1909, contained in the *Bulletins* of the Aerial Experiment Association No. 37, page 46. Curtiss mentions:

I found Mr. Herring quite anxious to close up the deal with me, and I finally made him an offer, a little bit better than his original proposition, which was verbally accepted . . . The announcement was made at the Aero Club Wednesday evening of this con-

solidation. Mr. Bishop (Cortlandt Field Bishop) represented the moneyed interests . . .

In the letter is the statement that:

Mr. Herring showed me a great deal, and I would not be at all surprised if his patents, backed by a strong company, would pretty well control the use of the gyroscope in obtaining automatic equilibrium. This seems to be about the only road to success in securing automatic stability in an aeroplane.

If the deal goes through I will be manager of the Company and everything will go on just as it has, except that we will have Mr. Herring's devices on the machines which we may build, which, by the way, recalls the fact that I accepted an order from the Aeronautical Society for an aeroplane to be delivered in the Spring at Morris Park, N.Y. I did this on my own responsibility with the idea that if the consolidation was made with Herring it would be turned over to the new company, or if a commercial organization

Charles F. Willard, pilot, seated in the *Golden Flier* at the Domingues Field meet in Los Angeles, 1910. *Willard Collection*

The Curtiss engine installation in the Aeronautic Society *Golden Flier. Curtiss Collection*

The *Golden Flier* takes off at Hammondsport, 1909. *Curtiss Collection by H. M. Benner*

Letterhead of the Aeronautic Exhibition Company, founded by the Aeronautic Society to promote aviation. *Original courtesy Charles Forster Willard*

succeeded the Experiment Association the order would be turned over to them. If neither of these materialized, the Curtiss Co. would endeavor to fill the order itself.

Later, in a summary titled "The Outlook on Aviation" by F. W. Baldwin, contained in No. 38, page 51, of the AEA *Bulletins*, Baldwin makes note of the fact that:

The final papers of the Herring-Curtiss

Syndicate have been signed (March 27, 1909) and it is understood that the new concern will take charge of the Curtiss works immediately.

The machine which Curtiss will deliver and exhibit before the Aeronautic Society in May is described in *Aeronautics* as having a spread of twenty feet with a depth of four feet. The supporting surfaces will be parallel and spaced five feet apart. The vertical rudder will be placed in the rear and there will be a horizontal rudder both in front and rear. A new and partly automatic device for maintaining equilibrium will be employed consisting of moveable surfaces between the supporting frame. The surfaces will be made of the same rubber silk which is used on the *Silver Dart*.

An automatic steering wheel will be used on which is located a spark advance and a throttle. Pushing back and forth on the wheel raises or lowers the horizontal control.

The engine will be a 25 H.P. four-cylinder motor driving direct a 6 ft. laminated wood propeller of new design, pitch equal diameter, at 1200 revolutions per minute. The engine has double valves in the head and a single push valve.

In *Bulletin* No. 1, "An Epitome of the Work of the Aeronautic Society from July, 1908, to December, 1909," page 19, there appeared a curious comment as follows:

On Jan. 21st, 1909, a contract was made with Curtiss, and $500 was given to him on signing the contract; and he was to have a total of $5,000. At Curtiss' request, the existence of this contract was to be kept secret until he had severed his connection with Dr. Alexander Graham Bell's Aerial Experiment Association the first week in March.

In the matter of that request the Society kept its part of the promise absolutely. But, as with the invitation to Delagrange, the fact leaked out. The result was as before. The force in opposition to the Society arose, and did its utmost to deprive the Society of the credit of its enterprise.

The disclosure of the arrangement between Curtiss and the Aeronautic Society is balanced

Drive an Aeroplane

¶ The operating of an aeroplane, readily handled by the amateur, is now an assured fact.

¶ In the number of aeroplanes already purchased Europe is far in advance of America. This was likewise true with the introduction of the automobile.

¶ Our Paris correspondent writes us that hundreds of aeroplanes have been sold to private individuals in Europe. One manufacturer, alone, has sold 112—many of the early deliveries at large premiums.

¶ A substantial interest has also begun to arouse Americans. A great wave of enthusiasm has set in, and, although more different makes of heavier-than-air machines are to be had abroad, to America belongs the distinction of producing the lightest, speediest, and most practical aeroplane yet designed.

The Herring=Curtiss Aeroplane

amply demonstrated its supremacy at the recent Rheims international meet by winning the coveted International Cup, which brings to America next year the big world's contest.

¶ We invite those interested to favor us with a call. Americans desiring to enter the international contest next year should order machines early to secure prompt delivery, so as to be ready for the different events.

¶ A special inducement will be made to those ordering now for delivery after Jan. 1st, 1910.

Every HERRING-CURTISS AEROPLANE is demonstrated in flight before delivery to the purchaser.

Call or write to Aeronautical Department,

Wyckoff, Church & Partridge

1743 Broadway, at 56th St., New York City

A copy of the original advertisement placed in *Life* magazine, November 18, 1909, by the sales agency Wyckoff, Church & Partridge.

by the fact that a number of historical firsts were in the making. The *Bulletin* continued:

There can be no question that this step by the Society, viewed even in its simplest form, as a business transaction only, was an historic and most interesting event. This commission constituted the first purchase of an aeroplane ever made by an aeronautical society. It was the first commercial transaction of the sort ever made in America. The machine to be so built would be the first flying machine ever made to order and for sale in this country. It was probably the first time in the history of the world that money had been advanced upon the order for a flying machine just as in any ordinary business proposition. It was in fact the actual beginning of the aeroplane industry in the United States. It was further noteworthy that, while it started this industry in the Empire State, it was New York men who took the lead, and it would bring the first machine of the new industry to the Metropolis. The circumstance was certainly one of quite unusual interest, and it is appropriate that the names of the men who contributed to the purchase of this historic aeroplane should be recorded in this record of the Society's achievements. The list is as follows:

Lee S. Burridge, Herbert C. Smyth, William J. Hammer, C. W. Howell, Jr., Frank O. Burridge, E. T. Tandy, R. E. Sabin, C. W. Howell, Frank G. Smyth, Jr., E. W. Cameron, C. F. Blackmore, James M. Fisher, Carlos de Zafra, Thomas A. Hill, E. T. Birdsall, Fred A. Scheffler, O. A. Danielson, J. P. Stoltz, E. L. Jones, Michael A. Whalen, George Bold, Albert Huth, Wm. A. Kelley, Dr. S. B. Battey.

In a letter to the author, dated January 13, 1968, Charles Forster Willard, the pilot selected by the Aeronautic Society to fly the *Golden Flier*, noted that the machine was christened the *Golden Flier* in the presence of a lot of people.

The name resulted from the golden yellow silk surfaces and the orange shellac coating on the wood and bamboo.

He also noted that following the Rheims race:

Curtiss brought the Rheims machine to

Los Angeles for the meet Jan. 1910* and also a second machine in general like *Golden Flier* with a larger engine . . .

Curtiss had agreed to teach two members of the Society to fly. The two selected by the Society were Charles F. Willard and Alexander Williams. On July 18, 1909, after a toss of a coin to determine who would make the first flight, Williams got in and the plane was released. He pulled back on the elevator control and froze. The plane took off, climbed and slipped over to the right, landing on the right wingtip and front control. The front control surface struck the ground first and caused the airplane to turn over with the engine still running. Williams was rushed to the Mineola hospital with a fractured left arm and thumb. After he regained consciousness, he decided that flying was not for him. There were no spare parts with which to repair the *Golden Flier* and Curtiss was busy with the construction of his Rheims machine, which had first call on parts. In the meantime, Willard went to Coney Island each evening and tried all the rides. Speed was a common sensation to Willard, a racing driver, but he wanted to experience movement in the air. The experience paid off. The rest of his "training" consisted of sitting in the damaged machine, with his eyes closed, and working the controls. It was not until Tuesday, August 3, that the plane was repaired, at which time Curtiss made several short flights. The following morning it was planned that Willard would take his lesson and, on Thursday, Curtiss would sail for Europe to participate in the Rheims race. Curtiss instructed Willard: "Don't go too high, just up and land; and for God's sake, don't break it up again, it is not all paid for."

Willard made four short flights on August 7, and five more on the eighth. On the ninth, he continued trials, spending most of his time in practicing turns and landings. Following this, Willard made a series of flights and did, in fact, teach himself to fly the Aeronautic Society machine, the *Golden Flier.* He had proven to be a very apt pupil.

On the final payment of the $5,000 for the *Golden Flier,* Curtiss formally handed over the machine at Mineola before sailing for Europe. Curtiss had, in fact, shrewdly delayed the formal transfer in order to practice in the machine as long as possible before his departure.

---

*First aviation meet held in the United States, Domingues Field, Los Angeles, January 10–20, 1910.

Following the official hand-over, Willard made a sensational cross-country flight, but while he was at considerable height in the air, the camshaft of the engine broke, forcing him to land. Later, at Toronto, he flew above Lake Ontario, becoming the first aviator in this country to fly over a large body of water. Three times Willard received thorough duckings. At Cincinnati, November 12–14, 1909, he flew in a contest against Curtiss and beat him, winning trophies for both speed and altitude.

It should also be noted that during his trial flights over Mineola, Curtiss established some preliminary records, eventually remaining in the air for 31 minutes.

On July 17, Curtiss made official flights for the Scientific American Trophy and the President's Prize of the Aero Club of America.

The first try was for the President's Prize. The distance flown in competition was 1.35 miles, which was covered in 2 minutes 32 seconds. After making the first circuit, Curtiss started out again and made nineteen more rounds of the course, covering a total official distance of 25.002 miles in an official lapsed time of 52 minutes 30 seconds. The official average speed was 28.68 miles per hour and the average height was 20 feet, with a maximum of 40 feet. The Scientific American Trophy was offered to the aviator who made the greatest distance during the year 1909, covering a minimum of 25 kilometers.

To the observer, certain features of the *Golden Flier* stand out for ease of identification. The first and most apparent detail is the relatively long moment arm of the fore and aft horizontal surfaces. This is followed in prominence by the biplane forward elevator, which had a triangular-shaped vertical stabilizer surface reaching a point about 12 inches above the upper surface, at which point it is connected by a bamboo pole back to the steering column to provide the necessary leverage for pitch control. The single horizontal rear stabilizer was rigidly fixed to the frame. The rudder, at the rear, was a relatively small rectangular surface, but because it was in the propeller blast, was a powerful control.

The 4-cylinder upright engine provides another distinctive identification point on this airplane, as does the tapered portion at the outboard extremities of the wings.

Perhaps the most positive identification of this machine is the hinging of the ailerons to the midpoint of each of the forward outboard in-terplane struts; and the ailerons themselves having a tapered form in the plan view, the widest portion at the front, with a cutout to clear the bracing wires at the rear-center of the ailerons. All models that followed had the ailerons hinged to the outboard rear interplane struts.

Not so readily apparent was the single-fabric surface of the wings and the fixed rear horizontal surface. The ailerons, rudder and front elevator were all double-surfaced (fabric on both sides, upper and lower, of frames).

Several features unique to this machine included direct control of the engine. A small pedal operated by the left foot closed the throttle, which is normally wide open. The pedal on the right, which operated the brake on the front wheel, also short-circuited the magneto and stopped the engine as the landing was made. This was a single-place airplane.

The single-surface fabric was stretched as tightly as possible and its rigidity was improved by the use of spruce and ash ribs. These ribs were enclosed in pockets sewn to the upper side of the fabric. The ribs extended beyond the rear spar to form a trailing edge through which a wire was run for bracing and tension purposes.

The fore and aft outrigger frames extended 10 feet 6 inches from the edges of the main wings. The ailerons, hinged as they were, on the forward outboard plane struts, had marginal control response in the roll axis or lateral direction. The mounting of these ailerons in this manner tended to throttle the gap between the wings and thereby interfere with the lift efficiency of the wings, at the same time restricting the efficiency of the ailerons and causing a noticeable increase in head resistance (drag). Because of this, the portion of the ailerons on the *Golden Flier* extending beyond the outboard tips of the wings probably provided the only effective lateral control.

Directional control (yaw) was accomplished by turning the wheel left or right, moving the small but powerful double-surfaced rudder. Ascent and descent (pitch control) was accomplished by fore-and-aft movement of the control column. Roll of the machine was accomplished by leaning to one side or the other, thereby operating the ailerons through the shoulder yoke system. The shoulder yoke consisted of shoulder-high "arms" that were free to shift from side to side as the pilot leaned right or left. These arms were linked to the interplane ailerons to produce a banked condition of the aircraft or to recover from a banked position. The wheel control in front of the pilot controlled the vertical rudder. Using the two controls together, the pilot could produce a coordinated turn or recover from a turn. A further refinement in the interest of safety consisted of a strap attached to each seat arm at the forward part, passing over the front of the aviator's shoulder, around the back of his neck and forward of his other shoulder to a fixed point on the opposite seat arm. This made an effective "seat belt," restraining the pilot in rough air or violent maneuvers, which became a standard part of the exhibition pilot's repertoire. This shoulder yoke was one of the characteristic features of the Curtiss method of control.

Specifications of the aircraft were as follows: The wings had a 28-foot 9-inch span with a 4-foot 6-inch chord and a 4-foot 6-inch gap. The spars were made of eastern silver spruce. The wings were covered with yellow Baldwin rubber silk consisting of two sheets of very thin silk fabric with rubber cement pressed between. This, plus the orange shellac on the bamboo outriggers, accounted for the name Golden Flier. The wing area was 258 square feet. There were twenty-two ribs constructed of steam-bent spruce and laminated ash that were spaced 15 inches apart. The angle of incidence measured 4 degrees 14 minutes with the aircraft in a ground position. The front controls were also a biplane structure, 2 feet by 6 feet, the total area being 24 square feet. They were pivoted 10 inches back from the leading edge of the control. The rear controls consisted of a single horizontal and a single vertical surface. The horizontal surface was 2 feet 3 inches by 6 feet and the vertical rudder was 2 feet by 3 feet 4 inches. The horizontal rudder was pivoted 8 inches back from its leading edge. The balanced ailerons were mounted between the wing panels attached to the forward interplane struts. They measured 6 feet wide at the front and 5 feet 5 inches wide at the rear; the front to rear dimension was 2 feet.

The structure of the aircraft was primarily of clear Oregon spruce, with bamboo outriggers fore and aft. Total weight was 550 pounds.

The engine was a 4-cylinder vertical (upright) water-cooled engine with a bore of 3¾ inches and a stroke of 4 inches. The cylinders were of cast iron with welded copper jackets. Lubrication was by a force-feed system. The pump was a separate unit. The oil was in a tin container under the engine and was delivered to the engine through a tube. A larger tube returned the excess oil back to the oil tank. The crankcase was of aluminum alloy Macadamite and the crankshaft was of vanadium steel. The pistons and connecting rods were of aluminum alloy Macadamite. Both valves were in the head and actuated by a single pushrod and cam. The weight of the engine, including oil and water pumps, was 85 pounds. Ignition was by a Bosch magneto, which weighed 12½ pounds; the power developed was 22 horsepower, though it is generally rated at 25 horsepower at 1,300 rpm with the maximum speed of 1,800 to 2,000.*

Weight of the complete power plant, which consisted of the motor, the radiator, magneto, oil and water pumps, was about 192 pounds. The thrust line of the propeller was about on the line drawn between the pivot point of the front elevator and that of the rear elevator; it was about 2 feet 3 inches above the rear spar of the lower wing. The propeller was 6 feet in diameter and 7 inches wide at its extremity and 4 inches at the center. The structure was primarily silver spruce; engine beams were laminated ash and spruce and the main brace from the rear of the engine bed to the front wheel was ash.

In a letter to the author in March 1968, Charles F. Willard notes that after the flights at Mineola, Long Island, he took the Golden Flier on the road to demonstrate it to the public. The first exhibition was at Athens, Pennsylvania; then Richmond, Virginia; and Toronto, Canada, where he twice alighted in the water. These were followed by an exhibition at Letonia, Kentucky, and on to Los Angeles's Domingues Field for an aeronautical meet on January 10–20, 1910. While at Los Angeles, the airplane was sold to a carnival for a static tent exhibition.

One possible reason for confusion regarding the machine is the fact that after its sale several near copies were made and put out on exhibition in late 1910. It is recorded in the December 1909 issue of Aeronautics that ten machines were to be completed by the Hammondsport factory by December 1909; four of these made to order for A. C. Triaca. The third machine built, after the Golden Flier and the Rheims machine, was the first one sold to a private individual, A. P. Warner. It was sold by Wyckoff, Church and Partridge, a distributing agent.

*Charles F. Willard, pilot of the Golden Flier, wrote that this engine developed only 22 horsepower and only one or two of this specification were built. The second group of 4-cylinder engines had a bore of 4 inches and a stroke of 4 inches and were rated at 40 horsepower.

The *Rheims Racer,* August 1909

The event for which the Rheims machine was constructed was the Gordon Bennett Race, or the Coupe-Gordon-Bennett, which, in 1909, was to be held at Rheims, France. In his haste to build the machine and get himself and the machine to Rheims in time for this event on August 29, 1909, Curtiss had very little time in which to practice with it or learn its characteristics. In *Aeronautics* for September 1909, we find:

CURTISS SAILS FOR EUROPE

Glenn H. Curtiss sailed on La Savoie, with "Slim" Schriver, to represent America in the international flying machine contests at Rheims during the last week of August.

On the same steamer went an exact duplicate of the aeroplane bought by The Aeronautic Society, with the exception that it has 30 in. less spread and is fitted with a more powerful motor, about which there is much secrecy. Some say it has four cylinders, some say eight; employees of the Curtiss plant shut up like clams when the motor is mentioned.

Entry has been made by Curtiss in the Gordon Bennett Aviation race over a 10-kilometer course, twice around. The fastest time takes down $5,000 in cash to the aviator and a $2,500 cup to his home club. There are still other contests for a purse totaling $40,000.

Since Curtiss was the only American representative present and had only one airplane and one engine with him, his strategy was to fly only the minimum time necessary, thereby guarding against any mishaps.

The Rheims events of 1909 were otherwise known as *La Grande Semaine d'Aviation* (The Great Week of Aviation). It was the first Grand Aviation International Tournament. It took place from August 22 to 29 on the Bethany Plains in the Champagne district of France. During this meet aviation history was made more rapidly than in any other aviation contest ever held. Records made on one day were broken the next. It marked an epic in the history of mechanical flight.

The four principal prizes to be awarded were the Grand Prix de la Champagne, the Gordon Bennett Aviation Cup, the Prix de la Vitesse and the Prix de Tour Piste.

The Rheims meet was outstanding in many regards: there were a large number of contes-

The Rheims machine at Hammondsport prior to shipment. Note the extended "spars," which were pruned off after the airplane demonstrated its ability to fly with reduced wing area. Ailerons are still hinged to the forward interplane struts and the horizontal stabilizer is still a fixed surface. The engine is the first of the liquid-cooled V-8 engines producing 50 horsepower that proved to be such a surprise to other contestants at Rheims, France.

Specifications

The *Rheims Racer*, August 1909

Span	26 ft. 3 in.
Length	30 ft. 4 in.
Chord	4 ft. 6 in.
Gap	4 ft. 6 in.
Area	118.125 sq. ft. (225 sq. ft.—*American Aeronautics*, p. 68, Sept. 1909)
Weight gross	700 lb.
Power plant	8-cyl. V, water-cooled, 51.2 hp @ 1,475 rpm; bore 4 in., stroke 4 in.; prop., wood, 6 ft. 0 in. (Willard states that this was 4 in. by 4 in.—first of this type built.)

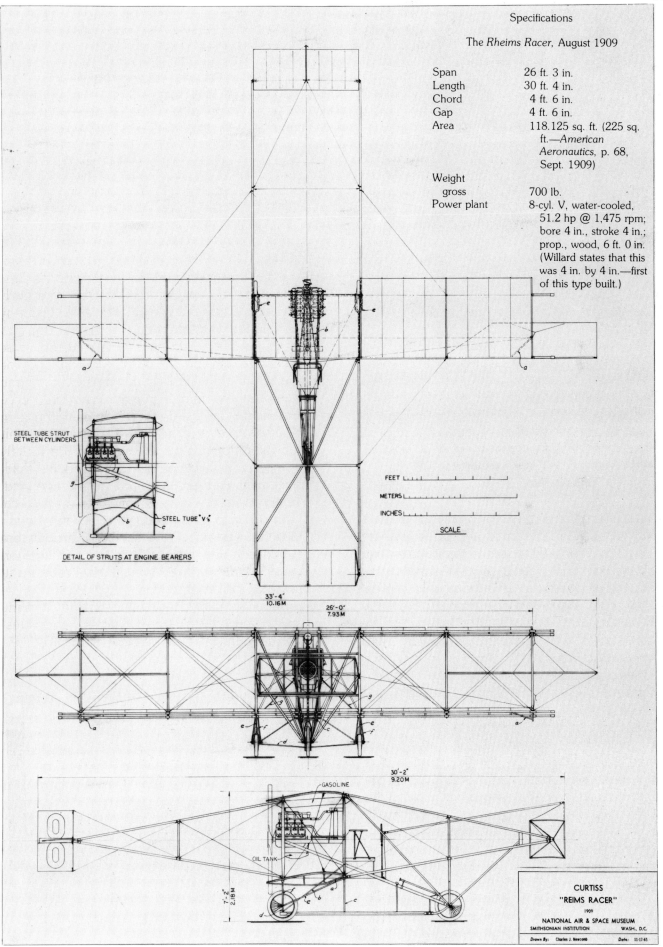

STEEL TUBE STRUT
BETWEEN CYLINDERS

STEEL TUBE "V's

DETAIL OF STRUTS AT ENGINE BEARERS

FEET

METERS

INCHES

SCALE

33'-4"
10.16 M

26'-0"
7.93 M

30'-2"
9.20 M

GASOLINE

OIL TANK

7'-2"
2.18 M

CURTISS
"REIMS RACER"
1909
NATIONAL AIR & SPACE MUSEUM
SMITHSONIAN INSTITUTION   WASH., D.C.

Drawn By: Charles J. Newcomb   Date: 11-17-65

An aerial view of the very rough "flying field" at Rheims, France, August 1909. Though the quality of this picture is poor, it is one of the earliest aerial photographs, and the packed grandstand shows the enormous interest Europeans showed in the feats of the earliest fliers.

tants, the weather was exceptionally good and a vast wildly enthusiastic public swarmed over the grounds to witness this series of great events. The management and organization of the meet were quite exceptional; there was not only a great display of flying, but it was unmarred by any serious accident. The accommodations for the machines, as well as for viewers, were both ample and convenient.

Rheims did have some bad features, however. The ground was a large plain of cultivated land stretching almost as far as the eye could see. The course was almost too big, for the aircraft, when flying at the far end about two miles away, were almost beyond the range of unaided vision. The roughness of the cultivated ground was a considerable surprise to the aviators as the machines racked and rolled over stubble and root crops. In many places wheat sheaves were stacked about on the ground, providing a further test of the structural integrity of the participating machines and the skill of the pilots. The conditions were so severe that out of a field of thirty-eight entrants, only sixteen could be classified as having made successful flights. Many ran around on the

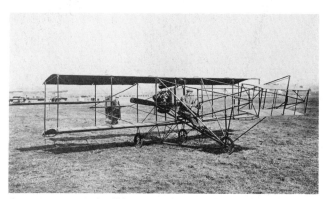

Curtiss tries out the Rheims machine. The spars have now been shortened to their final form.

ground, unable to rise, and some never left their sheds.

The entrants assembled for the meet were all Europeans except Curtiss, who was representing the Aero Club of America. The Aero Club representative was competing for the Gordon Bennett Cup. He was to be the cup's custodian and receive a cash sum of $5,000. The club that won the trophy three consecutive times would be the permanent winner. The cup was offered by an American, James Gordon Bennett, the sagacious proprietor of the *New York Herald*. One of the conditions of his gift was that the first cup competition was to be held for speed, in France, over a closed circuit of 20 kilometers, about 12.43 miles.

In order to compete for the Gordon Bennett Cup, it was necessary for the Aero Club of America to designate the aviator or aviators who would represent the American team for the defense of this trophy. Having witnessed the performance of the Aeronautic Society airplane, and being fully aware of Curtiss's competitive abilities dating back to his bicycle and motorcycle days, the board of governors of the Aero Club of America invited Glenn H. Curtiss to become the first member of the American team. (The Wrights

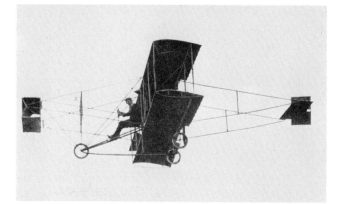

Glenn Curtiss in the Rheims machine flying for the Gordon Bennett Cup, 1909.

A close-up of engine and shoulder yoke controls of the Rheims machine. This was taken before the "spars" were pruned.

were then fully occupied with government contracts and Wright types, built by Europeans, were entered by their pupils.) After accepting this invitation, Curtiss found himself in a rather difficult situation with regard to time. He had agreed to deliver the *Golden Flier* and to train two pilots to fly it. The almost immediate crash of the *Golden Flier* by Williams, one of the pilots selected for training, made it necessary to await the repair of the aircraft before commencing with the instruction of Willard. In the interim, Curtiss had received the invitation from the Aero Club and was hard pressed for time in which to build and test a machine for the Gordon Bennett Race at the Rheims meet. Curtiss did, however, manage to construct a second machine, his *Rheims Racer,* in less than four weeks. It was, in a practical sense, a copy of the first machine, with suitable modifications for the intended contest. It was necessary to work day and night, right down to the last minute, to complete the machine and have it crated in time to arrive at Rheims for the competition. As a result, it was tested only very

briefly before being crated for shipment. Curtiss did not have an opportunity to try the machine before he, Tod Shriver, his chief mechanic, and Ward Fisher sailed for Europe on August 5, 1909.

The "Rheims machine," as it was known to the Curtiss people, varied from the *Golden Flier* in several important respects, the most notable of which was the installation of an 8-cylinder, 51.2-horsepower, V-type engine (similar to that used in the *Silver Dart,* but, in fact, a completely new design). In addition, during the building stages, the constructors thought that a reduction in wing area might reduce the drag, thereby enhancing chances of winning the race. In order to determine whether their theory was correct, they built the machine with spars the same length as those on the *Golden Flier,* but left the fabric off the outboard tip portion of the wings. The airplane was tested briefly in this configuration at Hammondsport and the theory proven correct. After this had been established, the spars were pruned off flush with the outboard interplane strut fittings, giving the *Rheims Racer* its characteristic shortened span and square wing tips.

With his keen competitive instincts, Curtiss made only qualification flights for the Grand Prize of Champagne, reserving his main efforts for the crucial flights that came later. The big day for Curtiss was the seventh day of the meet, August 28, 1909. The entrants were Le Fabre, Bleriot and Latham of France; Cockburn of England and Curtiss of America.

Curtiss started first and impressed everyone with his speed. He made two rounds of the 20-kilometer course in 15 minutes $15^3/_5$ seconds at a mean speed of 73.6 kilometers per hour, or 47.06 miles per hour.

LeFabre made the circuit in 20 minutes $47^3/_5$ seconds; Bleriot then came in in 15 minutes $56^1/_5$ seconds. He was followed by Latham, who made several turns of the course; his time for the two turns was 17 minutes 32 seconds.

Curtiss had won the Gordon Bennett Aviation Cup!

On the eighth day, August 29, 1909, Curtiss entered a three-lap race, which he won, and also entered a one-lap race in which he placed second. He had thus entered and won two races and taken second place in a third race.

Curtiss received $5,000 for winning the Gordon Bennett Race, at a speed of 47.06 miles per hour. He received $2,000 first prize for speed for the 30-kilometer race and $600 as second-place winner in the single-lap speed race of 10 kilometers. All in all, it had been a very successful meet for Glenn Curtiss.

The *Rheims Racer,* as noted earlier, was a very close copy of the Aeronautic Society machine, the *Golden Flier,* except that it was powered by an 8-cylinder, V-type, water-cooled engine. It had a bore of 4 inches and a stroke of 4 inches and developed approximately 51.2 brake horsepower and 1,475 rpm. It used a 6-foot straight-line propeller with a pitch of 17 degrees, and developed a thrust of 235 to 280 pounds.

The aircraft had a slightly different airfoil curvature of less camber than that used on the *Golden Flier.* This reduced span and camber resulted in a slightly slower takeoff, but a higher speed after the aircraft was in the air.

The wings were shorter than those of the *Golden Flier,* having a span of 26 feet 3 inches (a dimension that became standard for the D-type machines) and a chord of 4 feet 6 inches. The whole machine weighed slightly over 700 pounds.

Another interesting detail that distinguishes this machine from the *Golden Flier* is that the *Rheims Racer* was covered with gray-colored silk, which would hardly give one cause to confuse this airplane with the *Golden Flier.*

At Rheims the Curtiss racer was assigned the No. 8 race number. Curtiss found himself faced with competition from the best pilots of Europe and, certainly, the best airplanes, some of which were at least equal to his machine. Among them was Bleriot with his monoplane. In the final tabulation, Curtiss bested Bleriot by a scant margin of 5 seconds. His best performance was 30 kilometers in 24 minutes 15 seconds, at a speed of 75.7 kilometers per hour. He won the Prix de la Vitesse on August 29, in addition to the Gordon Bennett Cup.

The winning of the Gordon Bennett race by Curtiss determined the site of the second race for this trophy. After winning, Curtiss was deluged by offers for engagements to fly in Germany and Italy. A big meet was organized at Brescia, Italy, and Curtiss went there directly from Rheims. At Brescia, he carried the aircraft's first passenger, the celebrated Italian poet, author and soldier, Gabriele D'Annunzio, whose colorful career was by no means finished with aviation.

At the Brescia meet in Italy Curtiss won the Grand Prize and the Altitude Prize and was awarded a cash prize of $7,000. He later received numerous offers to make additional flights. The throngs of people who had crowded the meets at Rheims and Brescia were encouraging to him, and he returned to the United States full of enthusiasm for the future of aviation. Shortly after his return to the United States, Curtiss took the Rheims machine and his No. 3 machine, one similar to the *Golden Flier* but powered by a 4-cylinder engine with a bore of 4 inches and a stroke of 4 inches, slightly more powerful than that installed in the *Golden Flier,* to Los Angeles for the first meet at Domingues Field, January 10–12, 1910.

The Rheims machine was subsequently leased by Charles K. Hamilton to take on a tour of exhibitions. Hamilton's tour was short, unfortunately, for on March 12, 1910, he crashed the Rheims machine into the water at Seattle. The airplane itself was a total wreck, but the engine was salvaged and overhauled at the Curtiss plant and subsequently leased to Charles F. Willard for exhibition purposes until late in 1910.

The Hudson-Fulton Machine

The final aeronautical event for the year 1909 was the Hudson-Fulton celebration. The Hudson-Fulton Planning Commission had set aside the sum of $25,000 for contracting with various aviators to display their aircraft in flight in conjunction with the celebrations commemorating the discovery of the Hudson River by Henry Hudson, and the historic voyage of the Fulton steamboat up the same river. As envisioned, the aircraft would fly back and forth across the river over the pageant and proceed up river. There would also be numerous static aeronautical displays, among them models of the Langley Aerodrome, the restored original Wright machine, and the model of the Stringfellow machine that was in the Smithsonian collection. The Aeronautic Committee sought to interest and acquire the services of a number of aviators of that day, among them Capt. Thomas Scott Baldwin and his airship, Charles F. Willard flying the Aeronautic Society machine, the Wrights and Glenn Curtiss.

Curtiss went almost directly from his triumph at Rheims to this event, where he had a brand new machine that had been manufactured at Hammondsport during his absence in Europe.

The machine was generally of the type that had been purchased by the Aeronautic Society, with some special modifications for the anticipated overwater flights of the Hudson-Fulton celebration. The machine differed in several respects from the Aeronautic Society machine, having a pyramid-shaped float mounted between the wheel landing gear immediately above the central skid. In addition, the forward biplane control had the small triangular vertical surface removed, and the upright control horn of the elevator had been lengthened substantially. An additional feature was the larger ailerons, which now extended from the second inboard strut to a distance of 40 inches beyond the outboard struts. In addition to this, it was planned to install a metal gasoline tank beneath the second inboard struts. The radiator had been placed further forward, and the water pump for the engine had been moved to a position in front of

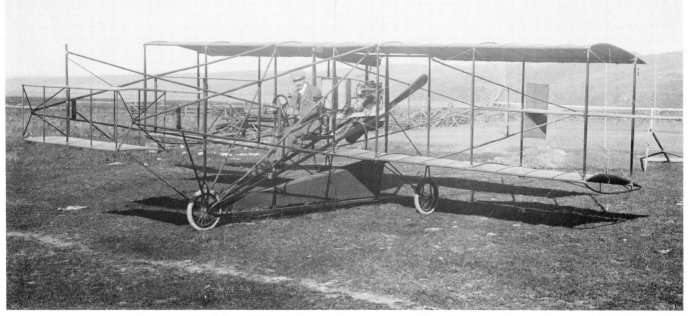

Curtiss poses in the pilot's seat of the Model D-4 Hudson-Fulton machine. Note the triangular flotation gear installed on the landing gear. The ailerons are still attached to the forward interplane struts.

The Hudson-Fulton flotation gear and "front wheel brake." The other pedal is the throttle.

the gear case instead of at the rear, as had previously been the case. Another refinement, which was not readily discerned from photographic records, is the fact that the wires to the vertical rudder were now run through fairleads along the bamboo outriggers all the way to the junction of the vertical struts and the outriggers at the trailing edge of the wing, and from here they ran over pulleys up to the steering wheel.

Curtiss and the Curtiss machine did not arrive in New York until September 27, 1909, having only returned from Europe on September 21. He was able to set up the aircraft in record time. Within two hours after arrival, the airplane appeared to the public to be ready for flight.

On the morning of September 29, Curtiss made one short attempt to test the machine. Because of the very early hour, 6:00 A.M., and foggy weather conditions, very few people were present to witness the "flight." Jerome Fanciulli, who was one of those present, states that the flight did not take place.

By way of explanation, contemporary accounts of the Hudson-Fulton event indicated that the weather conditions were far from ideal and allowed only two or, at the most, three days for aeronautical participation.

The outstanding flight of the celebration was the flight by Wilbur Wright from Governors Island, off the southern end of Manhattan Island, out past the Statue of Liberty, and up the Hudson to a turn made over the British warship *Drake* moored opposite Grant's Tomb, and then back to Governors Island. The distance of the flight had been in excess of 20 miles with an elapsed time of 33 minutes 33 seconds.

With the exception of the day of October 4, abnormally high winds prevailed and only two favorable days were available for the aviation part of the celebration.

The second part of the aeronautical program consisted of an airship competition for the $10,000 New York-to-Albany race. The participants were to be Capt. Thomas S. Baldwin, George L. Tomilson and John Roeder. The Baldwin and Tomilson airships were almost identical, both having been built by Baldwin and both powered by Curtiss engines. Captain

A quartering front view of the Hudson-Fulton machine showing the bamboo shaft connecting the elevator to the steering wheel.

Baldwin had acquired a special water-cooled engine for this airship and Tomilson had acquired from Baldwin the air-cooled Curtiss engine formerly used by Baldwin in his own airship.

On the morning of September 29, at about 10:00 A.M., Tomilson got away from the flight square at Riverside Drive and proceeded upriver toward Albany. When Tomilson was nearly out of sight, Baldwin took off, headed out over the Hudson River and turned northward along the course of the river. After passing Fort Washington, about four miles from the departure point, two top longerons of his airframe broke just behind the engine. Baldwin considered it dangerous to continue with the flight and descended.

Tomilson fared only a little better, for he had to make a forced landing when in the vicinity of White Plains, a distance of about 20 miles from the departure point. It was necessary for him to descend because of an oil tank leak.

Like Curtiss, Captain Baldwin had agreed to fly in the St. Louis Aviation Meet and he departed before Roeder appeared on the scene.

No record has been found of Roeder's participation in the airship competition.

Much criticism resulted from Curtiss's brief attempted flights and his departure for the St. Louis meet. The success of Wilbur Wright undoubtedly intensified the criticism, but Wilbur was not scheduled to perform in St. Louis.

In terms of chronology, it appears that the machine used by Curtiss was also described as the Plew machine. James E. Plew purchased a Curtiss machine No. 4, which was contracted for on September 23, 1909, and delivered on November 30, 1909. It is entirely possible that its shakedown period included the Hudson-Fulton event.

By the end of 1909 the Herring-Curtiss Company had produced at least nine aircraft as follows:

1. The Aeronautic   Late May 1909
   Society machine
2. Rheims machine   August 1909
3. A. P. Warner   September 25, 1909
   machine

4. James E. Plew   November 30, 1909
   machine
5. Arnold machine
6. DeRiemsdyk   December 18, 1909
   machine (first
   foreign sale of a
   Curtiss machine)
7. ?
8. Frank H. Johnson
   machine
9. Henry Wemme   February 1, 1910
   machine

Specifications

The Hudson-Fulton Machine

Specifications same as *Rheims Racer,* with the following exceptions:

Upright posts on front elevator lightened, triangular vertical surface removed, ailerons lengthened—40 inches beyond outer strut to second strut inboard. Inverted pyramid-shaped pontoon mounted fore and aft on center skid. Gasoline tanks strapped under second strut inboard from each end of wing. Engine bed larger and of laminated spruce. Shoulder brace hinged to seat. Rudder control cables run along the bamboo outriggers.

1910 Prelude:
The Herring-Curtiss Problem

The Aeronautic Society of New York changed its name to the Aeronautical Society of New York on April 7, 1910. As previously noted, the Herring-Curtiss Company was incorporated by the Department of State of New York on February 19, 1909. It will be recalled that the terms of the agreement included two significant contributions. Curtiss was to turn over the complete manufacturing company, as well as his Hammondsport property, which was his personal contribution, and he was to assume duties in the new corporation as vice-president and general manager. As his part of the transaction, Augustus M. Herring was to place his alleged patents that, at this time, were only patents "applied for" in the hands of the newly formed corporation. One major fact is difficult to ignore: the Herring patents were, in the final analysis, not granted and, therefore, did not become tangible material for Mr. Herring's part of the transaction.

After having entered into this agreement in good faith, with an eye toward keeping out of the clutches of the Wright brothers' lawyers at this stage in the proceedings, Curtiss in effect jumped out of the frying pan into the fire. In addition to the patent litigation that was begun by the Wright brothers at about this time, Curtiss soon found himself in legal troubles with Herring. Curtiss, therefore, was beset by two legal barbs constantly harrassing him during the formative period of his company.

In one form or another, Curtiss found that he was obliged to defend himself constantly in the courts of law. Insofar as the Herring-Curtiss Company is concerned, the company was not formally dissolved until March 10, 1926.

Curtiss had been carried away by what appeared to be the big money deal that Herring offered. He also believed that Herring really had the patents he claimed he had, predating the Wright patents. Curtiss believed the Herring patents would help in fighting the Wright litigation, which had opened in September 1909. The facts were that Herring had applied for patents in 1898 and had been rejected by the Patent Office. A second application was made in 1910 with similar results. Herring kept putting off giving Curtiss and the rest of the board a listing of the patents. Finally Curtiss did what he should have done in the first place—checked the patents. No patents were found, nor did Herring advance the working capital he had agreed to provide. At the same time, Herring was maneuvering to get voting proxies to win control at the stockholders' meeting. Fortunately for Curtiss, he, Thomas S. Baldwin and Monroe Wheeler constituted a majority on the board of directors. They obtained an injunction to prevent Herring from voting his stock at the stockholders' meeting scheduled for January 1910. In a series of legal maneuvers the company was declared bankrupt, placed in receivership and bought at auction by Wheeler acting on Curtiss's behalf.

In the course of a personal letter to the editor of *The Aero,* Curtiss said:

The papers, as usual, have things somewhat mixed. Our business is in the hands of a receiver, but is not shut down.

Our trouble is due to our connection with Mr. Herring, who organized the company, but did not put in any money or goods. He, however, acquired a controlling interest, and threatened to assume control of the business last fall. In view of this, no money could be raised to carry on the business, and, together with the undesirable publicity from the injunctions, we were unable to meet our bills, and were forced into the hands of a receiver.

The injunction of the Wrights, however, was not issued, and I have been making flights right along. The matter is now in the Court of Appeals, and if the misrepresentation by Mr. Herring in regard to his inventions do not prove too damaging we will without doubt finally win the case.

The G. S. Curtis you mention is another man, and I have seen in the papers that he is to fly a Herring-Burgess machine, in which production Mr. Herring is now interested.

It was typical of Curtiss's modesty that, although this letter was written only four days after his great Albany–New York flight, he never so much as refers to his own performances, except in the passing reference above.

The Pfitzner Monoplane, 1910

The Pfitzner monoplane, while not a Curtiss aircraft in the strict sense of the word, was constructed at the Curtiss facilities at Hammondsport and designed by a Curtiss associate, Alexander L. Pfitzner. Pfitzner, an automotive engineer employed by Curtiss as superintendent of the Curtiss engine department, set out to design an original monoplane to prove that it was not necessary to copy anyone to produce a successful aircraft. The result was an unusual machine employing a novel system to provide lateral control. These interconnected control surfaces, known as "equalizers," varied the area of the wings by sliding spanwise.

The aircraft had a number of interesting and novel features in addition to the "equalizers." Among these features was a quadricycle landing gear, with brakes on the two rear wheels operated by a lever on the pilot's left side, a "dep"-type control system that focused all control movements, including the rudder, in one control unit similar to the James Means control.

This control system was the second most interesting feature of the machine, since most control systems up to this time had involved hand, foot and body movement of the aviator, making the piloting of an airplane a contortion act of the first magnitude. The Pfitzner control and the Means control that preceded it made use of instinctive movements of the pilot to maintain the control of the aircraft.

Unlike his contemporaries, Pfitzner placed the rudder, as well as his elevator, in front of the pilot, feeling that the pilot should be able to observe the reaction to all movements of the controls. The throttle was mounted on the axis of the control wheel and an ignition button was attached to the right-hand spoke of the wheel within convenient reach of the pilot, enabling him to stop the engine. This was similar to the control system of the Johnson brothers' monoplane of 1909.

Construction took place in January and February of 1910 and the first flight was made in February, resulting in damage to the aircraft when Pfitzner struck a tree. A number of flights followed, during which the builder gained experience in handling the machine, but more often than not the flight ended with damage to the aircraft. It was exhibited at the Sportsmen's Show at Buffalo and also at the local country club. On April 5, thirteen successive flights were made, one of them demonstrating the efficiency of the equalizers when a gust of wind upset the

Results of one of several bad landings suffered by Pfitzner during the testing of his monoplane. *Curtiss Photo Collection*

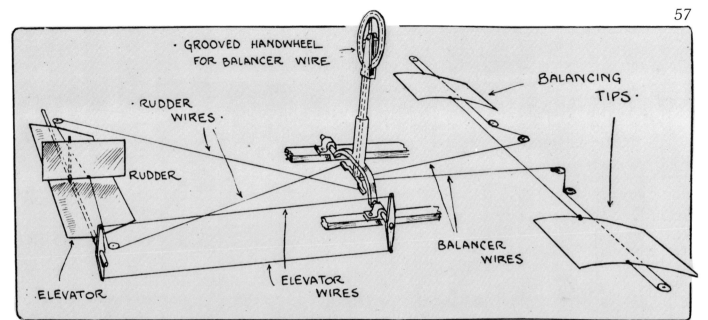

· GROOVED HANDWHEEL
FOR BALANCER WIRE

· RUDDER
WIRES ·

BALANCING
TIPS ·

· RUDDER

BALANCER
WIRES

· ELEVATOR

· ELEVATOR
WIRES

Diagram of the Pfitzner control system from *Flight*, March 12, 1910.

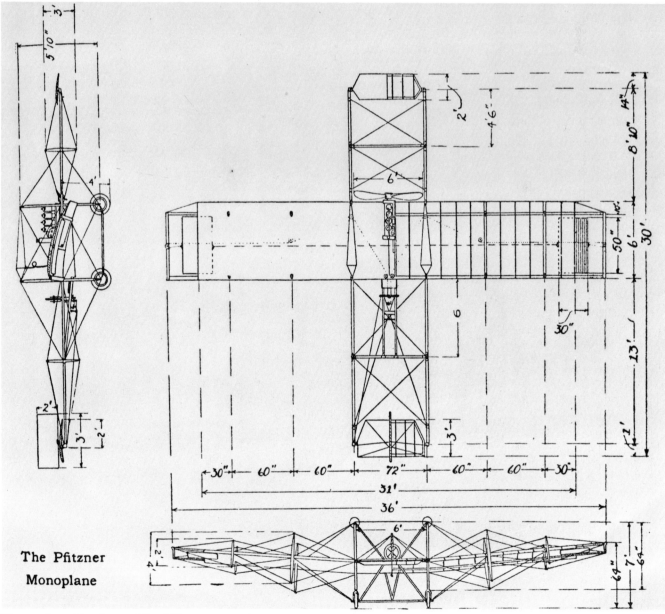

The Pfitzner
Monoplane

Plan and profile views of the Pfitzner monoplane.

1006

machine during the landing. Pfitzner's quick reaction with equalizers and engine resulted in a recovery without damage.

After Pfitzner severed his connection with Glenn Curtiss, he was employed by the Burgess Co. and Curtis (Greeley S. Curtis, spelled with one "s") and took his monoplane with him. It was acquired by the company and offered for sale at a price of $4,000, equipped with its 4-cylinder, 25-horsepower Curtiss engine.

Pfitzner himself came to a tragic end when he took his own life on July 12, 1910. His monoplane was exhibited at the Harvard-Boston meet, October 3–16, 1910.

Specifications	
The Pfitzner Monoplane, 1910	
Span	36 ft.
Length	30 ft.
Chord	6 ft.
Engine	4 cyl., water-cooled, 25 hp
Weight net	430 lb.

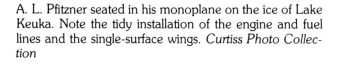

A. L. Pfitzner seated in his monoplane on the ice of Lake Keuka. Note the tidy installation of the engine and fuel lines and the single-surface wings. *Curtiss Photo Collection*

The D-II Canoe Machine, 1910

Following the early trials with the *Loon*, events had moved at a rapid pace and included the Rheims meet, the Hudson-Fulton celebration, the St. Louis meet and the Albany flight, all of which consumed most of Curtiss's time. However, the Albany flight and a couple of water landings by exhibition pilots Willard and Hamilton redirected Curtiss's attention toward developing a water machine.

The Canoe Machine of 1910 marked the beginning of Curtiss's long development of waterborne aircraft. First thoughts along these lines dated back to the AEA *Loon*, a modification of the *June Bug*. His first record of ideas along these lines appeared in the AEA *Bulletin* as follows:

Hammondsport, N.Y., Aug. 19, 1908: I have read the last two *Bulletins* with great interest. The scheme of starting a flying machine from and landing on the water has been in my mind for some time. It has many advantages, and I believe can be worked out. Even if a most suitable device for launching and landing on land is secured, a water craft will still be indispensable for war purposes and if the exhibition field is to be considered, would, I believe, present greater possibilities in this line than a machine which works on land.

An arrangement of floats to support the flyer when at rest would be necessary. Then small hydroplanes to carry it up out of the water and to catch the shock of landing. I do not think the problem is difficult.

For work on land, I would submit the enclosed sketch of a new launching device. The one fixed wheel is used entirely for starting and alighting, the skids only acting as supports while standing. Balancing on the one wheel can be easily secured with the moveable wing tips and the front horizontal rudder as when flying in the air. If we have the opportunity would you advise trying this on the *June Bug*?

G. H. Curtiss

Curtiss persisted in his pursuit of a waterborne aircraft. He contended that if an airplane could

Launching the Canoe Machine, Lake Keuka, May 1910. *Curtiss Collection*

fly at all, it could fly more successfully from water than from land. The unobstructed area of Lake Keuka, in the midst of the hills of upper New York, prompted him to continue his experiments in the knowledge that water surfaces were unobstructed, reasonably smooth and a ducking was about the worst one could expect in the event of a wreck.

The Canoe Machine was assembled from a standard "school" machine used for pilot instruction, a D-II configuration with a standard canoe belonging to F. W. Baldwin that was handy for the experiment. Small wing-tip floats and planing shingles were attached to the wing tips at an angle and height determined by trial. The purpose of the test was to determine how the airplane could be balanced on a single float and how it would maneuver on the water. The canoe was braced internally and covered with canvas to prevent its being swamped. The aircraft-canoe combination was never intended to fly. It was a standard single-place school machine powered by a low horsepower (33

horsepower, 3¾-inch bore, 4-inch stroke) 4-cylinder engine. It had been conclusively demonstrated during training operations that it could not lift two persons.

The taxi tests were conducted by Curtiss during early May 1910 and, to his satisfaction, proved that he could maneuver as expected. This project was laid aside to devote full energies to the preparation of the *Albany Flier* for the Albany–New York flight. Following the successful Hudson flight, Curtiss returned to Hammondsport where he undertook a number of additional tests affixing hydrofoils to the bow of the canoe. After he had completed these experiments, this machine was exhibited at Atlantic City as a static display on July 4, 1910. Following this, the wheel chassis was reinstalled and the aircraft returned to flying status.

The pontoon for the first hydro-aeroplane was built and installed on this, or a similar model, in order to determine the center of buoyancy. This was a static test and soon afterward, in November 1910, this pontoon was shipped to

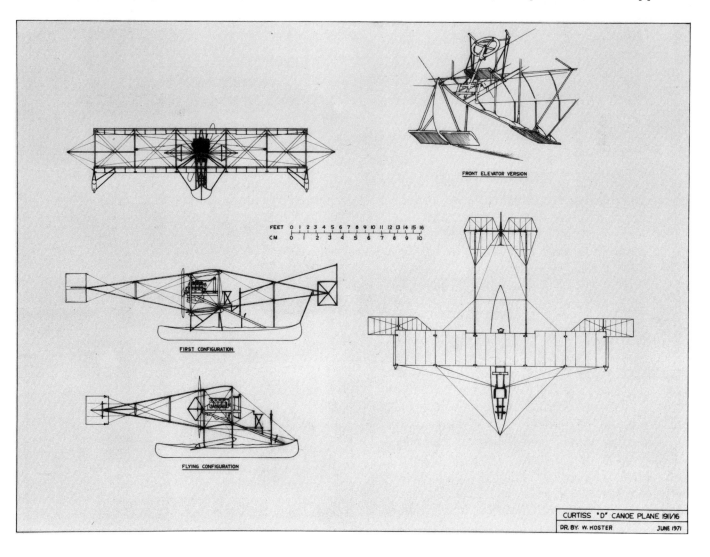

FRONT ELEVATOR VERSION

FIRST CONFIGURATION

FLYING CONFIGURATION

FEET 0 1 2 3 4 5 6 7 8 9 10 11 12 13 14 15 16
CM 0 1 2 3 4 5 6 7 8 9 10

CURTISS "D" CANOE PLANE 1911/16
DR. BY. W. KOSTER   JUNE 1971

In spite of the failure of the *Loon* in 1908 and some earlier failures with the D-4 Canoe Machine in 1910, Curtiss persisted with this hull form, probably to prove it could be accomplished—for litigation purposes. Details of the later D-8 Headless Canoe Machine are shown here.

San Diego for the tests that led to the first hydro.

Henri Fabre, who is credited with having made the first hydro-aeroplane flight, had made a three-point suspension for his *Hydro Avion*, using two floats mounted very widely spaced beneath the wings and a third float at the front. Curtiss had not considered the catamaran construction as the best means for making water flights. He felt that if the machine, in making a landing, struck one pontoon first, it would have a tendency to spin about this point and probably wreck itself, whereas the single central float would be the last thing to leave the water and the first to come in contact with it and would be a much more practical device.

Another disadvantage of the laterally displaced floats was the possibility of one float taking on some water, thereby upsetting the balance of the machine on the water and in the air. He considered the single float much better for this reason; in the event of leakage it would still be able to fly so long as it would carry the load. A further advantage of the single float was in maneuvering on the water, since it allowed the airplane to pivot in a relatively short distance.

Drawing on his bicycle experience Curtiss reasoned that if he could balance a single float, he would be able to ride on the water pretty much in the same manner as one would ride a bicycle on land. The only major problem was to find a way of balancing upon this single float while at low speed and at rest. This was accomplished by means of the end floats, or wing-tip floats, which supported the wings while the machine was at rest, and which were also the means of balancing the airplane while gaining speed and getting to the surface of the water before taking off.

Later, in 1916, an attempt was made to get the "canoe configuration" airborne. The canoe was fitted by Henry Kleckler in accordance with Curtiss's instructions. Curtiss then took it out on

Success! The only known photo of the D-8 Canoe Machine airborne, proving that this hull form could get off the water. The V-8 engine produced about 50 horsepower greater power than the D-4 of 1910.

Lake Keuka and, after a number of test runs, got the machine in the air at an altitude of 6 to 10 feet. The substantial increase in power from 30–35 horsepower of the 4-cylinder engine to the 100-plus horsepower developed by the V-8 made this test flight possible. Recollections by Kleckler indicate that the same canoe was used with a 4-inch-wide strip fixed to the keel from bow to stern to give a planing surface. Also, tests were conducted with hydrofoils fore and aft to see how the craft would balance when under way. In this configuration the flight components were mounted considerably higher to avoid the spray and the outboard floats were canister or tank-type floats with conical end closures.

While much has been written about the ability of an unstepped hull to rise from the water, there is photographic evidence to prove that this second variant did get off the water and, according to Kleckler's testimony, flew for about one thousand feet.

The transcript of the Janin case furnishes interesting details about the second canoe machine:

Q. Have you ever flown a canoe machine from the water?

CURTISS. Yes, sir.

Q. Where was this done?

CURTISS. Near Hammondsport, on Lake Keuka.

Q. Do you remember what canoe machine it was that you flew from the water?

CURTISS. It was a duplicate, as near as it could be constructed, of the original canoe machine, with the exception of the motor. The motor used was an 8-cylinder O.X.X. 110 horse power.

Q. And how about the canoe itself? Do you know whether that was the original canoe or a different one?

CURTISS. It was the original canoe.

Q. And will you please state how you are able to—how you were able to get that machine out of the water at that time?

CURTISS. I got the machine out of the water in very much the same manner as any of the short float type. The canoe was a flat bottom, and had rounded bilges, a pointed stern, which came up by the bow nicely, and in spite of the curves in its construction; the high power of the motor enabled me to pull it out of the water, I recollect distinctly a great acceleration of speed as the stern of the canoe broke loose from the water.

Q. In the original canoe, I notice the longitudinal balance was such that your center of gravity was well aft in your canoe. What was the location of the center as reconstructed?

CURTISS. It was the same, as near as we could, as it could be determined.

Q. You are shown sitting here more forward in this canoe flown in 1916 than you apparently were sitting in the original canoe in 1910—is that correct?

CURTISS. Yes, that was necessary to offset the added weight of the motor, which was back of the center of pressure.

Q. And due to the short length of the tail back of your wings, you were able to get this canoe out of the water with this excessive power?

CURTISS. Well, this was three times, approximately three times the horse power that we had in the machine which we made the experiments with some years previous. We had no expectation of taking that machine from the water.

Q. What happened to that machine when you tried to land with it?

CURTISS. Well, it developed that the canoe was not strong enough to withstand the shock of landing, because this machine was very heavily loaded, and landed at unusually high speed, and the bottom of the canoe was crushed on the landing.

Q. Are there any special features about that canoe machine which enable you to identify it as the original canoe?

CURTISS. Well, I know it was the original canoe, because of the fact that I had seen it several times, knew where it was kept, knew of the stern decking being cut away, and knew of some splits or checks that were in the planking of the canoe, and had been repaired at the time it was first used. So that I am positive it was the same canoe.

Specifications	
The D-II Canoe Machine, 1910	
Span	26 ft. 3 in.
Chord	4 ft. 6 in.
Gap	4 ft. 6 in.
Power plant	4 cyl., 33 hp

The Albany Flier, 1910

The Albany–New York flight was, by all standards, a success. The disappointing performance of almost all aeronautical participants at the Hudson-Fulton celebration from September 25 to October 2, 1909 was well recorded in the newspapers of the time. When Curtiss left New York City in the fall of 1909, the public and the press were impatiently waiting for a flight up the Hudson. Wilbur Wright had stayed on and made a 20-mile flight up and down the lower river. Curtiss left early due to a previously made engagement to fly at St. Louis. Because of public skepticism and press antagonism, Curtiss made a public announcement of his intention to fly down the Hudson from Albany to New York.

In characteristic fashion, Curtiss built a special machine (probably the unidentified No. 7 machine) at Hammondsport and made several trips up and down the river by train and boat, visiting some of the adjacent land areas in search of suitable landing fields.

To succeed it was necessary to overcome a number of obstacles, not the least of which were the turbulent air currents along the river. These currents, careening off the bluffs and around bends of the river, promised an eventful trip at the very least. Coupled with this was the fact that the hydroplane was still a thing of the future and as no really good landing sites were available for much of the course, it made a ducking or drowning a distinct possibility.

The *New York World* posted a $10,000 prize:

To the first person who on or before Oct. 10, 1910, makes the boat flight from New York to Albany, or from Albany to New York in a mechanically propelled airship, either lighter or heavier than air, the *World* will pay $10,000. The trip must be made within 24 consecutive hours, two landings being allowed between start and finish, to replenish gasoline, etc. This offer is made

Curtiss takes off from Inwood, the only landing en route from Albany to Governors Island, New York.

with no other conditions whatever, except that the starting point must be within the limits of Albany, or New York, and that intending competitors must give twenty-four hours notice to the *World* and to the Secretary of the Aero Club of America, of their intention to start. The twenty-four hours notice is required only (in order) that proper official records may be made. There are no conditions other than these, and no entrance fee is required.

Curtiss chose to start from Albany to avail himself of any prevailing wind that would speed him along, and it would be easier to make preparations at the Albany end. He chose Leslie Island just above Albany as his starting point.

In preparation for the flight, Curtiss made the trip from New York to Albany by riverboat, observing the details of the river and its peculiarities. En route Curtiss discussed details of the course with the unbelieving captain and first mate of the boat. Until Curtiss posed the question about the merits of flying over or under the Poughkeepsie Bridge, his questions were greeted with casual response or outright disbelief.

It was at Poughkeepsie that Curtiss had an amusing encounter. He was looking for a good landing field when he accidentally strayed on a piece of property belonging to the State Hospital for the Insane, which was situated just north of the city. While on this location, Curtiss encountered a man who inquired why Curtiss was there. Curtiss informed him that he was looking for a suitable place to land a flying machine. The man then remarked that Curtiss had come to the right place but he should be on the other side of the fence as that was where men like Curtiss were kept!

Curtiss later met Dr. Taylor, the superintendent of the hospital, who showed him around the grounds. When the doctor was informed that Curtiss intended to make a trip from Albany to

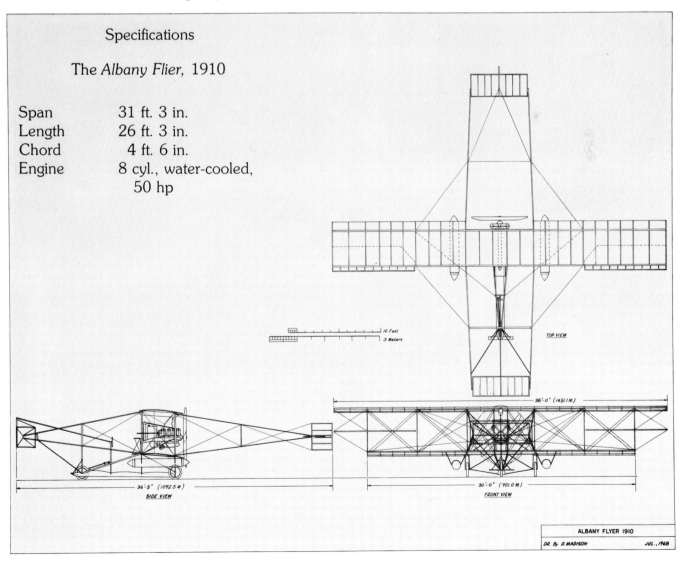

Specifications

The *Albany Flier,* 1910

Span	31 ft. 3 in.
Length	26 ft. 3 in.
Chord	4 ft. 6 in.
Engine	8 cyl., water-cooled, 50 hp

SIDE VIEW

TOP VIEW

FRONT VIEW

ALBANY FLYER 1910

DR. BY D. MADISON   JUL., 1968

New York in a flying machine and would have to land in that general vicinity if the doctor would allow him, the doctor replied that this would be possible as all flying machine inventors eventually landed in that institution.

However, a more suitable landing field was later found near Camelot.

There was only one other stop between Albany and New York that was really suitable for a landing field and if Curtiss had to land elsewhere it would have to be in the water. To add a small margin of insurance, he had the airplane equipped with two metal canisters and attached a board on the keel of the landing gear (which extended from the front wheel to the rear wheels) upon which was fastened a large canvas bag filled with corks.

The plane was transported to Rensselaer Island, where it was assembled and checked thoroughly. This was completed on May 29, 1910. The press, which had been waiting patiently for several days for the weather conditions that Curtiss considered favorable, became impatient and let it be known in their columns. As a

THE EXACT LINE THAT CURTISS FLEW FROM ALBANY AND THE ALTITUDES HE REACHED AT DIFFERENT POINTS.

THE WORLD: TUESDAY, MAY 31, 1910.

The accompanying diagram shows the course of the Hudson Flier, Curtiss's aeroplane, from Albany to New York, with the various towns which he passed on the way.

The dotted line marking the course is punctuated with indicators of the heights that Mr. Curtiss attained, or the levels to which he dropped, in the course of his long flight.

For quite a distance in the neighborhood of Peekskill the aeroplane was only fifty feet or so above the water, while at other points it rose to a height of 1,000 feet.

Crossing the Poughkeepsie Bridge it was more than 600 feet in the air, or 400 feet higher than the bridge, and running down from Inwood, where the landing was made in New York City limits, to Governor's Island, past the city skyscrapers, the Hudson Flier flew at an average of about 800 feet.

GREAT PRAISE FOR WORLD FOR OFFERING $10,000 PRIZE.

Scientists, Aviators and Inventors Say That Was the Stimulus Needed to Spur Aviation Here—Flight...

A map of the flight from Albany to New York City.

A close-up showing the complete flotation equipment. *Curtiss Collection*

result, a number of derogatory articles appeared.

On Sunday morning, May 29, all conditions were favorable and at 7:30 Curtiss took off. A special train, chartered by the *New York Times,* had been standing by on a side track, with steam up, awaiting the takeoff. The signal for the start was a small white flag hoisted from the Standard Oil Company building. The train consisted of one of the best engines and four coaches, one of which was a baggage car from which a *Times* photographer planned to take photos of the flight en route. The passengers on board were:

Mr. Frost, *New York Times* representative; H. E. Brown, assistant superintendent of the railway division; C. D. Van Schoick, special inspector of motor power; Charles Lewis, engineer; Henry Kleckler; M. Gillaran, fireman; Joseph Martin, conductor; the *Times* photographer; Augustus M. Post, secretary of the Aero Club of America; Mrs. G. H. Curtiss and Mr. and Mrs. Jerome Fanciulli.

The airplane got away and was well along the course before the train started. As soon as the Twentieth Century Limited passed the siding, the New York Central officials had arranged for a clear track for the special. Curtiss climbed to about a thousand feet and headed downriver to New York. En route, he stopped at Camelot near Poughkeepsie for fuel and again at 214th Street and Broadway for oil. His final destination was Governors Island, where he touched down at 12:00, landing in front of a hangar built for the Hudson-Fulton celebration. After rolling the airplane into the hangar, he was greeted by Mrs. Curtiss, who had rushed across the city by taxi,

and William J. Hammer, who, as secretary of the Hudson-Fulton Aviation Committee, had severely criticized Curtiss the previous year for departing before the celebration was completed.

The flight had covered 150 miles in 2 hours and 46 minutes, at an average speed of 54.18 miles per hour, enabling Curtiss to win the *New York World* prize of $10,000 and, for the third time, the Scientific American Trophy. The third win gave Curtiss permanent possession of the trophy. The trophy, now a prized specimen in the National Aeronautical Collections of the Smithsonian, was first won by Curtiss flying the *June Bug* over a one-kilometer course on July 4, 1908. The second win was for flying the 25.002-mile triangular course on July 17, 1909, and the third was for this spectacular flight down the Hudson.

Not generally recorded, but of equal and far-reaching historical significance, is the later use of this same aircraft, the *Albany Flier,* to make the first flight from a ship. This historic event took place at Hampton Roads, Virginia, on November 14, 1910, when Eugene Ely flew from a specially constructed platform mounted on the cruiser U.S.S. *Birmingham.* Taking off in inclement weather and with the cruiser barely under way, Ely dipped down toward the water, 37 feet below the deck, to gain the necessary flying speed. Recovering barely in time to avoid disaster, Ely did contact the water with his wheels, throwing up a spray that damaged his propeller. With his propeller split, Ely headed for land, Willoughby Spit, and effected a safe landing to complete the first flight from a ship at sea.

The *Albany Flier,* its undercarriage submerged, being towed across Keuka Lake.

The *Albany Flier* at Atlantic City before its historic takeoff from the U.S.S. *Birmingham* on November 14, 1910.

The Willard-Curtiss *Banshee Express, 1910*

The Willard-Curtiss machine was built to specifications laid down by Charles F. Willard, the pilot trained on the Aeronautic Society machine known as the *Golden Flier*. It was decided by the Society to send the *Golden Flier* on tour to popularize aviation. Willard was the pilot. During its relatively short career, Willard flew the aircraft in several meets, during one of which, the Domingues Field meet, January 10–20, 1910, Willard and Curtiss flew in competition with each other. Curtiss was flying the more powerful Rheims machine. Experience gained with the *Golden Flier* prompted Willard to lay down specifications for this Willard-Curtiss machine that was assembled at the Aeronautical Society shed at Mineola, Long Island, on August 11, 1910, and flown for the first time the following day.

The most notable changes from the *Golden Flier* were the increase in span, with an attendant increase in wing area and an increase in power by use of the 51.2-horsepower V-8 engine, instead of the 4-cylinder upright that had actually produced about 22 horsepower.

These two improvements were important to the safety of the pilot and survival of the aircraft. To sponsors or promotors of demonstrations, any field, no matter how small or rough, was considered satisfactory for use as an "airport." As a result, Willard and other demonstration pilots often found themselves confronted with inadequate "airports" and a potentially hostile audience that, after having paid admissions in advance, were determined to get their money's worth by one means or another.

It was therefore necessary to have a machine with sufficient lift to make the best of a bad situation. This Willard-Curtiss was the result.

The first test flight of this machine occurred on August 11 and lasted for seven minutes. On the thirteenth, Willard made several flights, one a 12-mile cross-country flight; and on another, Willard carried two passengers, his brother, Harry Willard, and J. C. "Bud" Mars. On the fourteenth, Charles Willard established an American record when he took up with him three men, R. F. Patterson, Harry Willard and A. Albin. The total gross weight with fuel, oil and

The Willard-Curtiss *Express* at the Walla Walla, Washington, aviation meet, April 27, 1911. *Photo from C. F. Willard*

water was 1,200 pounds and the total supporting surface was 320 square feet. The record flight, at 15 feet altitude, was for a distance of a quarter-mile.

The Willard-Curtiss machine offers a good example of how easily a researcher can be led astray. *Aeronautics* of October 1910 mentions the "Latest Curtiss Design" at the Boston-Harvard meet, and prominent among the changes was the addition of four inset ailerons. Checking this with Willard, it was soon aparent that the Willard-Curtiss was the machine described here and again in *Aero*, December 3, 1910. At the Boston-Harvard meet, September 3–16, 1910, Curtiss and Willard were the Curtiss "team." Willard had his *Banshee* in which was installed the Rheims-Hudson engine, a V-8, 51.2-horsepower, water-cooled engine, as the reader will recall. Willard, in a letter to this writer on February 28, 1970, states:

G. H. had ailerons on the struts (mid point, rear struts), mine were on the rear beams (spars); the first such use of ailerons. Remember I am the leading and first Curtiss pilot and everyone took what I flew as being Curtiss produced. Do not believe all that those people write, because they did not know, and like all writers were looking for being the first with the latest.

Willard's comments are as valid today as they were in 1910.

Aeronautics, October 1910, states:

The Curtiss machine which participated is reported to have used the same 8-cylinder engine used in the Hudson Flier (or one like it). This Boston-Harvard machine had several modifications, designed to reduce drag and produce more speed.

The cambre of the wings was reduced though the wing area remained the same as the Hudson-Fulton machine.

The most prominent change reported is the installation of four ailerons set into the outboard trailing edge of the wings and operating upward and downward differentially rather than just downward as in the case of the Farman ailerons. These four ailerons were adjusted to maintain the line of the airfoil, to avoid drag.

The front control had been reduced to a single surface with a diamond shaped vertical stabilizer mounted stationary half above and half below the single forward elevator. The rear horizontal surface on this, and others up to this date, was a fixed immovable surface. The outer panels of the wing were now covered on top and bottom surfaces though only the upper surface of the center section was covered.

Contemporary reports state that a machine with ailerons on upper and lower surfaces on both sides was also used by McCurdy. Shortly afterward, on January 30, 1911, McCurdy made a spectacular overwater flight, departing from Key West with Havana as the intended landing place. Unfortunately, McCurdy was forced to alight on the water about 10 miles from Havana after completing 89.78 miles in 2 hours 11 minutes. The pilot and machine were picked up by the U.S.S. *Paulding,* and taken to Havana. In spite of the unfortunate accident, McCurdy received a $5,000 prize from the Havana *Post* and a $3,000 prize from the City of Havana. It was the longest nonstop flight up to that date and was a world record for overwater flying. It was probably the most spectacular flight since Bleriot's 1909 cross-channel flight and more than four times the distance.

The possibility that this was the same machine, the *Banshee,* is discounted by Charles F. Willard and his doubts are confirmed by a photo that shows McCurdy readying himself for the Havana flight. The ailerons were of standard Curtiss design and installation.

Specifications

The Willard-Curtiss
Banshee Express, 1910

Span	32 ft. 0 in.
Length	not available
Chord	5 ft.
Gap	5 ft.
Engine	8-cyl. V, water-cooled, 51.2 hp
Weight	
net	not available
gross	650 lb. approx.

The Curtiss-Gordon Bennett Monoplane, 1910

The 1910 monoplane shown at the Gordon Bennett Race was the first monoplane built by Curtiss. Reportedly built for Charles Willard, the machine was considered too flimsy. During a meet at San Antonio, Curtiss asked Willard what kind of machine he wanted. Willard was flying a 4-cylinder D model and knew he wanted more power and less head resistance. The result was the monoplane.

Eugene Ely appeared with it at the Belmont Park International Aviation Meet, October 22–31, 1910, but no mention of its participation is recorded. Though the machine was associated photographically with Eugene Ely at the Belmont meet, the flimsy appearance, including spars with 1⅛-inch depth, discouraged even the most experienced pilots. No mention is made of flights by the monoplane in published records of the meet. That the monoplane did not fly has been confirmed by Willard in a letter to this writer dated March 2, 1965. Willard refused to fly it. The engine for the monoplane was rated at 51.2 horsepower.

Curtiss's construction details were retained, including the standard tricycle frame with pusher engine mounted in the usual manner. Bamboo outriggers support the aft fixed stabilizer and rudder and the forward elevator control. Two triangular pylons attached to each side of the engine and extending upward support the outboard panels by wires. A short auxiliary airfoil connects the apexes of the pylons. All airfoils, wings, rudders, auxiliary airfoil and horizontal control surfaces are double-surfaced (Baldwin fabric on upper and lower surfaces). The surface area of the wings was 224 square feet and the empty weight was 600 pounds. The propeller was 6 feet in length with a 6-foot pitch.

Specifications	
The Curtiss-Gordon Bennett Monoplane, 1910	
Span	26 ft. 3 in.
Length	25 ft. 0 in.
Engine	8-cyl. V, 51.2 hp
Weight gross	600 lb.

Eugene Ely poses in the pilot's seat of the monoplane racer, a drastic departure from the usual Curtiss structure in 1910. No record of its participation in the Gordon Bennett Race exists. Reliable persons believe that flights consisted of short, straight hops. Charles F. Willard and others refused to fly the machine because of the apparent structural weakness of the spars.

The Standard Model D, 1911

The year 1911 brought with it an almost feverish pace in the evolution of Curtiss aircraft. During this year, variations of the basic D model led to the first of a series of Curtiss water-based aircraft: the Curtiss "hydro-aeroplane," the tractor hydro, the Triad, a second variation of the hydro, the first flying boat, and the first of the E-series aircraft.

Events of the year occurred in rapid succession and make strict chronology impossible. In published statements (*Flying,* December 1913, page 30), Curtiss said:

We made tractor hydros with one propeller and tractor hydros with two propellers; hydros with the motor in the pontoon, and other hydros with the motor between the planes; and bob-tailed machines like those the English call "bat-boats." Every way we turned there were prospective opportunities for improvements. Without outside data all these things had to be built and tried out; then adopted or discarded. If all these experimental machines had been built one at a time, the three years leading up to the present flying boat would have stretched out to double that time; but often we had two, perhaps three experimental machines in course of construction at the same time. These experiments included various types of lateral control, different curvatures in the planes, different surfaces, gaps, elevators, methods of balance, and what not. Only a few days ago we had an expensive conflagration at Hammondsport. More room was needed. To secure it we cleared out the storehouse where discarded experiments had been kept. The mass made a pile as high as the boiler house, and the smoke that drifted across the valley must have cost $100,000.

This reference applied to Hammondsport only, and did not take into account the fact that other developments were taking place in Ham-

mondsport and simultaneously at the Curtiss winter camp at North Island, San Diego.

During 1911, the D model became fairly standardized. Prior to this time, the aircraft had a number of variations from the 1909 Herring-Curtiss D. Because each had participated in events of historic record in the embryo aviation industry, the name of the event overshadowed the designation of the machine. Examples of this are the preceding machines: the *Golden Flier,* which was the first Model D, and other machines that followed: the Rheims machine, the *Albany Flier* and the Canoe Machine, to name a few.

In 1911, the United States government purchased a grand total of three aircraft from Curtiss. The navy purchased the first and second airplanes. They were E models, designated by the navy as A-1 and A-2.

The Wright brothers had, on July 30, 1909, satisfied the contract provisions laid down by the War Department for the purchase of an aircraft and had sold the first airplane to the United States government for military use. Curtiss concentrated his sales efforts on the U.S. Navy and, to this end, had offered to teach two naval officers to fly Curtiss aircraft. Lt. T. G. Ellyson and Lt. (J. G.) John H. Towers were detailed to this duty and became the first navy pilots. On December 23, 1910, Lieutenant Ellyson was or-

The Model D-II. Note the dual-surfaced forward elevator, the uncovered lower wing surface, the fixed horizontal stabilizer, the 20-by-4 main wheels and 20-by-2 nose wheel and the 4-cylinder engine. *Curtiss Collection*

dered to report to the Curtiss camp at San Diego; six months later, on June 27, 1911, Lieutenant Towers reported to the Curtiss flying school at Hammondsport. Ellyson was destined to become naval aviator No. 1. Following this offer, it became apparent that special efforts were necessary to adapt the airplane to navy use. As part of the program of developing such a machine, it was necessary to demonstrate the method or methods by which the airplane and the ship could be practically mated.

As mentioned earlier, Eugene Ely, a Curtiss pilot, demonstrated that a standard land machine could successfully take off from a navy ship—in a historic flight from the cruiser U.S.S. *Birmingham* anchored off Hampton Roads, Virginia, on November 14, 1910. To accomplish this, it was necessary to construct a platform on the foredeck of the cruiser. After preparation and waiting for good weather conditions, Ely took advantage of a lull in inclement weather and made his takeoff shortly after 3:00 P.M. on November 14, 1910.

Fog still hung close to the water as Ely took off, dipped down until he touched the water, rose and headed for land. He landed safely on Willoughby Spit five minutes later. The lack of wind

and a slight miscalculation had caused him to touch the water and the spray caused one of the propeller blades to split and loosen a small piece of the tip. Ely commented that it would be an easy matter to land on the deck of a modified battleship whether it was moving or standing still.

Following the test, plans were made in cooperation with the navy to test these proposals. The next year, on January 18, 1911, a second test was planned. The cruiser, U.S.S. *Pennsylvania,* under the command of Captain Pond, was fitted with a large inclined platform on the afterdeck. Sandbagged ropes were stretched across this platform and raised slightly above deck level by timbers that were installed parallel to the center line of the ship. To catch these ropes, a special series of hooks was fixed to the landing gear of Ely's machine. The after-turret had been covered by canvas, netting and other materials to protect Ely in the event he was thrown out of the airplane during the attempt. As an added precaution, Ely wrapped a pair of inflated inner tubes around his chest and shoulders.

After delays caused by weather, Ely appeared in flight about 11:00 A.M., made his approach from astern, and touched down at an estimated 55 miles per hour with the help of a 12-knot

Lieutenant Walker in S.C. No. 8, March 4, 1911. This D-III machine has a single-surfaced forward elevator, double-covered wing panels, a V-8 engine and a cutout at the trailing edge of the wing center section for propeller clearance. *Curtiss Collection*

wind. He missed the first few arresting ropes, but the others stopped him quickly. After a greeting by Captain Pond, Ely was escorted below deck to the wardroom for lunch. During lunch, the airplane was turned around, the platform cleared and then Ely took off. The crowds that had gathered ashore cheered him and whistles blew until he was out of sight. From a practical point of view, this marked the beginning of the development of the aircraft carrier, which was the backbone of the powerful task forces of World War II.

Aside from the specifications of the basic D model, several of its variants had important modifications. The D-II was characterized by a single front elevator control consisting of a bamboo pole connecting the control column to the top of the elevator. The ailerons were mounted to the rear interplane struts rather than the forward interplane struts. The wings were single-surfaced, i.e., uncovered on the lower surfaces. The rear horizontal stabilizer was still rigidly fixed and a slot was provided in the rudder to allow unrestricted movement. The wheels were still the same diameter, 20 inches by 2 inches. The trail-

ing edge of the center section had a cutout to provide clearance for the propeller. The wingspan was 26 feet 3 inches and the chord was 4 feet 6 inches.

The D-III appears to have been the most numerous of the D models and was characterized by ailerons pivoted from the rear interplane strut instead of the front struts as in the case of the earlier models. This was considered a decided improvement, since the aileron pivoting between the wings lessened the efficiency of the ailerons as well as the wings. The covering of both the top and bottom surfaces of the wing,

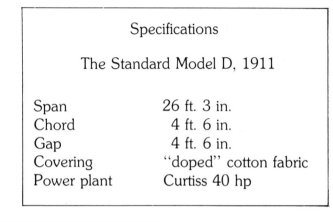

Specifications	
The Standard Model D, 1911	
Span	26 ft. 3 in.
Chord	4 ft. 6 in.
Gap	4 ft. 6 in.
Covering	"doped" cotton fabric
Power plant	Curtiss 40 hp

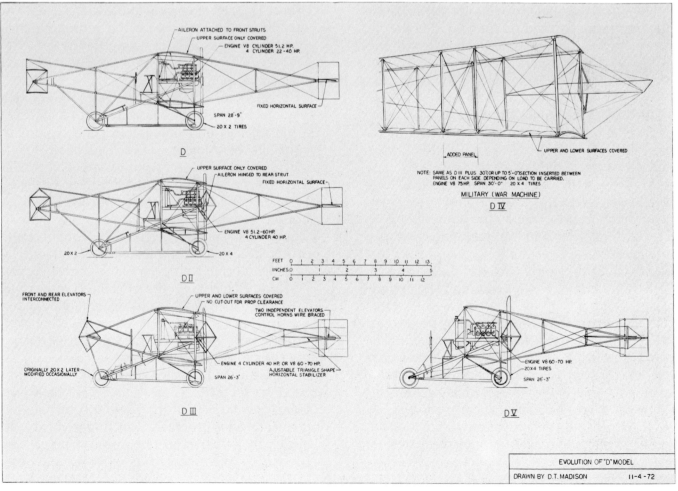

A group of army D-III machines, most of which are in transition to becoming "headless." The forward surfaces are missing but their supporting structure is still in place. Photo taken at the Curtiss camp, San Diego. *Curtiss Collection*

thereby enclosing the ribs and spars, improved the performance of the aircraft by an estimated 3 to 6 miles per hour.

The forward elevator was moved rearward and placed almost directly above the front wheel, or about 6 feet 9 inches forward of the wing's leading edge.

Technically, the most important change was the addition of two independently operated elevators, each having its own pair of wires, at the rear in place of the fixed horizontal stabilizer that was formerly used on the D and D-II. The two rear elevators operated in concert with the front elevator and were approximately 13 feet back from the rear edge of the main wings.

Two triangular-shaped horizontal stabilizers were used; their angle of incidence could be easily changed to correct for longitudinal (pitch trim) flight deficiencies. The D-III therefore had independently controlled elevator surfaces consisting of the monoplane forward elevator, which was connected to the pilot's control by an overhead bamboo pole linkage (on some, the pole was attached below hinge points), and two separate elevator surfaces at the rear connected independently by control cables to the lower portion of the pilot's control column. The rudder was placed between the two rear elevators and was pivoted 6 inches to the rear of the front edge. In addition, the rudder was operated by a tiller post extending forward from the rudder to which the steering wires were attached, giving more leverage than if the wires were attached directly to the rudder as had been done previously.

On the D-III, the engine was mounted 9 inches farther to the rear, making it unnecessary to cut-out the trailing edge of the wing to ensure clearance for the propeller.

One small but important technical detail was the addition of new operating controls, making it possible to bring the rudder wires inside the vertical post to the control wheel.

Gradually, as a result of tests begun at Hammondsport, the forward elevator was removed, resulting in the Model D-III Headless.

The Headless was developed quite by accident. According to Beckwith Havens:

L. Beachey was flying an exhibition date and hit a fence on landing, breaking his front controls. There was a lot of money involved in this engagement and Beachey was not about to lose it by a default so he flew anyway—without the front elevator. He was pleasantly surprised to find that the machine performed better than before. News of this improvement spread to Hammondsport where it was further tested. This was the beginning of the D "Headless." News of this change traveled by the "grapevine" and within a short time all existing exhibition machines were headless.

The D-IV variation in the D series is identified primarily by an extension to the wings consisting of a 30-inch insert between the outboard panels on each side, resulting in a wing area increased to 280 square feet. The overall span was now 31 feet 3 inches.

On March 7, 1911, the first Type IV, or "military machine," was demonstrated to a group of army officials and members of the diplomatic corps in Washington, D.C. The pilot, J.A.D. McCurdy, flew the airplane on two flights over the Potomac River. The airplane was designed for and intended to be sent to the Texas-Mexican border for use by the encamped army there. It was the first Curtiss machine to be bought by the army, the sale of which was negotiated by Jerome Fanciulli, manager of the Curtiss Exhibition Company. It was the same in all respects as the D-III, except for span. A major feature of the "war machine" was its ability to be "knocked down" into small sections for transportation. Each section of the wings was interchangeable. It had an 8-cylinder water-cooled engine rated at 51.2 horsepower. A passenger seat was provided directly behind the pilot, and the landing gear was now provided with three wheels, 20 inches by 4 inches in dimension. Spruce was used for the interplane struts, while the four posts at the corner of the center section were lami-

The first Model D-IV Military Machine was used by Eugene Ely to make the first "carrier" landing on January 18, 1911. Note the short 30-inch panels inserted in the wings.

nated ash and spruce. The center section of the structure was further strengthened by a system of double-cable trussing; the entire system of bracing in the center section was made of steel tubing in place of the wood structure formerly used. The ailerons, similar to those of the standard Model D-III, had, at their center section, a triangular tube structure to serve as control horns. Wings were still built on the sectional principle, though much improved in form with each section a complete panel with ribs and beams covered on top and bottom. The panels were interchangeable and fastened together without lacing. This system permitted the machine to be quickly assembled or taken apart and repaired in a very few minutes by substituting new panels to replace broken parts. The introduction of this small 30-inch section between the main outboard portions of the wing made it possible to vary the area of the wing in the field. It was first used by Eugene Ely on the first landing aboard ship on January 18, 1911. Photographic evidence indicated that this was carried to the ultimate by placing an entire third section of a 5-foot span on each side, making a total of six bays. This "war machine" photographed in Augusta, Georgia, on March 22, 1912, showed the additional large section, plus upper-wing overhang, which brought the wing area up to 325 square feet when it was desired to carry two passengers.

As in the case of the Model D-III, the elevators were hinged to the rear of the triangular-shaped adjustable horizontal stabilizer and were worked in unison by wires attached to vertical posts (control horns) braced to the center of each of the elevators and leading to the control wheel. The following appeared in *Aero,* March 30, 1912:

In demonstrating the new machine the pilot, Charles F. Walsh, made 53.1 mph, an excess of 8.1 mph. The specs required 45 mph. Endurance test was met with a flight of two hours 11 minutes at 300 ft and landings and takeoff from a ploughed field. In tests requiring the carrying of a passenger, Col. C. B. Wender of the Ohio National Guard accompanied the pilot. During these tests the aircraft was fitted with extra panels, the upper span increased to 43.8 and the lower wing increased to 39.8. The chord of 5'-0" gave the plane a lifting surface of 416.5 sq. ft. and enabled the plane to rise from the ploughed field with ease. The plane was knocked down for shipment in 33 minutes and reassembled for flight in 55 minutes.

Summarizing the features of the D-IV, we have the following:

1. Triangular-shaped adjustable horizontal stabilizers with independently controlled elevators attached.
2. A "knock-down" capability.
3. An 8-cylinder water-cooled V-8 engine of 51.2 horsepower.

The Model E Training Hydroplane. Lincoln Beachey, pilot, Glenn H. Curtiss on the launching ramp. Note the newly developed throw-over control that was developed for instructing purposes. *Curtiss Collection*

4. Inserts, one on each side, initially 30 inches in width, but adaptable to any spacing desired.

5. A double-wire system of trussing the center section, each wire having its own fitting and turnbuckle.

6. A single-surfaced front elevator almost directly above the front wheel. A bamboo pole connected from the lower arm of the upright yoke to the lower part of the forward elevator.

7. A second seat placed behind and slightly above the pilot.

8. The rear spar placed very near the trailing edge of the wing.

9. The engine moved further to the rear, eliminating the earlier characteristic cutout in the center section to provide clearance for the propeller.

10. The rear tires were 20 inches by 4 inches initially, the front wheels remaining 20 inches by 2 inches.

11. The center section was braced by steel tubing.

12. The ailerons were fitted to the rear interplane strut.

13. The plane was still built on the sectional principle, each section removable and interchangeable.

14. The wing surfaces were covered, both top and bottom.

15. The elevators had a small mast (control horn) mounted in the center of the elevator with guy wires to the four corners of the elevator both top and bottom.

16. The rudder was mounted vertically between the elevators with its axis 6 inches to the rear of the leading edge of the rudder and had a tiller projecting forward of the leading edge to which were attached the control wires.

17. The ailerons had triangular-shaped tubing with control horn wires braced to the four corners of the ailerons, both top and bottom.

During 1912, the structure of the standard machines went through a metamorphosis as the result of Lincoln Beachey's accident, which destroyed the forward control surface of an exhibition machine. At about the same time, navy pilots discovered rather quickly that the bow-mounted elevator on the navy's A-1 (an E model) was an impediment and removed it.

An interesting and amusing event occurred

Specifications

D-IV Military Machine

Width of planes overall	31 ft. 3 in.	Front elevator, single surface	24 in. by 75 in.
Width overall, including ailerons	38 ft. 1 in.	Two rear elevators, each having control cables for double safety and each having an area slightly over 5¾ sq. ft.	
Length overall, fore and aft, from tip to tip	25 ft. 6 in.		
Depth of main planes front to rear	48 in.		
		Diameter of pontoons for alighting on water	11 in.
Distance between front and rear posts (center to center) supporting main planes	42 in.	Diameter of propeller	7 ft. 0 in.
Height of posts	54 in.	Pitch of propeller	6 ft. 0 in.

Motor, 8-cylinder, 4 by 4, water-cooled, regular Curtiss type, equipped with Bosch magneto, Schebler carburetor, E1 Arco radiator

Height overall, from ground	7 ft. 4½ in.		
Total lifting surface of main planes	250 sq. ft.	Total weight, approximate	700 lb.
		Total weight packed in boxes, approximate	1,000 lb.
Aileron projection beyond planes on each end	41 in.		
Length of rear control bamboos	12 ft. 6¼ in.		
Length of front control bamboos	7 ft. 0 in.		

All vital parts double-wired. Beams, posts, ribs and propeller laminated. Push steering wheel operates front and rear elevators and rudder; balance controlled by shoulder yoke operating neutral ailerons.

A triplane hydro made from Model D and E components. *Curtiss photo from the A. R. Clemons Collection*

during the project to reproduce the A-1 for the fiftieth anniversary of naval aviation in 1961. As part of the project, engineers at the David Taylor Model Basin constructed a test model complete with the forward elevator. During the wind tunnel test, it was found that, under certain circumstances, the aircraft would be unstable, possibly even dangerously so. On learning of this, Norman Fresh, test engineer at the Model Basin, called Capt. Holden C. "Capt. Dick" Richardson, U.S. Navy (Ret.), former navy constructor and navy pilot No. 13, to report this condition. To Fresh's amusement, "Capt. Dick" replied that the pioneer navy pilots had discovered this on the first two or three flights and removed the forward elevator permanently.

For a period of time, the only change made was the removal of the control surface, leaving the supporting structure intact. The results were an ungainly looking machine. Finally, Curtiss redesigned the structure and began producing at Hammondsport the 1912 Headless D model. A specimen of this configuration is on exhibit in the National Aircraft Collection of the National Air and Space Museum.

On special order, triangular extension wing panels and braces were available for D and E aircraft that could be attached to the upper wing surface to give the aircraft added lift.

This was not a regular item of equipment and does not appear on our regular price list therefore it was charged at a net price ($100) barely sufficient to cover costs . . .*

The presence of or lack of these triangular-shaped extensions to the wings did not change the model designation of the aircraft on which they were installed. They were supplementary surfaces installed, when desired, on the D, E and even on the earliest F boats, as in the case of the army's first boat.

Specifications		
Models D and E (Standard), 1912		
	D	*E*
Span	26 ft. 3 in.	28 ft. 8 in.
Chord	4 ft. 6 in.	5 ft. 0 in.
Gap	4 ft. 6 in.	5 ft. 0 in.
Power plant	40/60/75 hp	40/60/75 hp

*Letter to W. I. Chambers from G. R. Hall, secretary-treasurer of the Curtiss Motor Company, dated September 12, 1912.

The Headless D Racer, 1912

The aviation industry was not prosperous during 1912 but it did have an aero show. The date was May 9–18 and the setting was the Grand Central Palace in New York City.

It brought together twenty-three airplanes and an equal number of engines from eight manufacturers. Curtiss brought the most exhibits of any single manufacturer, displaying three aircraft and two engines. Two of the aircraft, the standard land and standard hydro-aeroplanes have been recorded previously. The third machine, the 1912 Headless Racer, while not a radical departure structurally, was built as a racing machine to defend the Gordon Bennett Cup for the year 1912. The major difference was the reduction in wing area accomplished by reducing the span to 17 feet 3 inches. In other respects, it was a D-III, including the 20-inch-by-2-inch front wheel and 20-inch-by-4-inch main wheels. It was powered by the standard 75-horsepower V-8 water-cooled O engine and had an estimated speed of 85 miles per hour.

The Headless Racer, short-winged version of the standard Model D machine, photographed at entrance to Curtiss exhibit area at Grand Central Palace Aeronautical Show, May 9–16, 1912. It was intended for the 1912 Gordon Bennett Cup race.

Charles S. "Casey" Jones, Curtiss test and racing pilot, poses in the 1912 Headless. This specimen is in the collection of the National Air and Space Museum.

The Model D and E aircraft evolved into ''headless'' versions in the field, but were eventually manufactured in this form. The photo shows Lincoln Beachey flying a Headless D at Hammondsport.

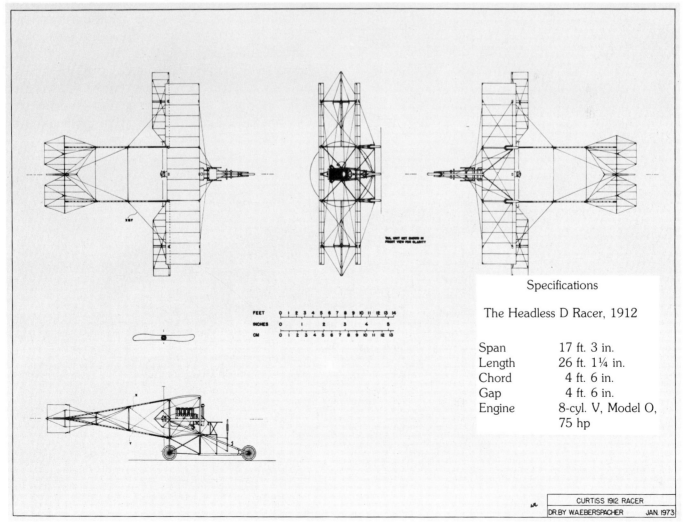

Specifications

The Headless D Racer, 1912

Span	17 ft. 3 in.
Length	26 ft. 1¼ in.
Chord	4 ft. 6 in.
Gap	4 ft. 6 in.
Engine	8-cyl. V, Model O, 75 hp

CURTISS 1912 RACER

DR.BY W.A.EBERSPACHER   JAN. 1973

The D Hydro

Probably the most significant and famous variation of the D model was a waterborne aircraft, the hydro-aeroplane. Most of the construction and trials of this machine took place at San Diego, and after a series of developmental models, Curtiss was successful in achieving a public flight from and on to the water on January 26, 1911, though the first flight had actually occurred several days earlier.

The standard D-type aircraft, along with a float landing gear, was shipped to the Curtiss winter camp at San Diego in December 1910 and, by a process of trial and error, was converted to a successful and practical hydro-aeroplane. Curtiss arrived at San Diego on December 2, 1910. The French constructor, Henri Fabre, had flown from the water prior to this date but, having accomplished this "historic first" on March 28, 1910, made no further attempts to develop the Fabre concept of hydro-aeroplanes. To give the reader a firsthand view of the process of developing the hydroplane, the following first-person recollections of the events that led up to this historic event have been extracted from testimony in connection with the Janin patent litigation.

Albert S. Janin, a cabinetmaker from Rosebank, Staten Island, New York, filed a patent application as early as January 26, 1911, for a main hull supported by two outboard floats. This was the main factor in his application, but he did not demonstrate its operation. The Curtiss application, dated August 22, 1911, included this feature but mainly dealt with the hydrodynamic features of the hull. As part of the proceedings Curtiss built an aircraft to the Janin patent specifications to demonstrate that it would not lift out of the water. The three-volume transcript of testimony resulting from the court action described the step-by-step history of early flying boat development. The depositions of Lt. Theodore G. Ellyson, U.S. Navy, Glenn Curtiss himself, and quotations from a narrative by Maj. George E. A. Hallett, three of the participants in

The Curtiss D airframe with floats in place of wheels. *From the H. R. Fitch Historical Collection, Title Insurance and Trust Co., San Diego, Calif.*

the tests, enable us to piece together the details of these events.

Starting with the question-and-answer testimony of Lieutenant Ellyson, we find the following:

Q. With respect to your first appearance at San Diego, which you state was about January 2nd, will you please state whether, when you reached there, there was a hydro-aeroplane on the premises, and if so, describe it as it appeared at that time, as well as you remember.

ELLYSON. There was a machine on the premises from which the land landing gear had been removed, and there were pontoons and floats ready to be fitted, but they had not been fitted at that time.

Q. As I understand your testimony, you then left San Diego a day or two after that date, and did not return until the 18th?

ELLYSON. I left San Diego on the 4th and returned there shortly before noon on the 18th.

Q. With respect to your return on the 18th, please state whether there was a hydro-aeroplane on the premises, and if so, describe it.

ELLYSON. There was a hydro-aeroplane on the premises, practically completely set up. What had not been done previous to our arrival, I personally helped to finish up that afternoon. The machine consisted of a Curtiss Standard Land Machine, fitted with a central float about five feet wide, a little over six feet long, and approximately fourteen inches thick at its thickest point. The bottom of this float was a hydro-surface. This was the main or supporting pontoon. The wing tips of the machine were fitted with paddles,* extending rearward from the front edge of the plane at an angle of about 45 degrees, to assist in the lateral balance

---

*As this hydro-aeroplane was tested, additional buoyancy was required while the machine was at rest. To provide this, inflated inner tubes were lashed to the upper side of these paddles.

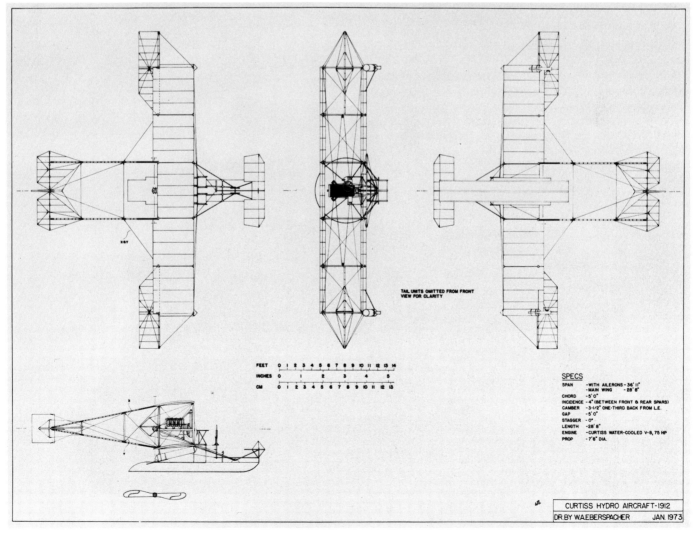

TAIL UNITS OMITTED FROM FRONT VIEW FOR CLARITY

FEET 0 1 2 3 4 5 6 7 8 9 10 11 12 13 14
INCHES 0 1 2 3 4 5
CM 0 1 2 3 4 5 6 7 8 9 10 11 12 13

SPECS

SPAN — WITH AILERONS — 36' 11"
— MAIN WING — 28' 8"
CHORD — 5' 0"
INCIDENCE — 4° (BETWEEN FRONT & REAR SPARS)
CAMBER — 3-1/2" ONE-THIRD BACK FROM L.E.
GAP — 5' 0"
STAGGER — 0°
LENGTH — 28' 8"
ENGINE — CURTISS WATER-COOLED V-8, 75 HP
PROP — 7' 6" DIA.

CURTISS HYDRO AIRCRAFT-1912
DR. BY W.A.EBERSPACHER   JAN. 1973

Towing the Curtiss D Hydro to the water at San Diego.

(on the water and on landing). There was a float approximately twelve feet in front of the aviator's seat. The dimensions of this float were approximately thirty inches long, fourteen inches wide, and four inches deep. The airplane was fitted with the Standard Curtiss ailerons, tail and front elevator.

Q. Was there any engine in the machine, and if so where was it located?

ELLYSON. There was a standard Curtiss eight cylinder engine, placed approximately over the center of gravity of the main or large float.

Q. Was there any vertical rudder on the machine?

ELLYSON. There was a Standard Curtiss tail, consisting of the tail braces, the vertical rudder, the horizontal rudder or rear elevator and the tail lifting surfaces.

Q. Did you ever see this machine . . . fly from the water into the air and alight on the water?

ELLYSON. Yes . . .

Q. That is, you saw the machine . . . fly from the water into the air and alight on the water?

ELLYSON. Yes. I can tell all the changes that were made, as I personally helped in making all changes, but the sequence may not be the exact sequence in which the

Curtiss poses in the Tractor Hydro.

different experiments were tried. When the machine was first run in the water with the engine stopped, it floated entirely upon the main pontoon with the front float at least twelve inches clear of the water. When the engine was started the thrust of the propeller buried this float, and although the machine was run over the water at about twenty-five miles an hour, it could not be made to leave the water. The angle of the front float was then changed in hopes that this would give more lift, but this did not

Launching of the third and successful version of the Curtiss hydro.

The Model E Hydro fitted with a test airfoil above the wing to conduct center of pressure experiments. *Curtiss Collection*

accomplish the desired result. The angle of the main float was accordingly varied and a small hydro-surface, a strip of wood about two inches wide was added to the rear edge of the main float. This served to raise the machine so that when it attained a speed the weight rested principally on the rear end of the main float, but the small float in front remained buried. Two forms of front elevators were used, first a single surface, and later a box type of elevator. Great difficulty was experienced from spray striking the propeller. To overcome this difficulty and to aid in starting, a canvas covered extension was placed on the main float, well braced, about two feet long, making the total length of the main float approximately eight feet. Trouble was still experienced, and then a small hydro-surface which consisted of a board about five inches wide and about five feet long was placed approximately three feet in front of the small float mentioned before. After trying this hydro-surface at various angles a position was found where the small float in front was held clear of the water as soon as the machine gained ten miles speed or over, and it did not touch the water at higher speed. To further increase the lifting in the front of the machine, a lifting surface similar to the front elevator was placed just to the rear of the front hydro-surface.

Q. Was this an air surface or a hydro-surface?

ELLYSON. This was an air surface. After these changes had been made the hydro-aeroplane attained a speed of from thirty-five to forty-five miles an hour, estimated, and apparently made short skips from the water. Two days before the first public flight was made, this machine made a short flight of from thirty to forty feet, attaining an altitude as high as five feet, sufficient to show that the machine was flying and not merely skipping from the top of the surface of the waves. When Mr. Curtiss returned from these jumps or short flights, I asked him why he did not make a longer and higher flight. His answer was that he wished to get the feel of the machine before attempting too much with it as it was a new type of which no one knew anything, and he wanted to make sure that he was accustomed to the feel of the machine before making long flights.

Q. How long did you say these flights, you have just spoken of, first occurred before the public flight?

ELLYSON. Two days before the public flight.

Q. Did this machine make any other flights before the public flight?

ELLYSON. On the same night that he made the first flights I helped to make a small change in the angle of the front

hydro-board surface. The following day he made several straight-away flights, attaining an altitude of from ten to fifteen feet and going distances of 100 to 150 feet. In these flights you could notice the slowing of the machine as he glided to landing showing the perfect control. After these flights on the day before the public trial no changes were made in the machine. Mr. Curtiss announced that the machine was perfect and that he wanted no changes made, as he wished to fly for the newspaper men the following day. I left North Island with the last of the men at dark on that night, and I was there before daylight on the day that the public flight was made, and when I arrived on the Island, no one else was there, so I am positive that no changes were made in the machine since the night two days previous to the first public flight when the angle of the front hydro-surface was changed.

In the same case, Curtiss himself testified as follows:

This machine was constructed very much like the former machine known as the canoe machine, except that this main supporting float was quite a different shape. It was about as wide as it was long, and to avoid the danger of heading over it was equipped with an additional float several feet ahead of the main float, a small additional float, which was bolted into the frame of the aeroplane at the point where the forward wheel on the land machine had been fixed. As the trials continued we added to this small forward float a planing board similar to the planing board I had used on the Hudson machine, and had alighted very successfully, to further obviate the danger of heading over on landing, and also to keep the bow up in starting, and offset the tendency of the propeller thrust to depress the bow of the craft.

Before we made the first trial at San Diego we extended that float about 2 feet, getting further forward by a rough construction of board and canvas. The float itself was

The Curtiss-Navy A-H (Model E) approaching the beach on March 30, 1911. The design is similar to the D-III type. Float gear was interchangeable with land gear and could be ordered at the time of purchase, or later, as an option that cost $500 additional.

William S. Lucky testing the stick stabilizer equipment. The fabric-covered disk mounted above the center section had the two transverse edges turned up about 10 inches, presenting a side area to any cross currents and thereby increasing the lateral stability of the aircraft much the same way that a dihedral does. This tended to return the aircraft to a stable flight path.

made of wood covered entirely with tin.

I learned, however, to steady the machine by the use of the horizontal rudder and I found that it was more controllable to give it full power and get on top of the water, get it planing as quickly as possible, and I soon found that it was quite easy to get off the surface of the water and fly along for 100 feet or more, and alight on the water. This I did a number of times, and to all practical purposes that was a flight. It showed we were able to get loose from the water and light back on the water safely; but having been in the exhibition business I knew that a flight, to the average man, meant getting up in the air where he could look up and see the machine from beneath, and that is why the first published flight, the first flight of which we kept any record, was made on January 26th, when we had a number of visitors and witnesses. At that time, I caused the machine to rise a considerable height and flew out over San Diego Bay and made a complete circle and returned and glided down and alighted in front of what is known as the Spanish Bight.

The following is an eyewitness account of Curtiss's first flight off water by Maj. George E. A. Hallett:

In January of 1911, Glenn H. Curtiss was experimenting here in San Diego with one of his regular eight-cylinder, 60 horsepower exhibition planes, which would normally operate from dry land, in an attempt to modify it so it would operate off the water and thus be of interest to the Navy.

At this time, I was working as a machinist from the Baker Machine Company on the waterfront of San Diego. Curtiss rented a motor boat from the shop to use as a ferry to North Island or, more exactly, to Spanish Bight, which then existed between North Island and Coronado. He also hired me, temporarily, to help make changes in the plane as the experiments progressed.

The plane was first assembled as brought from the Curtiss factory at Hammondsport on Lake Keuka, New York. Instead of the usual three-wheeled landing gear, there was a short, wide pontoon under the wings where the rear wheels had been and a very small pontoon where the front wheel had been.

When this rig was put in the water it was found it needed flotation on the wing tips to keep the plane from tipping over in the wind, so we added inflated motorcycle tubes to the ash "shingles" which acted as planing surfaces on the wing tips while the craft was taxiing on the water.

When we started the engine, it was found that the thrust of the propeller, which was about four feet above the water, pushed the nose down under the water. We then added a wood planing surface at the nose. With this combination, Curtiss could taxi slowly but water boiled over the top of the rear pontoon and the plane could not get up any speed.

On the front of the rear pontoon we next built a "snout" of wood and canvas, which prevented the water from flowing over the rear pontoon and added planing surface. With this combination, Curtiss could taxi a little faster; but, as he opened the throttle, the nose pontoon was pushed under water again. After that we put a wide planing surface out on the bamboo poles about six feet in front of the front pontoon.

When Curtiss tested this unwieldy rig, it actually got up on the surface of the water and moved along rapidly. He did not let it get into the air, but taxied around a little at a high speed and finally skidded sidewise, in a turn, and wrecked part of the pontoon on a mud flat.

The next day, after repairs, Mr. Curtiss

made several short flights a few feet above the water in this weird contraption.

That evening, Mr. Curtiss (or "GH" as we called him) went to his rented home in Coronado and sketched a single neat pontoon which was to replace all the conglomeration we had under the plane. This pontoon was detailed and built in the Baker Machine Company by Bob Baker (the late Captain R. H. Baker of Point Loma) and his pattern-makers.

Under the plane we put the new pontoon, which was built of thin spruce, and, after adjusting it to balance correctly, Mr. Curtiss made several flights several hundred feet high and all the whistles blew. This was January 26, 1911.

This was the flight of a practical hydro-aeroplane.

The new float designed by Curtiss was a simple straightforward affair. It resembled a flat-bottomed boat, planked with unlaminated spruce over a wood frame. The pontoon was 12 feet long, 2 feet wide and 12 inches deep. At a distance of about 3 feet back from the front end, the bottom surface curved upward forming a planing bow without any keel and a similar contour at the rear end with the curvature beginning at the top surface and trailing off to the bottom surface to form this float. The two contours, fore and aft, were so near the same contour that either could be used as a bow of the pontoon. The float was fixed to the aircraft in a manner to allow the weight of the engine of the aircraft to be slightly to the rear of the middle of the pontoon, giving the bow an upward tilt that assisted in making the airplane plane quickly as the power was applied. The weight of this new pontoon was about half as much as the apparatus that had previously been used in the experiments. In addition, this offered substantially less surface resistance to the water.

In *Flying* magazine, December 1913, Curtiss wrote:

We did not think when the hydroaeroplane made its initial flight that this was but the first step in the development of the water-flying machine. Rather, it then seemed, an end had been accomplished; aviation had been made as relatively safe as any other mode of rapid transit. Here was a machine we could offer to sportsmen with the assurance that with it they could enjoy the rushing exhilaration of flight without undue trepidation. The idea that water flying might be developed into not only the safest possible mode of very rapid travel, but at the same time the most comfortable of conveyances, did not suggest itself strongly until a year later.

During that first year of experimenting we awoke to the fact that the original hydro-aeroplane was, after all, only a makeshift. It did assure the pilot of a reasonably clear landing place at all times, but did not give him the liberty to fly exactly where he chose, on the water or over the water, with the freedom enjoyed now in the flying boat. In other words, with the hydroaeroplane one was obliged to fly above the water rather than on the water. For the standard pontoons were shallow, and if one attempted skimming along very close to the surface there was always the possibility of "stubbing your toe" in a wave or unseen swell, and that meant the probable upsetting of the machine with, at least, a consequent ducking. Another drawback to the hydroaeroplane, from a sporting or travel standpoint, was the relative discomfort of the exposed position. It was in overcoming these objections to the hydroaeroplane that the idea of the flying boat developed.

Specifications	
The D Hydro (first variant)	
Span	26 ft. 3 in.
Chord	4 ft. 6 in.
Gap	4 ft. 6 in.
Main float	7 ft. 1 in. long; 6 ft. 3 in. wide; 10 in. deep
Secondary float (for front wheel position)	2 ft. 6 in. long; 16 in. wide; 4½ in. deep; 6 in. deep side flanges
Power plant	Curtiss V-8-type, water-cooled, 4-inch-by-5-inch single rocker O type, 60 hp

The D-III Tractor Hydro, 1911

As related previously, the U.S. Navy was watching the development of the airplane with a view to making it a practical, tactical vehicle for use with the fleet. The presence of navy officers (and army officers) at the Curtiss camp and at Hammondsport gives ample evidence of the interest of the services. There was interest, but no purchase order.

In order to convince the navy of the utility of the airplane, it was necessary to conduct tests that would demonstrate the methods by which the airplane could be employed in naval operations. To demonstrate the method for operations, we have seen how Ely made a flight from ship to shore from the U.S.S. *Birmingham* at Hampton Roads, Virginia, on November 14, 1910, and again on January 18, 1911, at San Francisco, when he landed aboard, and took off from the U.S.S. *Pennsylvania.*

Still, even with these demonstrations, the secretary of the navy, George von Lengerke Meyer, was not convinced enough to order the first navy aircraft. To justify a purchase order, Secretary Meyer insisted that it be demonstrated that an

The Tractor Hydro ready for start. *Curtiss Collection*

aircraft could be launched and retrieved from a naval ship-of-the-line without impairing its combat efficiency. Having succeeded in producing a successful hydro-aeroplane, Curtiss undertook to demonstrate its utility. For this demonstration Curtiss used a tractor hydro. This machine was a basic D-III, possibly the same machine used for the test on February 2, but converted to a tractor configuration. The engine was mounted forward, in a tractor position, and the pilot's seat placed to the rear behind the trailing edge of the lower wing.

On February 17, 1911, Curtiss conducted the test in San Diego harbor, rising from the water, alighting on the water and arriving alongside the

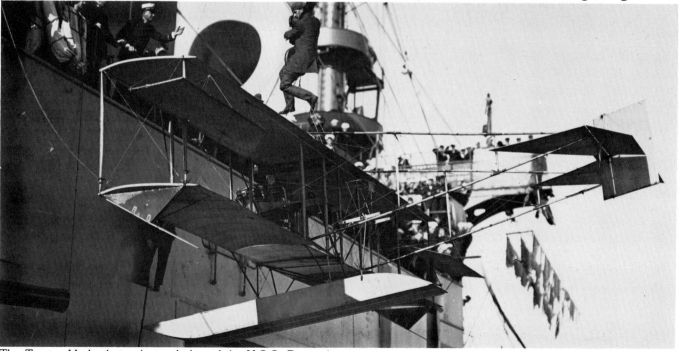
The Tractor Hydro being hoisted aboard the U.S.S. *Pennsylvania.*

A "hop" into the air. The Tractor Hydro did achieve momentary flight, which was reported for record purposes. However, this was about the maximum height attained, and the flight lasted only seconds.

cruiser U.S.S. *Pennsylvania*. The airplane and pilot were lifted aboard by a standard boat crane and placed on deck. Curtiss was invited to tea, after which he made ready to depart. While some contemporary articles state that Curtiss flew back to shore, Curtiss himself in his autobiographical book *The Curtiss Aeroplane Book* does not make such a statement. Waldo Waterman, a witness to the demonstration, stated positively to this writer that the outbound flight was, in fact, a very short hop, which ended in a stalled landing, the sound of which was clearly audible to viewers on the shore. After casting off from the cruiser, the airplane was taxied back to the Curtiss camp at high speed, never leaving the water. The tractor was obviously not properly balanced for flight operations. This tractor configuration was never revived, but did adequately demonstrate the ability to operate from a navy ship and probably was instrumental in selling the first airplane to the U.S. Navy. Photographs of the sequence of the test, including the "flight," were widely circulated in the press. Soon afterward the navy announced the purchase of the first navy aircraft. The tractor configuration was abandoned because of three factors: lack of forward visibility, discomfort resulting from exposure to propeller blast and damage to the pilot's clothing, the result of spraying oil.

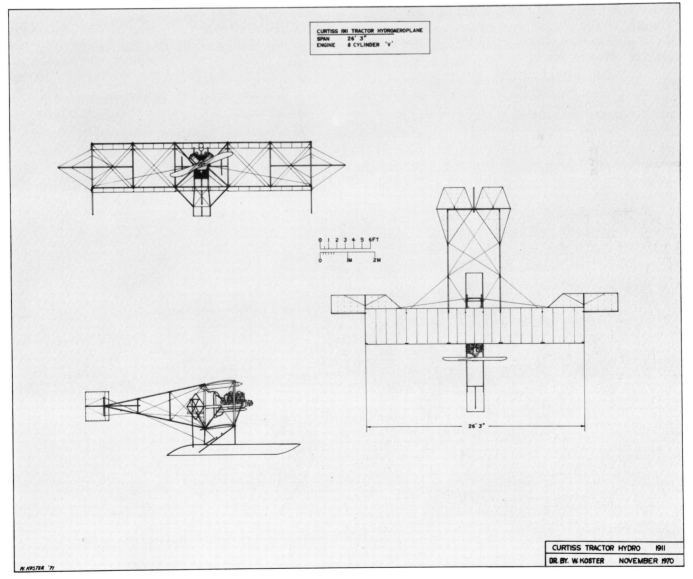

CURTISS 1911 TRACTOR HYDROAEROPLANE
SPAN 26' 3"
ENGINE 8 CYLINDER 'V'

0 1 2 3 4 5 6FT
0 1M 2M

26' 3"

M. KOSTER '71

CURTISS TRACTOR HYDRO 1911
DR. BY. W. KOSTER NOVEMBER 1970

The Triad, 1911

The Triad was perhaps the first successful amphibian aircraft as we understand them. The basic D Hydro was further modified by the addition of a retractable main wheel landing gear. As far as is known, the front wheel, mounted on bow of the main float, was fixed. Three of these machines were built, one for the navy; one for Al Engle, now in the Western Reserve Museum, Cleveland, Ohio; and one for Curtiss himself.

George Hallett states that larger, heavier versions (probably based on the E configuration) were delivered by himself and Charles Witmer to the Russian Black Sea Fleet at Sebastopol.

The first demonstrations of this type are reported to have occurred at San Diego on February 26, 1911, only one month after Curtiss had made the first public demonstration flights of the first Curtiss hydro. In the interim, he had tried the tractor version, developed a throw-over control for instruction purposes, and had the new main float constructed, all of this attesting to the rapid developments taking place and the inventive genius of Curtiss and his associates. Shortly after this first Triad flight on February 26, Curtiss took off from the water, flew to a nearby sand spit, landed, then taxied to the water for a second takeoff, ascended to a height of about 800 feet and made a second landing on the hard sand beach near the Coronado Hotel, stopping near the pier. Later the same day, he took off from the beach and returned to his hangar and alighted on the water of San Diego Bay.

With considerable doubts, this writer queried George E. A. Hallett about the accuracy of the above event. The capability of the small 2 inch tires on a sand beach gave me reason to doubt the description in the periodicals. In his reply, George Hallett confirmed the accuracy as follows:

In reply to your letter of September 18th, 1968, the beach near the Coronado Hotel is often so hard that the Curtiss first "Triad" of 1911 with its small tires, would hardly make a track on it. This is true when the tide is out, but if Curtiss had landed in the soft dry sand

The Triad taxiing ashore on North Island, San Diego. *Curtiss photo from the A. R. Clemons Collection*

G. H. CURTISS.
CONVERTIBLE RUNNING GEAR.
APPLICATION FILED NOV. 18, 1916.

1,269,570.

Patented June 11, 1918.
3 SHEETS—SHEET 2.

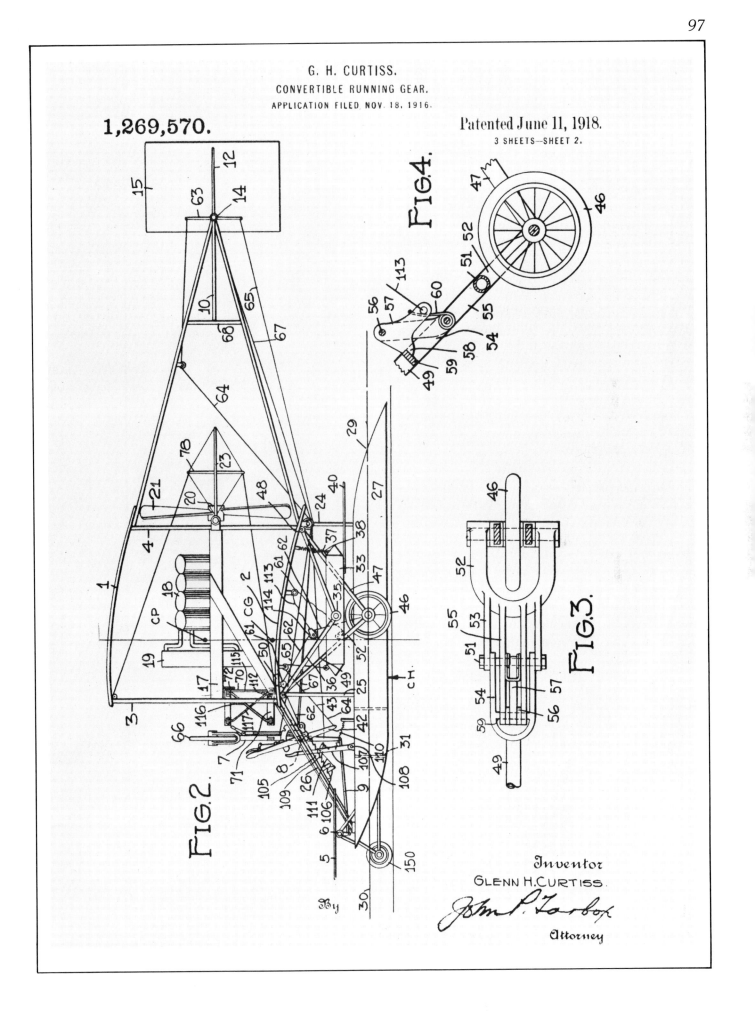

Fig.2.

Fig.3.

Fig.4.

Inventor
GLENN H. CURTISS.

By

Attorney

above the high tide mark, the tires could have sunk in enough to slow him up pretty fast. I believe he could have landed safely, even there, but would not have been able to take off from that part of the beach. He *could not* have landed in the water there because of the heavy surf. Curtiss had lived in Coronado long enough to know these things about the beach.

In his descriptive article, Capt. Paul Beck, U.S. Army, had estimated the wind velocity at 18 miles per hour.

During the same brief period of experimentation, the standard pusher hydro was tested as a triplane. During this experiment it was determined that the machine could lift an additional 200 pounds using the same power.

All things considered, the hydro development was an outstanding success. The now standard D model was available to purchasers in either the land version or the hydro version, the latter costing an additional $500. Prices at that date, 1911, were as follows:

Model D (III): 4-cylinder, 40-horsepower, water-cooled engine; speed 45 miles per hour; weight for flight 550 pounds; price $4,500.

Model D (III): 8-cylinder V-type water-cooled 60-horsepower engine; speed 60 miles per hour; weight 650 pounds; price $5,000.

Model D (III): 8-cylinder hydro, as above, with hydro gear, price $5,500.

Model D (III): 8-cylinder V-type water-cooled engine, 75-horsepower Curtiss engine; speed 70 miles per hour; weight 700 pounds; price $5,500.

Preparation for launching the U.S. Navy's A-1 (Model E Triad) from a cable device. This system was suggested by Ellyson in order to make the airplane compatible for use aboard ships. *Curtiss photo from Verville Collection*

Transition stage of the Triad without the front wheel. *Curtiss photo, A. R. Clemons Collection*

The U.S. Navy Triad (A-1), the first navy aircraft tested at Hammondsport by Curtiss and Lt. Theodore G. Ellyson, who became naval aviator No. 1.

The Model E, 1911

Development of the D-IV made it apparent that greater lifting area was a necessity, particularly for exhibition flying, where small unimproved "airports" were the rule rather than the exception. Charles F. Willard and other 'exhibition pilots had experienced numerous problems, not the least of which were irate crowds. The alternative, at times, was flirting with disaster in taking off and landing in marginal situations. Increased lifting capacity encouraged the carrying of passengers, which became a popular source of revenue after the novelty of pure "exhibition" flights wore off, and it would also permit operation from airports with higher elevations above sea level.

The Model E became standardized, retaining the same general details of the D-III, but the individual wing panels were enlarged to provide the additional lifting area.

The E model is referred to in the Curtiss catalog as "The Weight-Carrying Curtiss Aeroplane" and had a span measuring 28 feet 8 inches, 2 feet 5 inches greater than the D model. The overall length of 25 feet 9 inches remained the same and the overall height increased slightly from 7 feet 5½ inches in the D model, to 8 feet in the E model.

The specifications and prices found in the 1912 catalog of the Curtiss Aeroplane Company are as follows:

Model E-4: 4-cylinder, 40-horsepower water-cooled Curtiss engine; speed 40 miles per hour; weight 600 pounds. Price $4,500. (I'll wager not many of this version were sold.)

Model E-8: V-8 cylinder; 60-horsepower water-cooled Curtiss engine. Equipped with Curtiss alternating (throw-over) control system; speed 55 miles per hour; weight 700 pounds. Price $5,000.

Model E-8-75: Same as Model E-8, but with V-8, 75-horsepower engine; speed 60 miles per hour; weight 750 pounds. Price $5,500.

Model E-8-75: Hydro, same as above. Price $6,000. The hydro equipment weighed 125 pounds and could be fitted in two hours by experienced mechanics.

The first army "trainer" is recorded as a D-E, presumably a hybrid, using components from each model and powered by a 40-horsepower Curtiss engine. This was S.C. No. 6. S.C. No. 8 and No. 23, the third and sixth Curtiss machines purchased by the army, were designated as Scouts and powered by V-8 75-horsepower engines.

One of the variations that received wide exposure in the press of that time involved the removal and reinstallation of the forward elevator. It was mounted low, just far enough above the bow of the float to allow adequate movement. This was the state of the art when the U.S. Navy took delivery of the first navy machine, later designated the A-1, which first flew at Hammondsport.

When preparations for the fiftieth anniversary of naval aviation were undertaken, one of the projects was the construction of two reproductions of the A-1. One of these was intended to be a historically correct version for museum use (now in the National Aircraft Collection), and the second was to be a reproduction for flying during the celebration. An interesting fact about the reproduction for flying was the decision to substitute steel tubing for the bamboo outriggers in the tail section. Stresses and limits for steel tubing were known factors, whereas no stress analysis was available for selected bamboo. Charles F. Willard comments, ". . . bamboo had a marked advantage over wood in wrecks. It breaks, bends but does not sever. Beachey had destroyed three Curtiss Ds and was not speared. The bamboo stood up for three to four years of flying, so why bother with tubes? On one occasion, my crankshaft sheared and let the prop hit my tail bamboo. It bent and wrecked the propeller but did not sever the bamboo, . . . that's why bamboo was used."

One is tempted to wonder how much progress was made in ignorance and also to admire the courage of the early aviation pioneers who proceeded in spite of the many unknowns.

The A-1 probably was the best known and most used of the Triad-type aircraft, even though the landing gear was not fitted at the time of delivery and no photos viewed by this writer show the retractable gear installed.

The A-1, in the hands of navy pilots Ellyson, Towers, Bellinger and Richardson, was used for many experiments to find the means, methods and equipment required to adapt the airplane to the requirements of the U.S. Navy. Among the numerous experiments performed was a test of a cable-launching device intended to be used aboard ship. It was devised by Ellyson and successfully tested at Hammondsport. It consisted of a central cable plus two outboard cables parallel to the center cable stretched from a platform about 12 feet high to post "deadheads" sunk in the earth at the waterline of Lake Keuka. The center cable supported the main float of the hydro-aeroplane through a U-shaped channel fastened to the bottom of the float. Near the wing tips two rectangular frames were mounted, one under each wing tip, which would ride on the outboard cable if the aircraft should tip to either side. The aircraft was pulled up the cable to the platform and after ensuring that all was in readiness the engine was started and Ellyson took his place in the pilot's seat. The throttle was opened to full power and the aircraft started down the cable. So quickly did the aircraft accelerate that lateral control was immediate. Because of this the outboard cables were not even touched before the aircraft rose from the cable in free flight under full control. It was thought that a similar cable arrangement could be fitted from the mast of a ship to the deck level, making this one of the simplest possible launching systems for use aboard ship. Though the experiment was a complete success the idea was not developed further.

A catapult launching system tested at Annapolis on July 3, 1912, resulted in a ducking for Ellyson and destruction of the aircraft. A successful catapult launching was not made until November 12, 1912, at the Washington Navy Yard, with Ellyson at the controls of the Curtiss A-1. The first Triad, probably a D configuration, had a span of 26 feet 3 inches; the navy's A-1 was an E configuration with a span of 28 feet 8 inches.

The second of the unusual variations of the E model was the navy's A-2. It evolved from a hydro to an enclosed "bat-boat," a bobtailed flying boat (E-1) and finally to the first OWL (Over Water or Land) amphibian, designated the AX-1. In this latter configuration, wheels were installed in "pockets" in the bottom of the hull and were retracted into these pockets when water operations were under way.

The A-1 and AH series of naval aircraft produced by Curtiss were basically of the E type, but with modifications, some made at the time of construction, others made during their operating lifetime. Changes in flotation gear and extensions to the wings were some of the most apparent changes. These extensions were not standard equipment, but supplied on special order at a cost of $100 a pair.

The A-1 has special significance, being the first aircraft purchased by the U.S. Navy. The Wrights had succeeded in selling the first airplane to the United States government, the 1909 Military, NASM 1912-1. The navy, with more difficult operating conditions, delayed purchase of an airplane until it could be demonstrated that their special conditions could be met. Curtiss, with a long interest in water-flying operations, continued experiments at Hammondsport and San Diego and finally succeeded in making his first practical flight from water on January 25, 1911. Curtiss had made a series of short flights with the earlier float versions on the preceding three days. Refinements dictated by this historic flight were tested on a flight of February 2. The float design and position used on this latter flight became the standard for all Curtiss hydros for the navy and private owners for several years. Variations of this basic design were ordered as late as the end of 1915. These were the AH-8, 10, 12 and 18 aircraft.

In the papers of Capt. W. I. Chambers, a note dated January 17, 1914, indicates that the A-1 was originally ordered as a school machine "grass cutter" with a 4-cylinder water-cooled 40-horsepower engine, costing $2,750. Later, before delivery, it was modified into a hydroplane with an 8-cylinder water-cooled 70-horsepower O-type engine, the final cost being $5,600.

The A-2 (AH-2), E-1, AX-1, OWL was first a hydroplane, a Triad and cost $5,500. This was followed in 1912 by the A-3 (AH-3), the third navy aircraft, at the same unit cost of $5,500. Chambers's note further states (as does the log) that the A-2 was remodeled into the OWL boat (Owl I) at an additional cost of $2,000, at which time it was redesignated the E-1. The new hull had been designed by Richardson and built by Curtiss. Curtiss personnel were obviously unimpressed with the resulting performance, for in a letter of October 22, 1913, to Captain Chambers, H. C. Genung comments as follows:

In regard to our special boat. It was designed with a view to carrying your specified load of 450 lbs. live weight. In the tests reported to you, we exceeded this by 120 lbs. and still climbed 1420 feet in 11 minutes. It would therefore appear that some improvement has been made. We are not content to rest here, however, but are now making a change in propeller and motor speed, which we are confident will result in a climb of 2000 feet in 15 minutes with the 570 lb. load. I hope to be able to so report to you tomorrow.

This change noted above will also probably increase the maximum speed to some extent without materially affecting the minimum. If this be the case, the all-round efficiency of the machine will not be so bad. As a rough-water boat there are some beneficial changes which could probably be made, but as it stands, it would undoubtedly be more stable than a boat of the A-2 type under the same conditions. After all, however, its accomplishments are limited only according to the weight it must carry, and, therefore, won't your A-2 boat when it is finished be still heavier and accordingly handicapped in accomplishments when carrying an equal load?

The new A-2 hull as designed by Richardson is going to run into considerable weight, be even heavier, in fact, than our boat, all things considered. Then, if you also wish to carry the prescribed load, Model "F" surfaces become a necessity, and, accordingly climbing ability, speed and ease of handling are proportionally reduced. Cleanliness of design is, perhaps, worthy of consideration, and the A-2 type with independent tail can hardly equal our boat in this respect.

These various thoughts, and the fact that early delivery is essential, lead us to make the following proposals:

Six regular boats (presume you would desire those of the new English type) could be delivered quite promptly on account of the workmen in all departments being most familiar with their construction. Believe we could guarantee something like this:

One	—Nov.	15th
"	"	30th
"	Dec.	15th
"	"	30th
"	Jan.	15th
"	"	30th

Six boats as per our special design, but with such changes as you may suggest. Same schedule, but one week later:

Six boats of the A-2 type could be gotten out in about the same periods, except that deliveries could not begin so early. The present A-2 boat is scheduled for delivery on Nov. 12th, and as trials would have to be held after that, it probably would be Nov. 20th at least before work could be begun on the quantity. The land wheels (per drawing by Toms) we would place on any of these machines in any manner designated by you. This work we estimate would add one week to all delivery schedules, the time being consumed in the strengthening of the hull and the making and installation of the wheels.

To return to the matter of weight carrying: If this is not an essential point, we would very much appreciate learning how much this can be cut down. It is possible that the reduction would permit of our changing to Model "E" surfaces, in which instance we feel that we could in every way equal, if not better, the present performances of A-2. At any rate, we would like the opportunity to try.

The folding wheels, as at present fitted to our boat, can unquestionably be improved upon, but we still believe they would give quite satisfactory service. We base our decision upon the fact that a boat turned out by us about a year ago, with wheels similarly constructed, gave very good service. This boat was used here and at the Coast by Mr. Curtiss and landed about fifty or more times with no appreciable trouble or depreciation. We have not made any tests of these wheels here, because there seemed to be no object in doing so. Such tests might be interesting, however, from a business standpoint. We may go ahead with them later.

The U.S. Army Signal Corps was also active in a limited way in purchasing from the Wrights as well as Curtiss. Signal corps order No. 9597, dated March 13, 1911, was for the purchase of a Curtiss Speed Scout, manufacturer's No. D-38, powered by a 75-horsepower Curtiss O engine. It was to become S.C. No. 2 after delivery on March 17, 1911, at a price of $6,000. It was destined to have a short operating life, for it was damaged in the fatal accidents of Lt. G.E.M. Kelly on May 10, 1911 and Lt. J. D. Park on May 9, 1913. It was rebuilt, but finally condemned on June 16, 1914.

The second army Curtiss purchase was in 1911 and was S.C. No. 6, purchased on S.C. order No. 10141, dated June 27, 1911. This aircraft, a trainer or "grass cutter," was a D-E combination (manufacturer's No. D-E 39), and was powered by a 40-horsepower Curtiss engine. It was accepted on July 27, 1911 at a price of $4,500 at College Park, Maryland. It was condemned on May 20, 1914.

The Collier Trophy, donated to the Aero Club of America by Robert J. Collier, to be awarded annually for the greatest achievement in Ameri-

Specifications	
The Model E, 1911	
Span	28 ft. 8 in.
Chord	5 ft. 0 in.
Curvature (Camber)	3½ in., 33 percent (⅓ back)
Covering	Double-surfaced Goodyear cloth
Spars	1 in. by 1½ in.
Length overall	25 ft. 9 in.
Height overall	8 ft. 0 in.
Remarks	Drop of beams front to rear is 4 in.

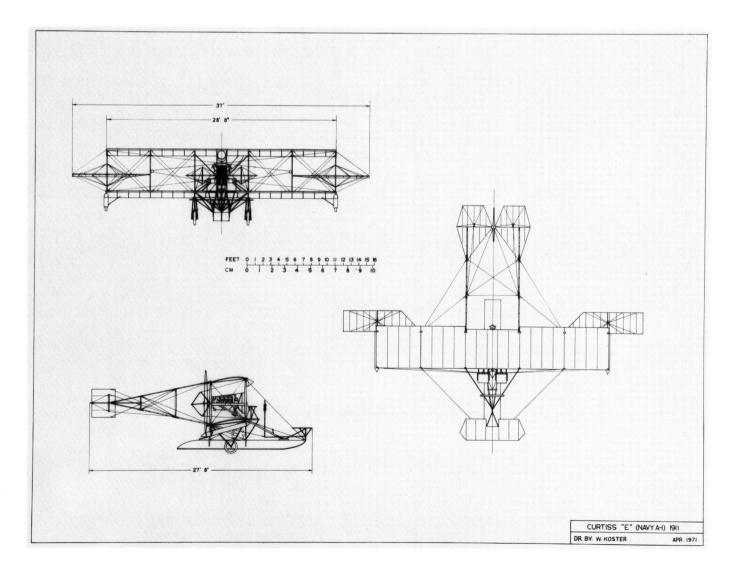

CURTISS "E" (NAVY A-1) 1911
DR. BY. W. KOSTER   APR. 1971

can aviation during the preceding year, was awarded to Glenn H. Curtiss for the year 1911 for the development and performance of the hydro-aeroplane.

Prior to 1911 a number of persons had tried to develop the hydro-aeroplane. Henri Fabre had given up when his machine crashed at Monaco in 1910. Curtiss's success in 1911 inspired French and British experimenters to try again and in 1912 a number of such designs, some of which were direct copies of the Curtiss machine, appeared at the Monaco meet.

In 1912 Curtiss succeeded in developing the flying boat, a boat with wings rather than an airplane with floats. By the end of 1912 no less than seven nations were adopting flying boats for their navies.

In 1912, Curtiss was again awarded the Collier Trophy, for development of the flying boat.

The year 1912 was a continuation of work on projects and aircraft types initiated in 1911, with emphasis on developing the designs into practical vehicles. The Model E was further developed, along with more powerful engines. The most important single development was the flying boat, which got its start near the end of 1911. From a rudimentary and unsuccessful example, the flying boat gradually developed, through trial and error, to the point where it was a successful patentable machine. It became the most important patent held by Curtiss, and is the development for which Curtiss is best known.

During 1912, the U.S. Army and the U.S. Navy took a serious look at this new technology and purchased increasing, though still limited, numbers of aircraft for training and experimental purposes.

A number of foreign exports from the Curtiss Company were recorded, with several aircraft being shipped to the Russian Black Sea Fleet, 2 to Germany, 3 to Japan and 3 to Louis Paulhan in France, who undertook the building of 12 more under license and introduced the hydro to England in collaboration with Claude Graham-White.

In spite of the interest by the military services, the aviation industry had a depression year in 1912. The established aviation industry produced about 46 aircraft. An estimated 100 additional aircraft were built by individuals, in contrast to a total of 750 aircraft built by the industry and individuals in 1911.

Curtiss produced the standardized D and E models with a variety of power plant options as well as landing gear options. The flying boat became a practical reality, and during this year the Model F was introduced. For more efficient training, fixed dual controls were developed and also a throw-over control that made it possible to operate the aircraft from either seat.

At the beginning of 1912, four military officers were in pilot training at Hammondsport. They were Lts. T. G. Ellyson and J. H. Towers of the U.S. Navy, Lieutenant Beck, U.S. Army, and Lt. J. W. McClaskey of the U.S. Marine Corps.

A second pilot training camp was set up at Miami, Florida, on January 1, 1912, with Charles C. Witmer as instructor-in-charge. Curtiss's exhibition activities extended to Europe and to Cuba during the early part of the year and Curtiss himself visited Europe in the last quarter of the year.

The Curtiss Exhibition Company was formed in 1909 to manage and supply aircraft and components for a select group of aviators who operated under the Curtiss name, with Jerome Fanciulli as manager.

The OWL, 1912-1914

The OWL I (Over Water and Land) was derived from the A-2, the second Curtiss aircraft purchased by the U.S. Navy. The A-2 was a standard E model ordered in May 1911 and delivered in mid-July 1911 at a cost of $5,000. It was powered by the new OX engine of 80 horsepower and had an average speed of 65 miles per hour with an occasional maximum speed of 70 miles per hour. Landing speed was about 40 miles per hour.

The OWL I went through a series of experimental modifications. The first modifications resulted in a redesignation of the A-2 to the E-1 in September 1913. It was later rebuilt in December 1913 and renumbered in March 1914 as the AX-1. It differed from the standard hydros in having a wider and shorter main float that incorporated a step similar to the flying boats. Instead of the seats being mounted at the level of the lower wing, they were mounted on the pontoon.

The OWL (for Over Water and Land) A-2 beginning its water test at Hammondsport.

The OWL after takeoff, showing the location of the wheels in pockets in the bottom of the float/hull.

A light framework covered by fabric was built up to shield the pilots. The result was a bobtailed boat of a configuration referred to as a bat-boat by the British.

The type was developed at the direction of Capt. W. I. Chambers, chief of aeronautics for the navy. It was his opinion that this configuration was an ideal type for use by the navy and marine corps and a necessary type for navy work, which required ships to operate off coasts where terrain and rocks or bad surf made communications with land-based operations impossible. The A-2 was amphibious, capable of operations at sea or on land by use of wheels fitted into pockets in the hull bottom. Unfortunately, as the log indicates, the performance left much to be desired.

In 1914, Captain Chambers resurrected the OWL concept (Over Water and Land). He persisted in his opinion that this represented an ideal type for use by the U.S. Navy and U.S. Marine Corps. The relatively poor performance of the earlier A-2 (OWL I) did not deter Captain Chambers. Photos, taken on December 24, 1913, show the almost completed OWL II in the construction shops. While improvement is evident in the design of the hull bottom, the wheel wells and the general hull design, no photos have been found to show the completed machine.

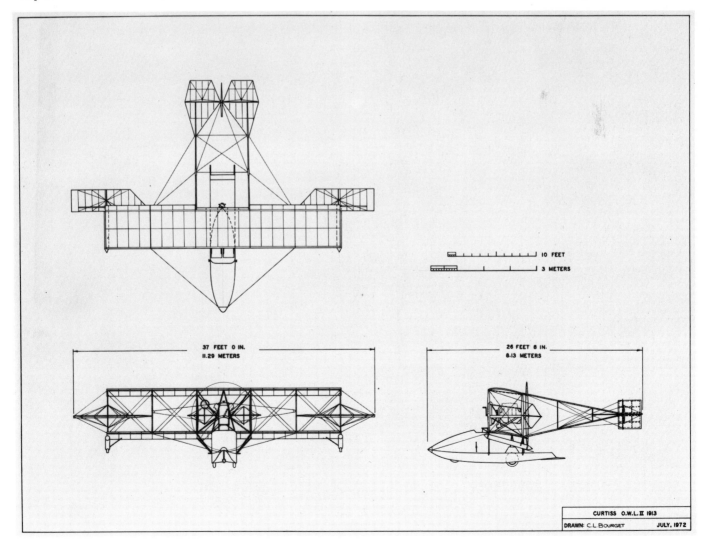

From the existing photos, it appears that E wing segments were fitted. Since one of the requirements for these machines was easy storage aboard ship, it is probable that E panels were fitted rather than F panels, which were about three times greater in panel span.

According to contemporary published information, the OWL II was a far more substantial machine than the first and embodied a **V** bottom and pointed bow. Metal-lined pockets housed the wheels, and heavy coil springs were installed on the landing gear. The brake system reverted back to an earlier ''grab hook'' design that could slow the aircraft on land or catch a cross wire in case of landing aboard the deck of a ship.

While it is a curious and possibly even logical design, based upon naval and marine corps concepts of the day, it was not an attractive aircraft and I have been unable to determine the disposition of this machine or if it was, in fact, purchased by the U.S. Navy.

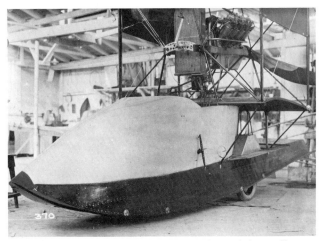

The OWL II was, in fact, an improved amphibious E-type hydroplane, as is evident in this front quarter view. *Curtiss photo from the A. R. Clemons Collection*

This profile of the OWL II shows its similarity to British bat-boats. Tail-supporting outriggers have not been installed at this date. *Curtiss photo from the A. R. Clemons Collection*

The OWL about to be launched on Keuka Lake.

The 1912 Model D Flying Boat

The first flying boat has been described in an article in *Aeronautics*, January 20, 1912, as follows:

The new Curtiss hydroaeroplane was given its first trial at the North Island ground of the Curtiss Company in San Diego Bay in California on January 10th. Mr. Curtiss made the flight himself in the presence of Naval officers, pupils and invited guests.

The new craft, which is equipped to carry a passenger and is driven by a 60 horsepower motor, made tremendous speed in contact with the water, estimated at about 50 miles an hour. It lifted off the water with ease and traveled at more than 60 miles an hour in the air. It differs in many respects from the Curtiss hydroaeroplane now in use by the United States Naval officers. There are two propellers instead of one and these are driven by clutch and chain transmission. The propellers turn both in the same direction. The motor is equipped with a new automatic starter, which Mr. Curtiss has

lately designed, and there is also a fuel gauge and bilge pump.

The boat, or hydro equipment, contains a bulkhead fore and aft, and is twenty feet long, with an upward slope in front and a downward slope in the rear. The great advantages claimed for the new machine are that it is safe, comfortable and quick to rise from the water in response to its control. The hydro equipment, which is more like a boat than anything yet designed and used on the aeroplane, will, it is claimed by Mr. Curtiss, be able to withstand any wind or wave that a motor boat of similar size could weather. The planes are standard model "D," 26 ft. 3 ins. spread.

A hood is used over the engine to protect it from the spray.

Waldo Waterman, an early pilot and aircraft designer, and a reliable contemporary witness to the trials, indicated that the trials were not the success described by the reporters. Waterman's recollections as told to this writer are borne out

The first flying boat resting in shallow water. One of the mechanics is standing on the extreme rear of the hull to balance the nose-heaviness of the design. Courtesy of *Lansing Callan, Curtiss Collection*

Testing the propulsion system for the first flying boat, Hammondsport. *Curtiss Collection*

Mrs. G. H. Curtiss poses sitting at controls of the first flying boat designed, before its shipment from Hammondsport to San Diego.

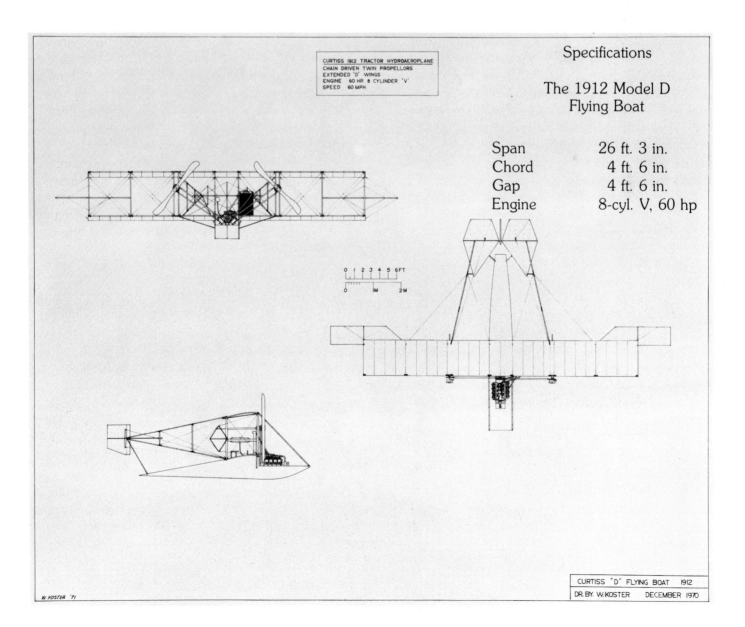

CURTISS 1912 TRACTOR HYDROAEROPLANE
CHAIN DRIVEN TWIN PROPELLORS
EXTENDED 'D' WINGS
ENGINE   60 HP 8 CYLINDER 'V'
SPEED   60 MPH

Specifications

The 1912 Model D
Flying Boat

Span	26 ft. 3 in.
Chord	4 ft. 6 in.
Gap	4 ft. 6 in.
Engine	8-cyl. V, 60 hp

0 1 2 3 4 5 6FT
0   IM   2M

CURTISS "D" FLYING BOAT   1912
DR. BY. W. KOSTER   DECEMBER 1970

W. KOSTER '71

NEW MODEL FLYING BOAT
CURTISS HYDRO AREOPLANES
MAKE FLYING SAFE

Learn to Fly at Curtiss Aviation Camp, North Island

THE FUTURE OF AVIATION

The future of aviation is no longer a matter of surmise. The value of the aeroplane as a commercial and pleasure vehicle has been demonstrated beyond question. Recent experiments have shown that passengers, mail, food or ammunition can be carried to remote parts of the world with great safety.

In the matter of speed, the aeroplane greatly out-distances the fastest express trains, and on account of this, and the ease with which great heights are attained, warfare has been revolutionized.

We recommend prompt action on the part of those anticipating taking up aeronautics as a vocation, as the earlier the entrance, the greater the remuneration and the more rapid advancement of the art.

TERMS

The tuition fee is Five Hundred Dollars, payable upon enrollment, and in case of the purchase of a Curtiss Aeroplane within six months from the completion of the course, this amount is credited against the regular price of the machine. The course is complete and thorough and covers fully, practical flying, and the care and operation of both the motor and aeroplane.

Address:—Curtiss Aviation School, San Diego, Calif.

An optimistic Curtiss sales brochure circa 1911, illustrating the first attempt at constructing a flying boat.

by several facts, the most important of which is that the design was never carried any further. Examination of photographs shows several interesting details. In the first photograph the machine sits level in the shallow water only because Lt. John W. McClasky is standing as far back on the hull as seems prudent. The second photo, from the album of J. Lansing Callan, shows the same machine with an additional bow section grafted on to the hull. This adds further substantiation to the statement of Waterman that the machine normally would float nose down at an angle of 30 to 40 degrees.

A premonition of its failure is recorded in a letter from Curtiss to Capt. W. I. Chambers on January 3, 1912, in which Curtiss writes:

> The experimental hydro is about ready but the chain transmission and complications do not look good to me. I like the direct drive for its simplicity and reliability. However, I will write you all about it when it is tried out.

On January 31, the assistant general manager of the Curtiss Exhibition Company wrote Captain Chambers:

> I have a letter from Mr. Curtiss in which he advises that the dimensions of the new boat are 2½ ft. deep, 2½ ft. wide, and 20 ft. long.

Curtiss, in a letter to Henry A. Wise Wood (later president of the American Society of Aeronautical Engineers) of New York, dated January 15, 1913, from Coronado, California, stated:

> Answering the question in your letter of January 9th, I do not recall when I first thought of combining the hull and the fuselage for water flying.
>
> We built the first one in the fall of 1911, at Hammondsport, N.Y., and shipped it to San Diego to try. This was equipped with two chain-driven tractor screws, but owing to repeated accidents to the transmission this machine was never taken in the air. We did, however, give it several runs on the water.
>
> This type of machine [flying boat] was first flown at Hammondsport in the spring of 1912. The second machine being constructed immediately on my return from California. The form of this second hull was changed many times before it would leave the water readily.
>
> A third machine was built embodying the improvements suggested and after some alterations this was adopted as standard and is the one after which the machines sold to the army and navy and those shipped abroad were modeled.

It remains, nevertheless, the first attempt at producing a flying boat and lessons learned from this were carried into later successful designs.

A front view showing engine installation and the double chain drive. This is one of the few times Curtiss used this, normally preferring to use a direct drive with the propeller attached directly to the engine.

The Beachey-Curtiss Tractor, 1912

The Beachey-Curtiss Tractor was a contemporary of the first Military Tractor. Both were under construction in the latter part of 1912 and reported in aviation journals in January 1913. Apparently, the Beachey Tractor was first tested on twin floats at Hammondsport, though a photograph shows the landplane gear fittings and tail skid in place on the uncovered fuselage. The floats were added on, seemingly, as an afterthought. The limited level land area at Hammondsport caused Curtiss to make test flights from Lake Keuka. In several cases (on the J and R, for example), floats were attached for the testing of these landplanes.

In a press release sent by telegram, Curtiss described the Beachey Tractor as:

the first tractor biplane for land use built by the Curtiss company and is unquestionably the fastest biplane in the world. Surfaces twenty-four ft wide and four feet deep (chord) speed seventy-five miles per hour. Lincoln Beachey under whose directions the machine was built made the trials.

The control surfaces and stabilizers were standard Curtiss types, slightly modified, but the wing airfoil section was substantially different. Instead of the usual thin profile double-cambered surface, the Beachey machine used a relatively thicker profile with the flat lower surface and cambered upper surface to accommodate the two spars, which were located 8 inches and 36 inches to the rear of the leading edge of the wings in contrast to the former Curtiss practice of making the leading edge serve as the front spar.

The landing gear consisted of two **V**-shaped struts. At the lower apex of these struts were two

Preparing the Lincoln Beachey Tractor Biplane for a test flight at Hammondsport, 1912. The fuselage is still uncovered and the machine is being mounted on a float for testing on Lake Keuka. *Curtiss Photo Collection*

vertical slots to permit vertical movement of the axle.

The pilot seat was located so close to the engine that the rear cylinders were almost between the pilot's knees.

In Curtiss's letter to Henry A. Wise Wood, dated January 15, 1913, he talks about a "second machine" constructed after the first flying boat, and this has come to be known as the "Freak Boat."

The title "Freak Boat" in one of my listings of Curtiss aircraft prompted one of the former Curtiss personnel to comment that Curtiss never built such a thing as a "Freak Boat." Nevertheless, in the list of captions for Curtiss negatives, the title is most definitely that of the "Freak Boat." Furthermore, the name was scratched into the negative bearing the number 667, and the date 1911–12 is also just discernible.

The photographs and the description by Curtiss, as well as certain mechanical characteristics of this "Freak Boat," make it virtually certain that this aircraft was the No. 2 configuration referred to by Curtiss. The tail surfaces were the same as those used on the first tractor boat. The wings were, in all probability, a D configuration and the control system appeared to be typical of the state of the art for that date. The major departure from the previous machine is the installation of an 8-cylinder engine mounted in the center section under the upper wing, high enough to allow clearance of the propeller over the hull and with the propeller plane of rotation located to the rear of the trailing edge of the wings. The lack of a "step" supports Curtiss's statement that several modifications were necessary before the aircraft would become airborne. No record or description of this "Freak Boat" has been available to the writer, though several photographs have been collected in the course of this research project.

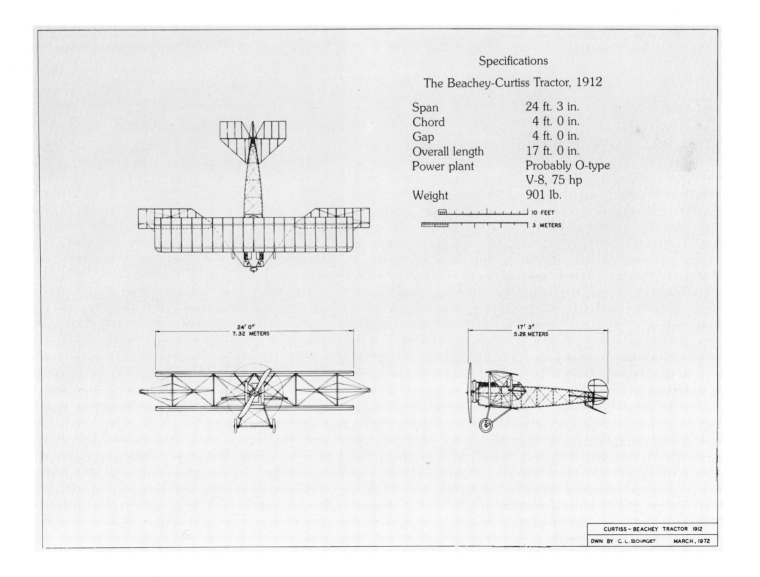

Specifications

The Beachey-Curtiss Tractor, 1912

Span	24 ft. 3 in.
Chord	4 ft. 0 in.
Gap	4 ft. 0 in.
Overall length	17 ft. 0 in.
Power plant	Probably O-type V-8, 75 hp
Weight	901 lb.

10 FEET
3 METERS

24' 0"
7.32 METERS

17' 3"
5.26 METERS

CURTISS – BEACHEY TRACTOR 1912
DWN BY C. L. BOURGET   MARCH, 1972

Beachey in the cockpit, restrained by the "ground crew." A shoulder yoke aileron control was used, but the brakes were not included in the design. *Curtiss Photo Collection*

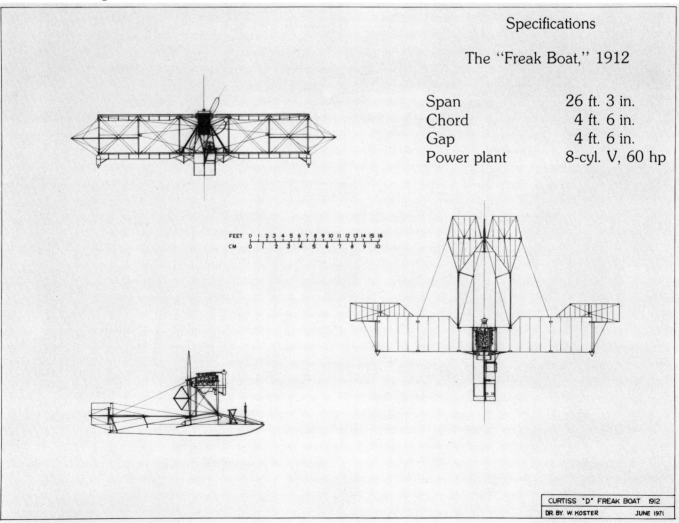

Specifications

The "Freak Boat," 1912

Span	26 ft. 3 in.
Chord	4 ft. 6 in.
Gap	4 ft. 6 in.
Power plant	8-cyl. V, 60 hp

FEET 0 1 2 3 4 5 6 7 8 9 10 11 12 13 14 15 16
CM 0 1 2 3 4 5 6 7 8 9 10

CURTISS "D" FREAK BOAT 1912
DR. BY. W. KOSTER   JUNE 1971

The "Freak Boat" on the shore of Lake Keuka. The first design followed the unsuccessful Tractor Boat of 1911. Model D type wings are still being used, but the engine is mounted high for a direct drive pusher propeller. *Curtiss Collection*

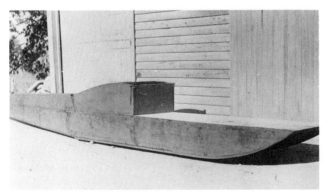

The hull of the "Freak Boat" showing the beginning of a "step."

The "Freak Boat" launched and ready for trials. Curtiss is standing beside the pilot's seat. *Curtiss Collection*

The First Successful Flying Boat
The 1912 Model E

On his return to Hammondsport from San Diego in the spring of 1912, Curtiss set to work building a second flying boat. The experience gained from the San Diego experiments proved useful, but still required refinement and additional development before success was assured.

The second variant, described previously as the "Freak Boat," was replaced by a third variation, which had a vertical rudder post at the rear of the hull instead of the horizontal termination as in the case of the two previous experimental flying boat hulls. Additionally, there was a break in the horizontal line of the scow bottom, though it could not be considered a "step" initially. By a series of modifications, the hull was changed to a "stepped" scow hull and finally "standpipes" were located immediately aft of the step to help break the suction of the water. Experience gained during these experiments contributed to the design's success, and also proved useful in later patent litigation, notably the Janin patent case.

The flight gear, wings, empennage, etc., were adapted directly from the then standard E-75 machine (28-foot 8-inch span). A greater "drop"

from the front to the rear beam or spar amounted to 5½ inches. The camber of the wing had increased marginally from 3½ to 3⅞ inches.

Wing panels were still quickly demountable, but only the panel over the engine was double-surfaced, i.e., covered top and bottom with Goodyear cloth. The outboard main panels were covered only on their upper surfaces. The chord was 5 feet 6 inches and the gap 5 feet 0 inches.

The fuselage was 26 feet ½ inch with the maximum hull beam located just behind the rear beam attachment point. Six watertight compartments were provided, any two of which could support the aircraft on the surface of the water.

A number of devices were tried to improve takeoff performance. One was a large forward elevator attached at the bow. The step was built into the hull and, as noted before, to increase the flow of air into the step area, vertical standpipes were installed.

Curtiss's efforts met with success in July 1912 and resulted in patent No. 114,2754, filed September 6, 1912, and granted June 8, 1915.

This aircraft was the first of a long line of flying

The first successful Curtiss flying boat. Illustrated is the early testing configuration with the bow elevator installed and wing-tip extensions added. Hammondsport, 1912. *Curtiss Collection*

The E Flying Boat in its second configuration. The forward elevator has been removed, leaving a tubular hole at the bow. The elevator was removed after it was discovered that it was a potentially dangerous control. This was confirmed in 1960 during wind tunnel tests when a reproduction of the A-1 was constructed for the fiftieth anniversary of naval aviation.

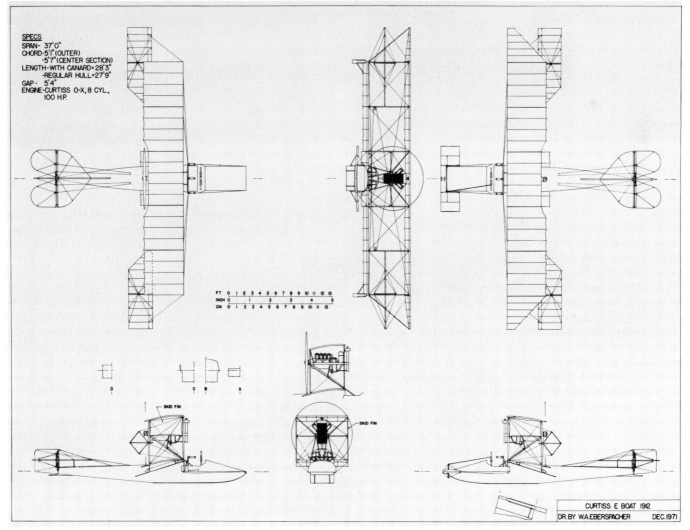

SPECS
SPAN- 37' 0"
CHORD- 5'1" (OUTER)
-5'7" (CENTER SECTION)
LENGTH- WITH CANARD= 28'3"
-REGULAR HULL= 27'9"
GAP- 5'4"
ENGINE- CURTISS O-X, 8 CYL.,
100 H.P.

SKID FIN

SKID FIN

CURTISS E BOAT 1912
DR. BY W.A. EBERSPACHER   DEC. 1971

The standard 1912–1913 E Flying Boat with wing-tip extensions, antiskid panels on each side of the engine bay, and canister-style floats. The step is still in its developmental stage. The aircraft is probably the Vilas machine or a sister ship. *Curtiss Collection*

Probably the final configuration of the first Model E Flying Boat was this amphibian form. The wheels enabled the plane to be taxied to and from the launching ramp.

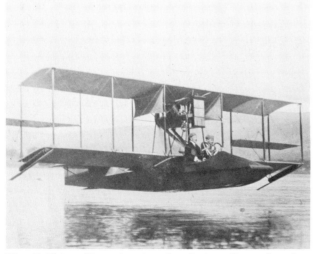

The E Flying Boat showing the first vestiges of a step. *Verville Collection*

Specifications	
The First Successful Flying Boat, the 1912 Model E	
Span	37 ft. 0 in.
Chord	5 ft. 1 in.
Gap	5 ft. 4 in.
Curvature	3⅞ in.
Length	27 ft. 2 in.
Power plant	8-cyl. V, Model OX, 75–100 hp

boats that made Curtiss famous. Developments proceeded at a rapid pace, resulting in training machines, sporting machines and aircraft for the army and navy. A great number of types and models resulted.

In a letter to Captain Chambers, dated July 17, 1912, Curtiss states: "The flying boat No. 2 is a weight carrier. I made a flight the other day with two passengers in the regular seats and a man lying on the boat between the main surfaces and the tail. No trouble at all getting out of the water."

On June 25, 1912, Curtiss wrote: "In the trials yesterday the 'Flying Boat' showed a variation of speed of from forty to fifty-two miles an hour. The speed with the new surfaces seems to be about fifty miles an hour. Our first trials have been with the end panels removed and with planes covered only on top. Now we have them completely covered and on all surfaces." On June 27, he wrote to Chambers: "We are trying hard to find a method of building the boats of metal, but we have not arrived at a satisfactory plan as yet. I think your idea for a semi-automatic elevator control is excellent. We may be able to try it on this machine."

On November 22, 1912, Curtiss again wrote to Chambers: "If you consider it advisable to have another man there for the trials of the boat and cannot come yourself, I would be pleased to have Mr. Richardson* come up, in which event he could pass on the construction of the boats, especially the part relating to the requirements for launching, and the new metal covered boat which we have already started."

*Holden C. Richardson, naval constructor, naval aviator No. 13.

The U.S. Navy C-1 (Curtiss E Type) Flying Boat, 1912

During the latter part of 1912, the U.S. Navy placed a contract for its first boat-hulled aircraft. The C-1, later redesignated the AB-1, was received on December 1, 1912.

Like the Vilas Flying Boat of 1913, the C-1 was an E type, fitted with overhanging outboard panels attached to the upper wing. The hull had a flat scow bottom with three batten strips fastened longitudinally on the hull bottom. The hull had a shallow step approximately in line with the trailing edge of the lower wing. The hull measured 25 feet overall, with a net length of 24 feet. The hull had a ribbed top, and ribbed bottom and sides. The rib frames were of ash, spaced on 3-inch centers. Eight watertight compartments divided the hull laterally, so that it was practically unsinkable. Any two compartments were sufficient to float the entire airplane. Longitudinal battens were spaced on 4-inch centers and made of 1-inch ash. The first of three sheathings was of $^5/_{16}$-inch mahogany. This was covered by heavy canvas set in marine glue and covered by an outer planking of ¼-inch mahogany.

Over the bow, and extending back to the cockpit, was a hood serving as a wind and spray shield. The covering was waterproofed aircraft fabric finished in aluminum. The cockpit was 42 inches wide. A double steering wheel permitted operation by either occupant and each had a foot throttle. A safety starting handle for the engine was within reach of either occupant.

After taking part in the catapult experiments at the Washington Navy Yard, the C-1 on May 8 was flown down the Potomac River from Washington and then up the Chesapeake Bay to the Naval Academy at Annapolis, Maryland. The pilots were Lt. John H. Towers and Ensign Godfrey de C. Chevalier. The distance was approximately 169 miles and the flying time was three hours and five minutes for an average speed of nearly 50 miles per hour. They left Washington at 7:40 A.M. and arrived at Annapolis at 10:45 A.M. The altitude was approximately 1,700 feet, and this was the longest flight by service pilots to that date. They used 23.25 gallons of fuel (7.526 gallons per hour) and 1.625 gallons of oil.

After the successful flight of May 8, Towers entered the Great Lakes Cruise on May 13. The cruise, scheduled for July 8, was sponsored by *Aero and Hydro*, a leading aviation periodical of the time. The cruise course began at Chicago and ended 900 miles eastward at Detroit, Michigan. Due to the state of the art of flying boat development at this early date it was required

The U.S. Navy's C-1 (Curtiss Model E) Flying Boat. *Curtiss Collection*

that each pilot and aircraft pass a qualifying test. It was to be a contest between the best planes and pilots of the period. The list of pilots and aircraft, entered as of June 14, 1911, is in the accompanying table.

After a fairly short service life, the C-1 was transferred to the Naval Air Station at Guantanamo, Cuba, where it was struck from the active aircraft roll.

Aero and Hydro Great Lakes Reliability Cruise Entries to Date

Given in Order Received.

PILOT	ADDRESS	MACHINE	MOTOR
Tom Benoist	St. Louis	Benoist	80 H. P. Sturtevant
Antony Jannus	St. Louis	Benoist	
Hugh Robinson	St. Louis	Benoist	75 H. P. Roberts
Max Lillie	Chicago	Walco	80 H. P. Sturtevant
Frank M. Harriman	S. Glastonbury, Conn.	Harriman	50 H. P. Harriman
Lieut. J. H. Towers	Washington, D.C.	Curtiss	80 H. P. Curtiss
Weldon B. Cooke	Sandusky, O.	Cooke	75 H. P. Roberts
J. B. R. Verplanck	Fishkill-on-Hudson, N.Y.	Curtiss	80 H. P. Curtiss
Walter Johnson	Bath, N.Y.	Thomas	70 H. P. Kirham
G. M. Heckscher	New York	Curtiss	80 H. P. Curtiss
Glenn L. Martin	Los Angeles, Cal.	Martin	80 H. P. Curtiss
Roy Francis	San Francisco	Paterson-Francis	Hall-Scott

```
Specifications

The U.S. Navy C-1 (Curtiss E Type)
Flying Boat, 1912

Span            31 ft. 3 in., upper
                28 ft. 8 in., lower
Length          27 ft. 4 in.
Chord           5 ft. 0 in.
Gap             5 ft. 0 in.
Engine          8-cyl. V, Model O, 80 hp
Original Cost: $5,580; with changes, $6,500
```

The Model F, 1912

With the development of the flying boat, the days of the D and E exhibition machines were coming to a close. The novelty of the exhibition was wearing off and the airplane began to be viewed in more utilitarian terms. The Model F boat was the first step toward this end. The principal difference between the E and the F models was the wing construction. Instead of an assemblage of small panels, 5 feet to 5 feet 6 inches in length, fastened together by a series of interplane struts rigidly braced by wires, as in the D and E series, the F wings were constructed with the spars running the full half-span of the airplane wing. Because cantilever structure had not been developed at this time, the spars, which were very thin in cross section, required substantial bracing using flying, landing and external drag wires, as well as internal wires.

In catalogs and periodicals, the F-type wings were described as being used on flying boats and load-carrying aircraft. This new F series aircraft was very similar to the army's first flying boat.

Specifications	
The Model F, 1912	
Length	26 ft. 0 in. overall
Span	38 ft. 4 in. wings, 41 ft. 8 in. overall with ailerons
Chord	5 ft. 6 in.
Gap	5 ft. 6 in.
Covering	Rubberized cotton cloth, Goodyear
Power plant	8-cyl., Model OX, 100 hp

Curtiss received an order from the signal corps, GAO 48392, S.C. order No. 11610, dated June 19, 1912, for a land scout. The orders and specifications were subsequently changed by S.C. order No. 12117, dated October 10, 1912, for remodeling the aircraft to an F-type boat powered by a Curtiss 75-horsepower O engine for delivery at College Park, Maryland. It was, in fact, first tested on November 22, 1912, and accepted at Hammondsport on November 27, 1912, at a price of $6,000, which included an additional $500 to cover cost of remodeling. It was designated SC-15. It was damaged on February 18, 1913, in Lieutenant Goodier's accident and rebuilt. It was finally destroyed in an accident in which Lt. Rex Chandler lost his life on April 8, 1913. This was the first flying boat for the U.S. Army.

The accident of February 18, 1913, in which Lt. Lewis Goodier, Jr., was severely injured, resulted from an emergency landing during which one wing tip dug into the water. The aircraft then cartwheeled, breaking the hull and engine mounts, and pinned Goodier between the control wheel and the engine. Goodier suffered a fractured skull. Fortunately, the water was shallow and Curtiss and John D. Cooper, who witnessed the accident, rescued Goodier and returned him to the North Island hangars, where he was transferred to a waiting boat and then taken to Fort Rosencrans. This accident resulted in the addition of a structural member from the engine bearers to the hull, forward of the cockpit. This "Goodier strut" or "bow strut," as it came to be known, was a standard structural item on all subsequent F boats and a number of the later models, including the K models.

The acceptance tests of the army boat were conducted over Lake Keuka at Hammondsport and flown by Francis A. "Doc" Wildman and John D. Cooper, both experienced Curtiss pilots. On November 27, 1912, Curtiss wrote to Captain Chambers:

We have finished up the tests of the Army machine and the Board have recommended its acceptance.

As a result of these trials we have learned that the weight of the machine has been increasing and we were somewhat surprised to find it runs up over 1309 lbs., and I presume your machine (C-1) will weigh still more, as we have added a number of braces and increased the weight of several parts. This makes the climbing very difficult. In the Army machine, we had some trouble making the climbs, but as I have explained to Mr. Ellyson, we have been working toward a practical boat—one which would stand the strains—and have not paid so much attention to the weight.

A further interesting note in the same letter states:

We have a plan for three-propeller construction, which we would like to assemble on the metal flying boat, which we would like to build for you this winter. With this construction we expect to get considerable greater efficiency for weight carrying. A great advantage of the construction will be that either system can be used, that is, the machine can be driven by the direct-propeller by removing the two side propellers and chains, and, of course, fitting a propeller of greater pitch to the engine shaft.

The Sperry outfit* seems to require quite a good deal of adjustment, and it is difficult to say just when it will make a real successful trial.

---

*The Sperry autopilot that was then being evaluated in this flying boat.

The Model E, 1913

The E-type aircraft continued in limited production during 1913. The army acquired two Model E landplanes, one assembled from spares and powered by a 75-horsepower engine, which became S.C. No. 23, and the second, S.C. No. 22, powered by a 90-horsepower engine, delivered December 16, 1913.

The 1913 E boats were usually mistakenly identified as early F types. The E boats used the standard E wings with triangular extensions to the upper wing panels. An example of this model was the aircraft purchased by George von Utassy. Utassy, who was treasurer of a vast number of publishing ventures, including *Motor Boating* and *Cosmopolitan*, was a dedicated flying enthusiast. In company with his pilot-instructor, J.A.D. McCurdy, he constantly was flying around Long Island Sound exploring all the inlets and bays as well as New York Harbor in his E-type flying boat *Babetta*.

A second E-type flying boat achieved a place in history as winner of a $10,000 safety prize after demonstrating the Sperry gyroscopic stabilizer in January 1914. The Curtiss flying boat was flown by Lawrence Sperry to demonstrate the ability of the machine. The most

Henry Kleckler, mainstay of Curtiss's experimental work and a master innovator and mechanic, is shown working on the engine of the Navy C-1. Note the increased dimension of the bow "crash" strut. It is still installed too low on the engine mount to be effective in the event of a crash. *Curtiss Collection*

Among the most significant of the Model E flying boats was the first one purchased by the U.S. Army Signal Corps. This one, S.C. No. 15, was much modified during its operating life as experience was gained. S.C. No. 15 is shown on its launching dolly and track at North Island, San Diego, with the army "crew" servicing the aircraft.

spectacular part of the demonstration was when the pilot raised his hands above his head while his mechanic crawled out to the end of the wings.

An E-type flying boat was built in 1913 for L. A. "Jack" Vilas of Chicago. The hull of this aircraft still exists as a specimen in the collection of the National Air and Space Museum.

The description of the Vilas boat, appearing in *Aeronautics* of June 1913, read as follows:

An altogether different type of hull is represented in the flying boats built by Curtiss for L. A. Vilas of Chicago, J.B.R. Verplanck of Fishkill, N.Y. and the United States Navy. The wings mounted are the type E, spreading 31 feet 3 inches. In the Vilas boat an overhanging wing is attached at both extremities of the upper plane bringing the total spread of the upper plane to 40 feet. The separation [gap] is 5 feet 6 inches and the chord is 5 feet. The boat length is 26 feet, 4 feet 8 inches wide at widest point, 3 feet 6 inches at greatest depth and 30 inches in width at the extreme bow, and comes to a point at the rear.

. . . The steel braces of the engine section are changed from the earlier boat . . . The cockpit arrangement and construction of the forward end of the hull have been improved. The hood is hinged and opens forward and is covered inside with rubber matting which is also tacked on the bow, so that entrance is effected simply by stepping on the bow, walking over the hood and then closing the hood after one.

The elevator cables are attached to rocking levers at either extremity of a cross shaft running through the hull. The diagonal

Bulbous bow of the Sperry-Curtiss E Flying Boat housed the gyro control system of the first Sperry autopilot. Much test work was required to perfect this earliest version of the autopilot, and the flying boat provided an excellent platform for these tests. Courtesy *Sperry Gyroscope Co.*

brace from the end of the lower plane to the extension on the upper plane is arranged with a special device on the lower end so that by pulling on a cable from the seat this diagonal strut is immediately detached and the extensions fall down in a vertical position; this is to permit entrance into a shed narrower than the normal spread of the machine. A little lever throws open the outer members of the shoulder brace at the passenger's seat so that he may not be bothered with the side movement, or so that a student may not interfere with the pilot's movements in a ticklish maneuver. A big spruce diagonal strut runs from the engine bed braces to the bow of the boat. The motor is a Curtiss 90–100 hp, 8-cyl, 4″ by 5″ cylinders. By a different camshaft and valve action increased R.P.M. is obtained over the other eights.

Piping is run through the boat from the various compartments, converging under the pilot's seat to a valve and bilge pump. By turning a small knob around a dial, marked with numbers to represent the dif-

ferent compartments, any one compartment may be pumped dry. The engine is equipped with a starting crank. The forward end of the boat has a double wall 1½ inches thick. The weight of the boat alone is 390 pounds. The propeller is tipped with metal for a distance along the cutting edge. The armholes in the rear of the boat have been increased in number, there being two on the sides and two on top. The boat is wider at the top than at the bottom to shed spray. Watch, barometer and other instruments are provided.

Specifications	
The Model E, 1913	
Span	28 ft. 8 in.
Length	25 ft. 9 in.
Chord	5 ft. 0 in.
Engine	8-cyl. V, 60 hp or 8-cyl. V, 75 hp
Weight	
net	unknown
gross	700 w/60 hp
	750 w/75 hp

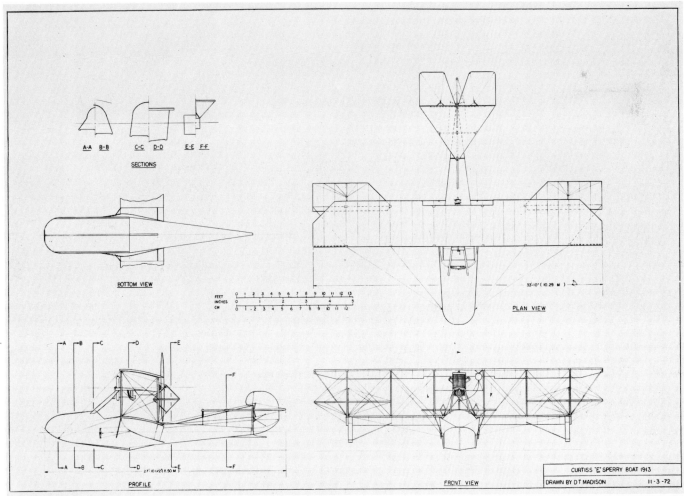

SECTIONS
A-A B-B C-C D-D E-E F-F

BOTTOM VIEW

PLAN VIEW

PROFILE

FRONT VIEW

CURTISS "E" SPERRY BOAT 1913
DRAWN BY D.T. MADISON   11-3-72

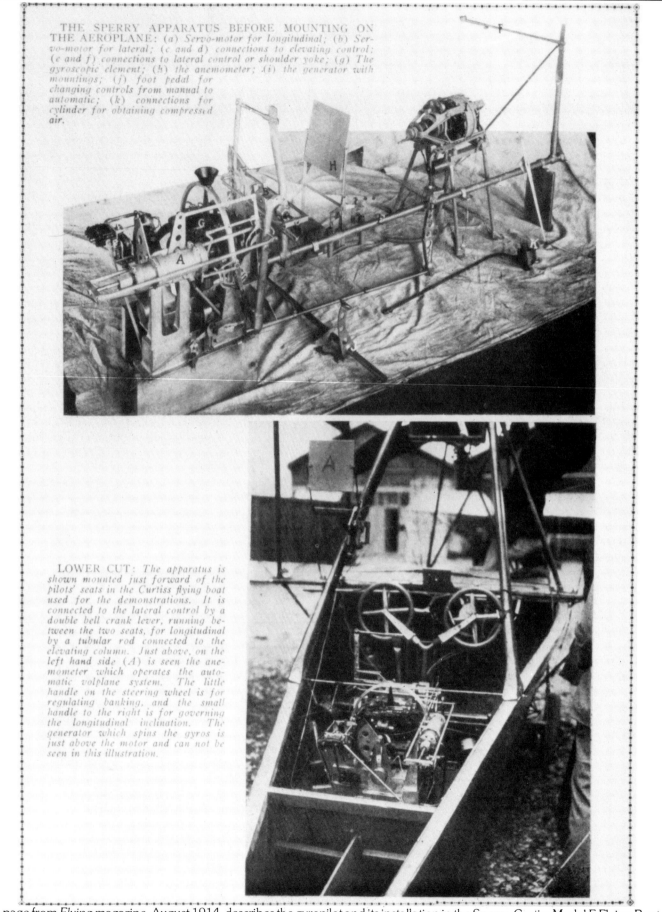

THE SPERRY APPARATUS BEFORE MOUNTING ON THE AEROPLANE: (a) Servo-motor for longitudinal; (b) Servo-motor for lateral; (c and d) connections to elevating control; (e and f) connections to lateral control or shoulder yoke; (g) The gyroscopic element; (h) the anemometer; (i) the generator with mountings; (j) foot pedal for changing controls from manual to automatic; (k) connections for cylinder for obtaining compressed air.

LOWER CUT: The apparatus is shown mounted just forward of the pilots' seats in the Curtiss flying boat used for the demonstrations. It is connected to the lateral control by a double bell crank lever, running between the two seats, for longitudinal by a tubular rod connected to the elevating column. Just above, on the left hand side (A) is seen the anemometer which operates the automatic volplane system. The little handle on the steering wheel is for regulating banking, and the small handle to the right is for governing the longitudinal inclination. The generator which spins the gyros is just above the motor and can not be seen in this illustration.

A page from *Flying* magazine, August 1914, describes the gyropilot and its installation in the Sperry-Curtiss Model E Flying Boat.

A view of the Sperry-Curtiss E Flying Boat showing the bulbous bow and the retractable beaching gear developed by Sperry.

Two Model E flying boats on the shore of Lake Keuka. The plane in the foreground was built for Marshal Reid. *Curtiss Collection*

Raymond V. Morris (in cockpit) and Beckwith "Becky" Havens (on ramp) pose with the Model E School Machine demonstrating the method of boarding the aircraft. Half of foredeck folds forward providing a boarding ramp. Note also the dual controls for student training. Havens was the first student enrolled in the Curtiss School. *Curtiss Collection*

The Model E Sport Boat at Hammondsport. The price of such a machine with an 80-horsepower Curtiss engine was $6,000 f.o.b. Hammondsport or San Diego. *Curtiss Collection*

Close-up of the special hull configuration of Marshal Reid's Model E Flying Boat. Reid poses in the cockpit. Note the shoulder yoke and the elevator controls on the outside of the hull.

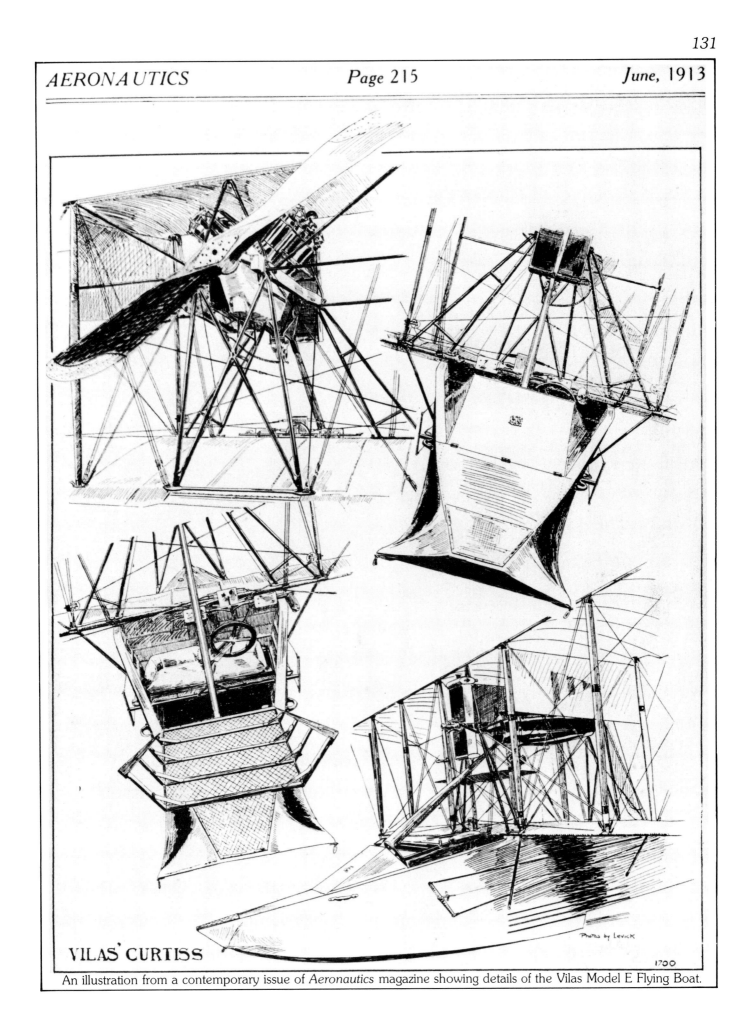

VILAS' CURTISS

1700

An illustration from a contemporary issue of *Aeronautics* magazine showing details of the Vilas Model E Flying Boat.

Illustration describing the operation of the special hatch developed for the 1913 Model E flying boats.

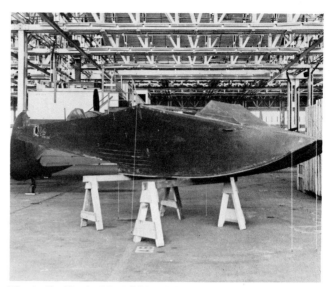

The hull of L. A. "Jack" Vilas's Model E Flying Boat in the collection of the National Air and Space Museum.

Specifications	
E-8 Vilas	
Span	40 ft. 0 in., upper
	31 ft. 3 in., lower
Length	26 ft. 0 in.
Chord	5 ft. 0 in.
Gap	5 ft. 6 in.
Engine	8-cyl. V, Model OX, 90/100 hp
Weight	
net	1,490 lb.
gross	1,890 lb.

Between the seats is a new style of Warner shaft-speed indicator, about as big around as a silver dollar. Other instruments in sight, are an aneroid barometer, for recording altitude; a plain barometer, indicating approaching weather changes; an automobile clock, oil and gasoline gauges.

The hull is painted, or enameled, in Nile green with gray trim around the coaming, making a nice contrast to the dark mahogany finish of the interior. The wings are covered in bright aluminum-finished Goodrich fabric. Just back of the seat is a swing door opening into a little cubby-hole where Vilas has his polished brass side lights and riding lights swinging cheerfully over his folding anchor. Everything is as handy as the pocket in a shirt.

There are two layers of planking on the bottom, one $5/16$, the second ¼ inch, between them a layer of heavy duck set in a marine glue. His fuel tanks have a capacity of more than forty gallons, which will keep his motor running for about six hours. He can travel approximately 400 miles without stopping.

A Curtiss Company newsletter of June 22–28, 1913, noted:

Jack Vilas, who recently moved to New York with his new Curtiss Flying Boat, seems to have created quite a sensation in the metropolis. After exhibiting the machine for a few days on the Astor roof, he made a number of passenger flights for the Westchester Club on Long Island Sound carrying a score or more of well-known people. The machine is at this writing packed for express shipment to St. Joseph, Mich., whence Vilas proposes to invade Chicago by flying across Lake Michigan.

A note on page 176 of *Aeronautics*, November 1913, records the following under the heading "The Flying Boat as a Dependable Vehicle":

L. A. Vilas kept a partial record of his summer's flying from June to October, and he estimates that he flew more than 3,500 miles. So far he has not had occasion to drop the lower half of the crankcase. The motor has not been overhauled since it left the factory. No breakage . . .

The boats for L. A. Vilas, J.B.R. Verplanck, Marshal Reid and the Navy C-1 were similar E types except for variations in hull design. The Verplanck boat had accommodation for three persons, instead of two as in the Vilas, and could squeeze in a fourth person.

The Reid E boat, delivered in May 1913, was powered by an 80-horsepower V-8 engine and featured an interesting foredeck and cockpit enclosure with flared sides in the area beside the pilot to permit lateral movement of the shoulder yoke aileron controls.

The S.C. No. 15 on its dolly headed for the barn after a day's operation. The starting crank and the first version of the diagonal "crash" strut from the engine to the hull are visible. *Curtiss photo, A. R. Clemons Collection*

The Model F Boat, 1913

Rapid development of the F boat continued during the years 1912 and 1913. Though it is virtually impossible to record the precise dates of the many changes, it is reasonable to state that the angular foredeck and hull of the F boat also characterized the earlier boats, which were also distinguished by canister-type outboard or wing-tip floats.

The single structural detail that distinguished the F types from preceding machines was the large half-span wing panels as distinct from the sectionalized or panel-style wings of the E aircraft. On the F model wings, the spars were deeper in cross section with some taper in the vertical plane as they extended further outboard. In addition, the drag bracing was accomplished by putting piano wire diagonal bracing inside the wing. With the passing of time and as experience was gained, the canister-style wing floats were replaced by more streamlined and efficient floats. Though the standard hull gradually took on a more rounded upper surface, a number of unusual variations appeared; among them were the Sperry, McCormick, S.C. No. 15 (F), Navy C-1 (E type), C-2 (F), C-3 (F), C-4 (F) and C-5 boats. The Sperry boat had a rather bulbous foredeck to accommodate the first of the Sperry autopilot mechanisms.

Within the framework of the F model were a number of variants, among them the aircraft delivered in 1913 to a number of sportsmen pilots.

Later in the year, the O engine was boosted to 100 horsepower, actually achieving 106 horsepower at 1,800 rpm. It was redesignated O+ or, as it became known, OX. One of the early applications of this engine was the so-called "English" flying boat, a four-passenger model that gained part of its increased lifting ability by adding an

The "English" F Flying Boat built for demonstration in England. Note the location of the ailerons attached to the trailing edge of the upper wing. This was used much later on the MF flying boats. This aircraft was powered by a 100-horsepower Curtiss engine.

extra wing area. This extra area was provided by an additional panel inserted in the center of the upper wing. The hull of the 100-horsepower "English" boat still retained the angular hull lines of the early standard F. This boat was developed for demonstration in European countries.

Another interesting modification was the installation of a special loading ramp. The rear half of the flat foredeck was hinged to enable it to be folded forward as a passenger walkway. The

inside of this folding panel was lined with rubber matting to make a nonslip walking surface.

The second of the "English" boats was the second aircraft purchased by Harold F. McCormick. The third of this variation was purchased by Barton L. Peck of Detroit.

The U.S. Navy C-2 was a Model F, shown here over Lake Keuka, flown by Lt. P.N.L. Bellinger.

Close-up of a 1914 Model F Boat showing its aerodynamic refinement and the fine finish of the planked hull.

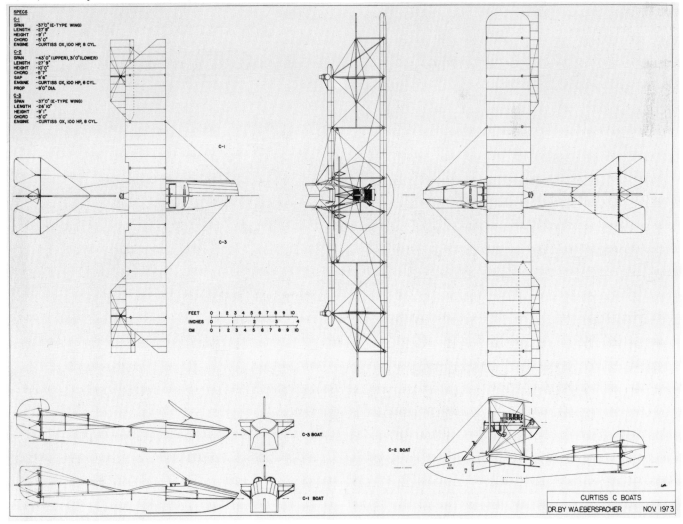

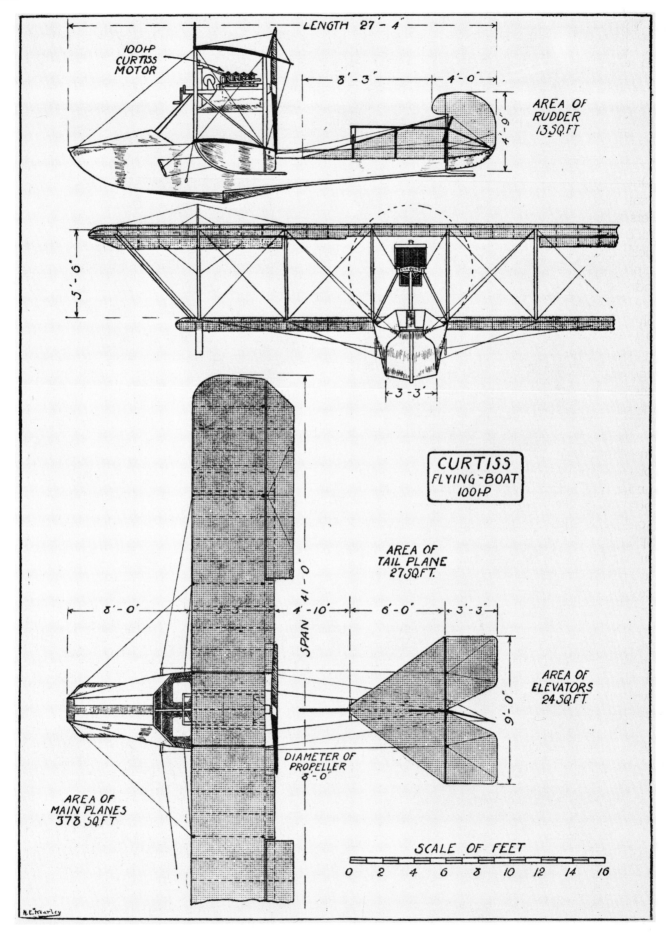

LENGTH 27'-4"

8'-3"   4'-0"

100HP
CURTISS
MOTOR

AREA OF
RUDDER
13 SQ.FT.

4'-9"

5'-6"

3'-3'

CURTISS
FLYING-BOAT
100HP

AREA OF
TAIL PLANE
27 SQ.FT.

8'-0'   3'-3'   4'-10'   6'-0"   3'-3'

SPAN 41'-0"

AREA OF
ELEVATORS
24 SQ.FT.

9'-0"

DIAMETER OF
PROPELLER
8'-0"

AREA OF
MAIN PLANES
378 SQ.FT.

SCALE OF FEET

0   2   4   6   8   10   12   14   16

A scale drawing of the 100-horsepower flying boat, as published in *Flight*, April 11, 1914, about the time this aircraft arrived in England.

The McCormick F Boats, 1913

One of the more interesting records of early aircraft design is contained in an exchange of letters between Curtiss and Harold F. McCormick of the International Harvester Company of Chicago. The letters are sometimes difficult to decipher because to save paper, the economy-minded Curtiss used the incoming letter as the place upon which to make the carbon copy of his reply. The exchange began on January 10, 1913, with an exploratory letter from Curtiss to McCormick, inviting him to vacation in San Diego and there learn to pilot one of his flying boats. McCormick's reply of January 15 stated in part:

I can say to you that nothing would give me greater pleasure than to accept your proposal and go to San Diego for a vacation and to learn to handle one of your flying boats. I have had my eye on your boat for some time and I thought that perhaps next spring or summer I would get one and under the care of one of your men I would learn to run one of these novelties. I am certainly interested ever so much in what you are doing and the accomplishments you are effecting. I am also appreciative of your frankness in stating to me one of the motives in your writing to me, and I should indeed be glad if I could reciprocate in any way your friendliness to me on several occasions.

With this encouragement, Curtiss on January 20 replied to McCormick:

A person could get better results and more fun with a flying boat on Lake Michigan after becoming familiar with it at a place like this [San Diego] where the water is as smooth as a mill pond almost every day in the month.

If . . . you decide, as suggested in your letter, to buy a machine, why not let us have your order now so we can build a special machine for you to incorporate all the latest improvements.

McCormick replied on January 25:

How long will it take you to build such an aeroplane as you suggest and what would be the improvements which you speak of embodying?

My idea would be to have a water boat which would not simply hold myself but one which perhaps would be driven at first by a professional with one or two extra seats for passengers. Then little by little, I can learn to drive this machine myself. Do you have any idea of building a machine that would carry three passengers or is two about the limit now? Would a water flying boat such as you would build be feasible to fly in and out from Lake Forest on good days on the water's edge?

At that time, Curtiss was just beginning the series of F boats, which had solid spars as their

First on the left is L. A. "Jack" Vilas and third from the left H. F. McCormick, at Hammondsport to inspect the second McCormick F Boat. The Vilas boat is in the background.

principal feature. Their passenger capacity, generally two or three, was largely dictated by the power of the engine. In reply to the above query, Curtiss wrote McCormick on January 30:

The flying boat we just recently delivered to the Navy carried a useful load of over six hundred pounds, which is equal to the weight of four average persons. The machine we would build for you, however, would have a somewhat greater lifting capacity than this, in order to accommodate a good supply of fuel and the auxiliary motor for running on the water in an emergency. . . .

If we should build you a machine, we will of course demonstrate it at our own expense and guarantee its performance. We want to demonstrate near Chicago next spring and I can think of nothing more desirable than to do it with a machine built for you . . .

We were recently awarded the Collier Trophy, for the greatest achievement in aviation in 1912, on the production of this type of flying boat.

This navy boat, incidentally, was the beginning of the four-place F boat that eventually became the *Seagull*. The limited public knowledge of flying in 1913 lead to questions that today appear naïve, as can be seen in McCormick's letter to Curtiss on January 31:

Does your flying boat fly close to the water, as well as higher up in the air—at an elevation of three or four feet? Do you consider it dangerous flying near the water? What is the elevation at which in traversing water, to be as near the water as possible and yet in the air, at which you think best results are attained, safety, speed and all things considered.

I have a country place about twenty-five miles from Chicago as reckoned along the shore-line. For example; call it twenty-six miles from the Chicago Yacht Club. What could I reasonably count upon in using a flying boat for service between these two points—in the morning and in the afternoon. Is twenty-five miles continuous flying too much to expect? On the theory I have, I could leave in the morning from Lake Forest, get down to the Chicago Yacht Club, and the flying boat could wait for me there till the afternoon, when I would fly back. I presume in order to feel fresh for the day's work at the office, and not blown to pieces, I should have some kind of a light suit which I would slip on, and a helmet over my head. I am sorry to be asking these detailed questions, but I am running the matter over in my mind, along these lines. Of course, the man who takes care of the flying boat and drives it for me, would stay with the boat in the daytime and go with me in the afternoon back to Lake Forest.

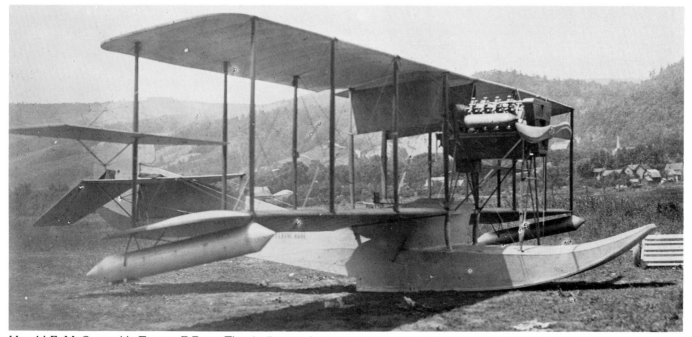

Harold F. McCormick's Tractor F Boat. The hull was designed to cause the bow wave to separate and flow to each side of the cockpit.

Further queries followed on February 4, 1913:

I had in mind having a hangar on the beach at the foot of a 74 foot bluff, which exists at that point. Our house is on the crest of the bluff and the beach is down below. A floating hangar might be very nice, but if it were located near to our house it would not be very much sheltered in case of storms which occur occasionally and there is no pier or breakwater in front of our property. Therefore, I had the idea of putting a hangar there and rolling the machine into the water, or otherwise getting it there.

The statistics you give me about the size of the aeroplane you have in mind are very interesting. The one thing I am thinking about is whether such a machine as you propose would be an experiment or an assured success. Would it not be better for me to start in with a two seated aeroplane or a three seated one rather than a four seated one?

I shall be glad to get from you more in detail the reliability which could be placed within reason, upon such an aeroplane to take me up and down the shore from Lake Forest to Chicago and return, fairly regularly if I desired it. Or would it be better to simply consider this aeroplane as a novelty and keep it up around Lake Forest and not expect to come into town with it? Of course, based upon what I have told you in the foregoing, this aeroplane would always be over the water, and for a vast part of the journey might skim along in only three or four feet of water, and it would only be as you approach Chicago, with the revetments

Specifications	
The McCormick I (Tractor)	
F Boat, 1913	
Span	38 ft. 4 in.
Length	26 ft. 0 in.
Chord	5 ft. 6 in.
Gap	5 ft. 6 in.
Engine	8-cyl. V, Model OX, 90/100 hp

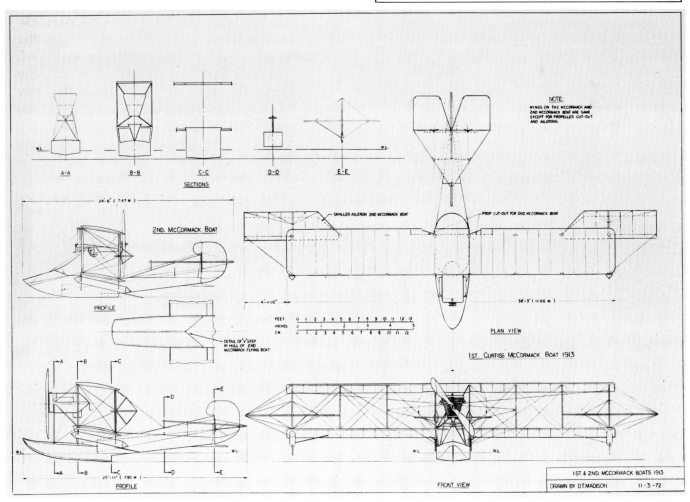

and embankments, that it would be sailing over anything like deep water.

Would the aeroplane you have in mind to carry four people be substantially bigger than a standard size for two seats? Would it have more power? Would it be more dangerous? Would it be more seaworthy in starting out in rougher water? Questions like these, I should like very much to have your opinion on.

Concerning these questions, Curtiss replied to McCormick on February 5:

Answering your first question "Does the flying boat fly close to the water as well as higher up in the air?" It does; in fact there is something peculiar about flying close to the surface of the water. Did you ever see a Pelican glide, as they sometimes do, for hundreds of feet and within a foot of the water, without any apparent movement of their wings. It is remarkable how the flying boat will glide along close to the water without much power, in fact with the throttle less than half open it will travel a long way without apparently dropping at all. It is particularly fascinating to fly in this manner and it can be done with perfect safety.

The flying boat has so much buoyancy and surface on which to alight, that a bad landing does not cause any damage. Of course it would be possible to smash the machine, but as compared with other aeroplanes or the old type hydroaeroplanes it is very easy to operate and easy to land.

The twenty-five mile flight, between your place and the Club House would be made in about thirty minutes and would be no tax on the machine. On days when the water is too rough for pleasure, you could of course make the trip by land although the boat could be flown on probably twenty-five days a month.

Test flight of the Spoonbill F, the McCormick Tractor F Flying Boat.

And in reply to a further question from McCormick, Curtiss replied on February 10:

If you think a three passenger equipment would be satisfactory, it would simplify the construction somewhat as [we] would use our standard eighty horse power engine and would need to make but very little change in the boat. This size boat (twenty six feet) is very seaworthy.

I hear rumors of a proposed hydro-aeroplane tour and contests about Great Lakes, in the spring. I think it would be great sport, if you have a flying boat to enter in such events. The machine being operated, if you wish, by the hired aviator.

As the project progressed, McCormick wrote Curtiss on February 27:

The question in my mind is whether there is any special danger in having the motor overhead as it is in your design, as against one placed lower down. I presume a motor placed lower down would destroy the question of distribution of weight. I notice in the blue print that you have the side elevators fixed as is usual in your type of machine, whereas in one of the photographs I thought I saw you had put on ailerons, somewhat as used in the Farman type.

I don't know that you mentioned what the price of this aeroplane would be, and how long it would take for delivery? This, I should like to know. It seems to me that in one of the photographs the body of the boat proper appeared to be deeper than that shown on your blue print. I presume such is not the case, however.

Would you propose to put on one of your new type motors or one of your regular ones of the past year? Has it a muffler, or not? I am very glad to learn that you think the plan of having a building on the shore and running the flying boat up on to this is better than a floating hangar, and I think this is also best, on the shore of Lake Michigan.

As to a man to run it, I presume I should have one of your best, as I would not want to run this machine myself until further on in the summer, when I would have plenty of time. In the meantime, I would like to have someone who could run it and care for it. Have you any suggestions to make as to the

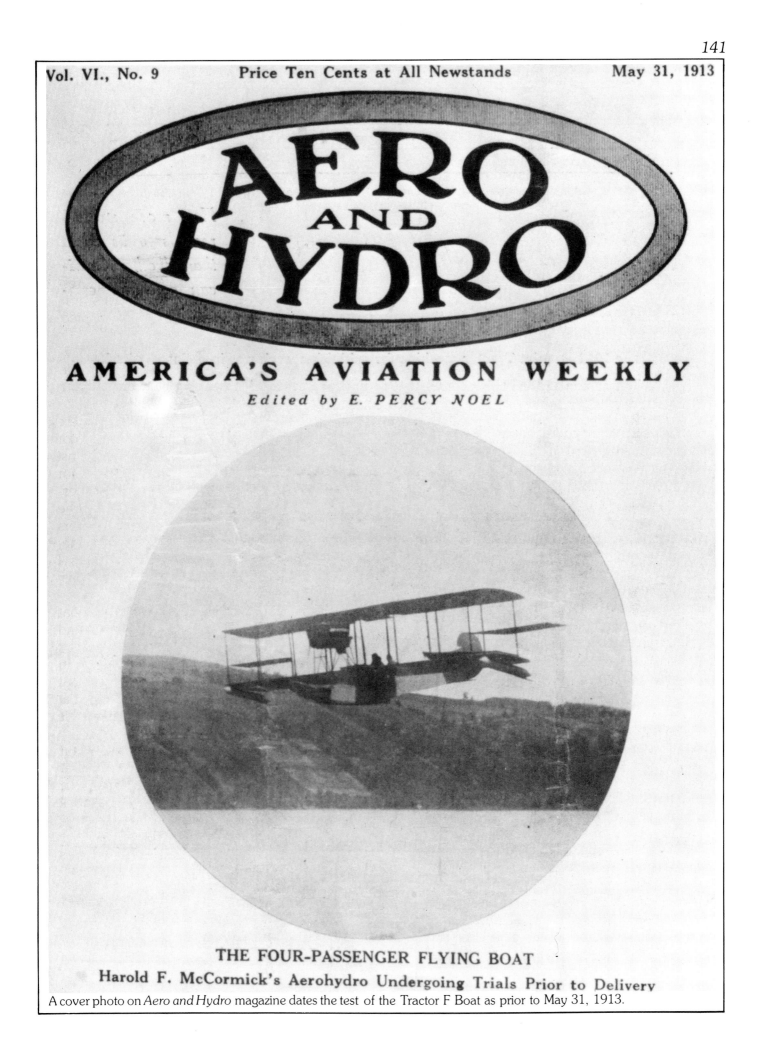

Vol. VI., No. 9   Price Ten Cents at All Newstands   May 31, 1913

AERO AND HYDRO

AMERICA'S AVIATION WEEKLY

Edited by E. PERCY NOEL

THE FOUR-PASSENGER FLYING BOAT

Harold F. McCormick's Aerohydro Undergoing Trials Prior to Delivery

A cover photo on *Aero and Hydro* magazine dates the test of the Tractor F Boat as prior to May 31, 1913.

man who should do this work, and about what his salary and expenses would be?

On March 6 Curtiss wrote McCormick:

I am in receipt of a copy of the blueprint sent to you. This drawing is very meager and does not contain all of the features which the machine itself will possess. One of the features will be a forward entrance, which enables operator and passenger to get in or out without going over or under wires or other obstructions. There will be a door in the hood for this purpose.

Landings may be made on the beach or wharf, head on. The wings of an aeroplane prevent landing broadside like an ordinary boat.

Our starting device works perfectly and we never start the motor by the propeller.

The bottom and some other parts of this boat will be made of duralumin, which is as light as aluminum and as strong as mild steel and which will not rust or corrode. We have been using this to excellent advantage for the past six months.

And on the same day Curtiss sent McCormick a second letter:

I believe that the high position of the motor is best. This keeps the center of weight up near the center of resistance, where it should be. Placing the motor in the hull of the boat and driving by chain brings the weight too low and affects the flying qualities of the machine, greatly. The low center of weight is not quite so objectionable where the propeller can be low also, as in the Farman, but where it is necessary to have the propeller high, as in a hydro-aeroplane, we get a very bad effect in fore and aft stability when the power is decreased or increased during flight or making landings. The pendulum effect on the lateral stability is also very bad in winds. This construction has been thoroughly tried by us.

As to the question of the position of the operator and passenger, in the sketch sent you, your point is well taken. In the drawing it looks dangerous but you get a different impression when you see the machine. The engine supports are strong and there is really no danger of the engine coming loose, even in case of a smashup.

Fact is, however, we have been planning a tractor, which will have all of the advantages of the present construction and some additional safety features. I will send you a sketch of this design and if it appeals to you, we would be glad to build a machine for you on these plans. We will guarantee its performance in every way.

We could make delivery May 1st, or any time thereafter to suit your convenience.

We would equip this machine with the new model O motor, which gives something like ten horse power more than the old motor. The list price would be six thousand dollars. . . . We have several good men who would be quite competent to take a permanent position with you, to operate and care for the machine as a chauffeur does an automobile. I have one man particularly in mind. A Mr. Hill, who is just finishing his course in our school. He is skillful and competent in every respect, being a thorough mechanic and very much of a gentleman. I expect a salary of fifty dollars a week would be about right for him. . . .

The pictures I sent you showing the ailerons attached to the rear beam of the upper plane was an experimental machine. It did not prove as satisfactory as the standard type.

The photos referred to were probably of the Model H in its original form. On March 10, Curtiss wrote again to McCormick:

I referred, in my last letter, to the Farman type ailerons. We will not use these as we prefer our standards which, being balanced, are easier to operate and more efficient.

I think the three seated machine will give you the best satisfaction.

We are constructing a set of planes with more surface than our standards. This will cut down the speed a little, but will make the machine arise quicker, from the water, and make it easier to alight in rough water. These new planes are built in one piece like the new military tractor. This facilitates quick and convenient assembling.

This correspondence led to a visit by McCormick to Hammondsport, and while there, to a flight in a two-place F boat.

The Curtiss proposal had been for the first four-place tractor flying boat. The unusual and awkward-appearing "spoonbill" flying boat was tested successfully on May 21, 1913.

Because Lake Michigan was never noted for its tranquil surface McCormick had asked that the boat have freeboard adequate to ensure that the passengers would not be immersed in spray. Consequently, the design provided a 4-foot freeboard and a pointed bow 6 feet forward of the passenger compartment. The bow was intended to break the waves and permit them to wash over the low foredeck. The approximate dimensions of the cockpit were 4 feet by 7 feet.

It was the largest and fastest aircraft produced to that date. Curtiss made the initial tests by himself, as he wanted to try out the controls and performances before taking any passengers. Among those who later accompanied Curtiss as passengers were L. A. Vilas of Chicago, Illinois, Charles Niles of Rochester, New York, and Marshal Reid of Philadelphia, Pennsylvania, all of whom were at Hammondsport to purchase aircraft of their own.

Charles C. Witmer, an experienced Curtiss pilot who had just returned from a demonstration tour in Europe, was hired to fly the aircraft for McCormick, and George E. A. Hallett was employed to maintain it.

The aerodynamic components, the same as those installed on the first military tractor and the navy's C-2, were known as F model wings. The hull was 4 feet wide with a single deep step in line with the rear spar of the lower wing.

Two silencers muffled the exhaust. In a weekly plant report by an unknown author, dated June 22–28, 1913, an interesting note appears:

While flying the McCormick boat last night Curtiss and Witmer amused themselves by rescuing a broken down launch. They were flying home about dusk with a thunder shower threatening when they noticed two men in a launch about a mile out, waving frantically for help. They explained that their motor (engine) was hopelessly stalled and wanted someone sent out to tow them ashore. Witmer sat on the tail of the big flying boat and held the painter of the boat while Curtiss towed them gently ashore. An attempt to speed up nearly flooded the boat. After seeing the motor boat safely stowed, Curtiss took the two sailors aboard with he & Witmer and brought them back to camp.

Construction details of the McCormick F, or the No. 1 flying boat were as follows: The wing span was 38 feet 4 inches, whereas the overall span of the machine was 41 feet 8 inches because the ailerons extended beyond the main panels. The wing chord measured 5 feet 6 inches and the wings were separated by a gap of 5 feet 6 inches. The wing panels were quickly dismountable. Their double-surfaced covering was Goodyear aluminum-coated fabric. The wing spars were laminated spruce. Canister-type floats were mounted under the wing tips.

The tail section consisted of an elliptical rudder, a vertical fin, two horizontal stabilizers and elevators. The rudder was 5 feet in diameter. The lower portion, made of wood, was bound with copper and was intended for steering the boat at low speed in the water; the upper portion was a fabric-covered piece similar in structure to the wings. The twin elevators were half-round sections operated by the control wheel in the conventional manner.

The overall length of the hull was 24 feet from bow to rudder post, and with the rudder it was 26 feet. The framework was built up with the integrity of a cantilever bridge. The bow top, sides and bottom, were ribbed with ash strips spaced on 3-inch centers, mortised at the corners and fitted with copper corner straps, and each frame was securely fastened with sixteen copper rivets.

The hull was divided laterally by eight watertight bulkheads, and any two compartments were sufficient to float the entire machine. The weight of the hull was 400 pounds.

Longitudinal ash ribs, or keelsons, 1-inch square were spaced on 4-inch centers. The bottom was triple-sheathed with $5/16$-inch mahogany planking over which heavy canvas was set in marine glue, and outer planking of $1/4$-inch mahogany diagonally laid as far back as the step in the hull, about 10 feet from the bow. At speed, the boat rode on only a few square feet of wetted surface just forward of the step.

The cockpit, 42 inches wide and 84 inches long, afforded ample elbowroom for four occupants. The two front seats were occupied by the pilot and a mechanic if one was carried. Dual controls, including a foot throttle, were installed so that either of the occupants of the front seat could handle the machine independently of the other, or they could handle it in unison for training purposes. Kenyon cushions for the seats served also as life preservers. All the metal fittings of the hull were of brightly polished aluminum or nickel-plated steel. The hull and exposed woodwork were finished in dark gray enamel.

The 100-horsepower Curtiss OX engine was mounted in tractor configuration together with the gas tank, radiator and propeller as a unit in a strong tubular frame forward and above the cockpit. Two silencers muffled the exhaust. The safety starting crank was within easy reach of either pilot. The main 40-gallon tank, providing fuel for six to eight hours flying, or 400 miles, was beneath the pilot's seat. From here fuel was pumped to a 3-gallon tank on the engine mount. Instruments consisted of an altimeter, tachometer and oil and fuel gauges.

Ailerons were positive-acting in both directions (in contrast to the Farman ailerons), and were operated by the usual Curtiss shoulder braces, interconnected for either operator. These "broke" open for the convenient entrance and egress of occupants. The rudder was operated by left or right rotation of the control wheel.

For clarity, it is well to identify the different types of machines produced by the Curtiss Company and their application at this time. There were three "types" in production in 1913—the D, E and F. Type D might have been equipped with either wheels or floats; it had a pusher configuration, and its wings were built up in sections.

Type E wings could be used with a boat hull, or with a pontoon or wheels, for sporting, military or passenger work. Both the D and E types were of pusher configuration, with one or two notable exceptions. The wings were composed of sections fitted together by bracing wires, brackets and interplane struts. The F wings, a new departure, for the time, were used only with the military tractor and heavy flying-boat hulls. These wings were one-piece and quickly demountable. The McCormick tractor flying boat was fitted with F-type wings.

The second flying boat produced for Harold F. McCormick, of a more conventional design, was one of three "English-type" boats built during the latter part of 1913. Another was sent to Europe for demonstrations and the third was purchased by Barton L. Peck of Detroit.

The aircraft was delivered to McCormick in July 1913 by pilot Charles C. Witmer and mechanic George E. A. Hallett. By September 28, the plane was ready for McCormick and his guests to indulge in a passenger-hopping party.

Specifications	
The McCormick II (Pusher) F Boat, 1913	
Span	38 ft. 4 in.
Length	23 ft. 7 in.
Chord	5 ft. 7 in.
Gap	5 ft. 6 in.
Engine	8-cyl. V, Model OX, 100 hp
Weight net	1,520 lb.

After an initial test flight with Hallett as passenger, Witmer began a long afternoon of joyriding. Starting with one passenger at a time he progressed to two, and each time the performance was repeated the plane exhibited the same ability to carry the load easily, planing after a short run and getting into the air gracefully and without effort. That it could carry four was certain, for a duplicate of this boat had shortly before carried five people at Hammondsport, though Witmer had not yet had an opportunity to do so.

Because of its better lines, this new boat produced a clean wake. No spray was thrown into the double cockpit and it was noticeably faster than the first, both on the water and in the air.

With winter approaching and Lake Michigan taking on a more fierce complexion, McCormick told Witmer and Hallett to take the boat south and operate it to "make expenses." They disassembled the machine and shipped it in a Wells Fargo Express car to Miami, where they set up operation in front of the Royal Palms Hotel in Miami Beach. Although they made expenses, corrosion took its toll, and it was necessary to replace all the metal fittings on the plane in the spring of 1914. They returned north by way of the Curtiss factory at Hammondsport, where Hallett completely rebuilt the engine. Then Witmer and his brother-in-law, Ben Thomas, proceeded to Chicago, where they operated the aircraft during that summer.

Like the contemporary E boats the engine and propeller of this machine were mounted in a pusher configuration. The wings were the then new F-type construction. A hull innovation, consisting of a **V**-shaped step incorporated in the lower hydroplaning surface, replaced the conventional box step. In this construction the apex of the **V** was in line with the center of pressure of the wings, while its rear tips, 5½ inches high, were in line with the rear spars. At speed, the boat rode on the few square feet of planing surface forward of the step, which was vented with two 1½-inch copper tubes that extended upward into the adjacent watertight hull compartment. Any two compartments could support the entire machine. The greatest width was at the cockpit, where the hull flared out to 44 inches. The beam at the planing surface was at its widest (34 inches) just ahead of the step, tapering to the rudderpost at the rear.

The hull, 20 feet 7 inches long, was built up almost exactly like the tractor boat and the dual controls were also similar. The hood over the bow was characterized by straight lines, rather than by the easy curves of the Vilas boat. Most structural details and furnishings were duplicates of those on the tractor boat. Metal fittings were finished in a gray enamel that pleasingly harmonized with the lighter gray hull and dark slate-colored wing surface. The hull weighed about 375 pounds.

The wings, similar to those of the army boat and the army tractor Model G, were of the F type, with continuous tapered spars. Each of the four main panels was 17 feet long, separated by a 5½-foot gap between upper and lower surfaces. The upper panels were attached to a 42-inch center section corresponding to the beam of the hull. The spars were spaced 4 feet 5½ inches apart and were carefully cross-braced with heavy wire. The rib spacing was 12 inches and the spruce interplane struts were braced by double aircraft wire with triple bracing for the engine bay. The wings, double-surfaced with high-grade Goodyear rubberized cloth, provided approximately 395 square feet of lifting surface. The chord of the center section was reduced to allow for propeller clearance.

The tail of the machine was standard Curtiss construction. A triangular vertical stabilizing fin, 9 feet 4 inches long by 2 feet 6 inches high, was fixed to the rear deck. The horizontal fixed stabilizing surface, also triangular in plan form, measured 6 feet fore and aft and 9 feet laterally. The rudder, elliptical in shape and partly balanced to facilitate its easy operation, had maximum dimensions of 4 feet fore and aft and 4 feet 8 inches vertically. The lower portion was made of wood, bound with copper. The empennage, easily demountable, was braced by steel tubes secured to the hull longitudinals.

The elevator was composed of twin surfaces, each measuring 4 feet 4 inches by 3 feet 3 inches. All the movable members of the rear control were operated by heavy cable through control arms of tubular steel acting both as levers and as king posts to truss the surfaces.

The rudder was protected by a heavy ash skeg at the extreme end of the hull. The hull forward of the step was also protected by three oak runners of substantial size.

The lateral control of the McCormick boat was by the standard Curtiss ailerons mounted midway between the wing panels and pivoted to the outermost two rear struts. The ailerons, positive-acting in both directions and practically balanced at the center of pressure for low angles of incidence, were operated by aircraft cable running over aluminum pulleys fixed to the strut fittings. They were 2 feet 6 inches wide and 9 feet long, the area of each being about 20 square feet.

The engine used was the then new OX 100-horsepower 8-cylinder Curtiss design. The engine and radiator were mounted as a unit upon a framework of large-diameter, heavy-gauge steel tubing securely cross-braced by additional tubing and steel ribbon. The fuel tanks were no longer mounted on the engine bed as before, but were slung from the struts next to the engine by steel straps. This method was thought to eliminate the destructive effects of vibration and it also placed the fuel tank away from the hot engine.

A single 8-foot pusher propeller was fitted directly to the engine crankshaft and turned at about 1,220 rpm. The power plant was mounted so that the propeller cleared the boat deck by more than 3 inches. A safety starting crank permanently attached to the engine was within easy reach of either seat.

The tank carried 15 gallons of gasoline and carried sufficient oil in the engine sump to last for about six hours.

A double, or dual, control provided for side-by-side operation. The wheel controlled the rudder; fore-and-aft movement operated the elevators, and shoulder yokes operated the ailerons, which were rigged to operate differentially but independently of each other. Should one fail, the other would still be operable.

A neat device was incorporated in this control that permitted "breaking" the yoke, thus allowing easy ingress and egress to the seats and also throwing either shoulder yoke out of operation or allowing both people to control the ailerons in unison.

The G Tractor Scout, S.C. No. 21, 1913

Some confusion exists as to the proper designation of this machine. *Jane's All the World's Aircraft* for 1913 illustrates this machine by line sketches and designates it as an F tractor. This may have been the initial designation, for it used F wings and an F boat empennage; however, it is carried on army records as a G model and its distinct difference from the F boats justified this change to G. It probably was an outgrowth of the army's first order for a tractor landplane, which was converted to an F boat (S.C. order No. 13045).

This Model G was the first military tractor built by Curtiss and it used a number of F compo-

nents, as described by Henry Kleckler in his letter of January 11, 1913.

Hammondsport, N.Y.
January 11, 1913.

Mr. G. H. Curtiss,
Coronado, Cal.

Dear Sir:

I suppose you will think by this time that I have neglected writing pretty seriously, but I have been more than busy every day and evening on the army tractor. It is coming

The Model G after modification by signal corp personnel at San Diego. Note that the hole intended for the propeller shaft is at the upper center of the radiator, and the tripod landing gear replaces the tricycle gear of the original. *Curtiss Photo Collection*

very nicely now, and certainly does look good as we get it together. We have it practically finished except wiring up controls, and fitting some of the body around the power plant. They are covering the last panel this afternoon, and the others are all fitted up ready to put in place and wire up. The tail is going to be especially clean on this machine. The stabilizers are on the center line of the fuselage, and curved on the inside to fit perfectly. The point is held by a quarter inch cap screw, which passes through the post of the frame to threaded plate fastened on the inside and three holes one and one-half inches apart are provided for adjustment of the stabilizers. The standard flippers and rudder are used except that the rudder does not have the wooden bottom as on the boat. It took considerable study to get a satisfactory shape for the radiator, but I think we have it all right. The radiator should be here on Monday. I was not able to get that ordered until we had the

machine partially set up, so that I could settle definitely on the exact shape.

We are putting in a forty (40) gallon gasoline tank under the seat and running forward in the center between the two operators' legs, and partially under the crank case so as to keep as much as possible of the

Specifications	
The G Tractor Scout, S.C. No. 21, 1913	
Span of top wing	37 ft. 4 in.
Span overall, including ailerons	38 ft. 4 in.
Chord	61 in.
Gap	66 in.
Length	24 ft. 0 in.
Approx. weight	1,050 lb.
Approx. speed	60 mph
Rate of climb approx.	200 ft. per min.

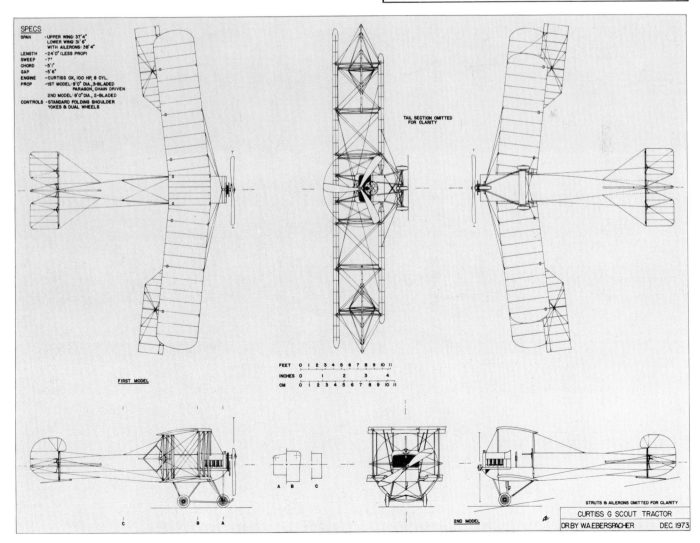

gasoline under the center of pressure. The top of the gasoline tank forms the seat, and saves any extra weight for this, the standard folding shoulder yoke being used. We are equipping this machine with an engine which has the new cylinder on and will ship along a muffler which you can use or not as you wish. We have been trying it with the muffler on the engine on the Lake here today and yesterday, also the three blade 8 ft. paragon. The muffler greatly reduces the noise of the engine, but the roar of the propeller is very prominent, so that the whole amount of noise is not greatly diminished.

The machine sounds like a planing mill in the air one-half mile away. . . . I think that the noise of the propellers is caused when the blades pass the edges of the surface, and this is proven by the fact that the three blade makes much more noise than the two blade, and gives the impression that the engine is running very fast.

When first installed Doc [Doc Wildman] insisted that the engine was turning fifteen hundred (1500), but a speed counter showed eleven hundred (1100). The first experiment was with the good 8 ft. propeller, which we have used on the flying boats on the standard hydroplane. This was a considerable improvement over the other propeller, which had been in use on that machine. The mile over the course with this propeller, and with the muffler on was made in 1.10 in one direction, and 1 flat in the other; a run over the same course with the three blade at a time when there was a little less wind gave readings of 1.10 and 1.8 so that the 8 ft. 2 blade shows slightly faster, and on climbing (without barometer) Doc could see no difference between the three blade, and our good two blade. We will try the three blade on the old flying boat tomorrow or Monday, and possibly it will show up better, and as that is the machine it was designed for, although there is so little difference in the speed of the two machines that I do not look for much difference in results.

The six cylinder motor has been running today, and acting pretty good, although it

A front view of the Model G packed for shipment. With narrow tread landing gear and wings folded, the G could be rolled into a railroad boxcar. *A. R. Clemons Collection*

does not throttle good enough yet, and they are having a little trouble with over lubrication. We have not taken any horse power readings yet, but it sounds good when running open, and also works very good. We will make some pictures before it is shipped, and send to you.

The drawings of the tractor, which we have been promising you for some time, I will finish up tomorrow and send them in my letter Monday. We work tomorrow on the tractor, and it should be ready to ship by Wednesday sure. This machine will be very convenient to set up as the power plant and running gear does not have to be taken apart. The wheels come off easily, and this leaves it narrow enough to come through the car door with lots of room to spare. The length of this crate will be six and one-half feet and the height six feet, width will be fifty inches at the bottom and narrower at the top. This saves a lot of complication in making the running gears so that it could be easily taken down. The machine will go in three crates, the power plant, wings and fuselage.

Will write more Monday.
Very truly yours,
THE CURTISS AEROPLANE COMPANY
Henry Kleckler

The G was built on speculation by Curtiss, but after an exchange of letters with Brig. Gen. James Allen of the signal corps, Allen's letter, November 15, 1912, to Curtiss read as follows:

Referring to your letter of the 10th instant, enclosing specifications for a military type Model "G" Curtiss biplane the Signal Corp is in need of a Curtiss aeroplane which will fulfill the requirements of our specifications for Scout type machines.

In case you construct an aeroplane of the proposed type and find that it fulfills our requirements, particularly the ascending tests with 450 pounds, please report the matter to this office with information concerning the selling price of such machines.
Yours truly,
Allen

In reply Curtiss indicated they were working on such a scout type and would report full particulars as soon as experiments had been completed.

On February 10, 1913, Curtiss wrote Capt. W. I. Chambers:

I am enclosing herewith prints of a tractor biplane, we have built for military purposes. This construction has many advantages for land work.

I have a letter from Mr. Ellyson, advising me of the demountable wings on the Burgess flying boat and telling me what an advantage they were for storing on board ship.

A profile view of the Model G Tractor Scout showing the flexible cockpit door, chain drive and the shoulder yoke aileron control still in use.

A year or two ago it was assumed that the aeroplanes would have to be stored below deck and the sectional wings were the only practical type.

We much prefer these one piece wings and if the machines can be stored above deck, they are no doubt better.

Please let me have your opinion on this, as we want to keep as well posted as possible on Naval requirements.

Very sincerely,
G. H. Curtiss

The Model G was shipped to San Diego, where it was tested and accepted on June 12, 1913. It was purchased by the signal corps on April 29, 1913. Delivery, on May 20, 1913, at San Diego was at a price of $5,500. *Aero and Hydro* magazine reported on the test flight on June 21, 1913:

CURTISS TRACTOR PASSES ARMY TESTS

San Diego, Cal., June 12—The 80-horsepower Curtiss military tractor successfully completed the Government tests this morning in the hands of John D. Cooper, chief instructor of the Curtiss San Diego school, and was accepted for the army by the inspection board which witnessed the tests.

The trials commenced early yesterday morning when Cooper made the endurance test. He remained in the air for two hours and five minutes, carrying a useful load of 600 pounds, which included pilot, passenger, gasoline and sufficient sand to make up the required weight.

This morning the speed, climbing, and landing tests were completed, with the same load as on the previous day. The machine made six laps of the prescribed course at an average speed of 52½ miles per hour. Later it climbed to 2,280 feet in the allotted ten minutes. In the landing tests Cooper landed successfully in the plowed field. The machine was then accepted and turned over to the Government, to be assigned to the San Diego Aero division.

The 80-horsepower engine was mounted low, on the lower wing, directly in front of the pilots, and was cowled in contrast to previous designs. The carburetor projected through the firewall/dashboard where it could be adjusted by either

pilot. The radiator was placed in front of the engine, automobile style, with the propeller shaft running through a hole in the upper part of the radiator. The crankshaft was fitted with a 22-pound flywheel and 16-tooth sprocket. The 30-tooth sprocket was fitted to the prop. Two bearings 24 inches apart supported the prop shaft above the engine, giving a rigid bracing against chain pull and prop thrust. The ¾-inch drive chain had a 1¼-inch pitch.

The G was much easier to assemble than the D or E. The fuselage and tricycle landing gear remained assembled with the main rear wheels 20 inches back of the center of gravity with a tread of 65 inches.

The nose wheel was mounted just to the rear of the propeller. The short coupling made it possible to turn in a short radius without assistance. Spring suspension was included in the landing gear design.

The fuselage was conventional for the time, using four spruce longerons spaced 42 inches wide at the cockpit and tapering to a vertical rudder post. It was fabric-covered to reduce drag. The field of view was very good. The side-by-side seating was standard Curtiss practice by this time with folding shoulder yoke, and dual control wheels though a single throw-over wheel could be installed.

The wings were standard F type, which probably accounts for its earlier F Land Tractor designation. The tail group was also derived from the F boats. Ailerons were still mounted between the outboard panels of the wings.

This plane was modified in the summer of 1914 after its acceptance as Signal Corps No. 21. Its new form included a tripod gear with two main wheels forward and a tail skid. The chain drive was dropped, as was the three-blade propeller, in favor of a direct drive two-blade propeller.

It is possible that it was further converted to the H configuration, though the report of two Hs (one with 75 horsepower, the other 90 horsepower) in the army's year-end report may have been just a simplification for accounting purposes. (See *Aeronautics*, December 13, 1913, page 201.)

After about a year of flying the G, No. 21 was fitted with floats and sold, minus engine, in Hawaii on November 12, 1914. Lt. Lewis Geiger, a pilot who had flown the plane extensively during its service life, accompanied the plane.

The H Tractor Scout, S.C. No. 22, 1913

While similar to the G tractor, the H differed in a number of details. Originally the top wing had a span of 41 feet with Farman-type ailerons inset in the trailing edge of the wing with outward-angled struts for supporting these extended panels beyond the 31-foot lower wings. The extra span of the upper wing was accomplished by insertion of a 7-foot 6-inch center section. The chord of both wings was 66 inches. The Farman-type ailerons were a distinctive departure from the standard Curtiss practice of using interplane ailerons; however, control was much less positive and interplane ailerons were installed with the outboard tips supported from the tip of the upper wings. A further modification was made, removing the center panel of the upper wing making it an equal-span biplane with interplane ailerons.

The Model H was produced to S.C. order No. 13404, dated April 22, 1913. It was powered by a Curtiss 80-horsepower O engine and delivered, flown and accepted on December 16, 1913 at San Diego. It was flown extensively because for a time it was the only machine available. Grover Loening related that when he arrived at San Diego in July 1914 to take charge of the Experimental and Repair Department of the signal corps, he condemned all the pusher aircraft then in operation.* This left the one lone Curtiss H (No. 22) and a Burgess-Wright Model H powered by a Renault engine that was geared down to swing a very large propeller. This latter machine was not looked upon favorably by the pilots. This circumstance left the training of about twenty aviators to Oscar Brindly and old No. 22, the Curtiss H.

When delivered, it had an O engine of about 80–90 horsepower, a top speed of 48 miles per hour and a landing speed of 46 miles per hour. It would fly comfortably with this light wing loading; the interplane ailerons and generous tail surfaces gave a somewhat soft control feel. It was clumsy but reliable.

Improvements were incorporated in the engine, increasing the power to 90–100 horsepower, with the OX driving a 9-foot two-blade propeller. The distinctive quadricycle gear was clumsy, requiring a flat touchdown; however, with a built-in shock absorber and a landing

*"Origin of Air Service Engineering" by Grover Loening, *Aerospace Historian* 2, no. 4 (October 1964): 93–100.

The Model H Tractor Scout had ailerons installed on the trailing edge of the upper wing. Experience showed the ailerons at this location to be less responsive than the standard Curtiss interplane ailerons. *Curtiss photo from the Shell Company Foundation, National Air and Space Museum*

speed of about 46 miles per hour, it presented no real problem. Ailerons were a generous 12 feet by 3 feet. The tail surfaces were the same as the ''English'' flying boat, a four-place F boat.

The landing gear was unusual, having three sets of heavy rubber shock absorbers on each side attaching the gear to fuselage. The wing spars of the F-type wings were heavy at the roots and tapered as they approached the tip, giving them strength in proportion to the load imposed on them. The wings were easily demounted by removing four bolts, one each from the top and bottom of each wing.

Overall width of the gear was 65 inches, with a tread of 56 inches, standard road gauge, enabling the machine to be towed along a standard road when necessary. Ailerons were individually connected so they could in an emergency be operated separately in case of accident to one or the other. The fuselage was covered to reduce air resistance. Pilots sat side by side, as in the G, with fabric removed from the lower wings out to the first rib (12 inches), making possible an excellent view. Like the G, the 40-gallon fuel tank was the

seat and the carburetor projected into the cockpit for adjustment. Also like the G, the fuel was pumped by an engine-driven fuel pump into a 2-gallon auxiliary tank on the dashboard. A window in this tank allowed a view of the fuel coming in from the pump and warned of impending fuel starvation. Like the G, the radiator was mounted on the forward fuselage directly behind the propeller. The engine was cowled by an automotive-type hood that extended back to the cockpit. A curved metal shield served as dashboard and deflected the engine heat away from the pilots.

While the letter H is generally associated with the flying boat series, beginning with the *America* and its successors, the H-4s, at least two sources clearly indicate the existence of the H landplane. The Ernest L. Jones chronology,* part of which was published in *Aerospace Historian* 13, no. 4 (Winter 1966): 64, is the most

*Ernest L. Jones, formerly editor of *Aeronautics*, and at the time of compilation of the chronology colonel (U.S. Air Force) on the staff of the Air University, Maxwell Air Force Base.

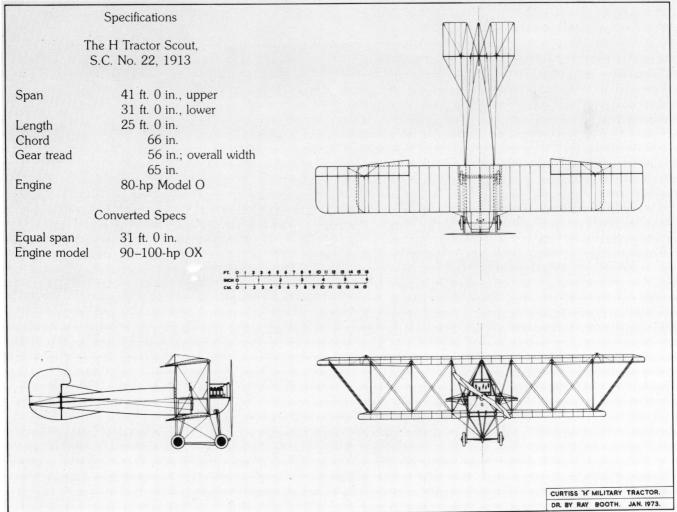

Specifications

The H Tractor Scout,
S.C. No. 22, 1913

Span	41 ft. 0 in., upper
	31 ft. 0 in., lower
Length	25 ft. 0 in.
Chord	66 in.
Gear tread	56 in.; overall width
	65 in.
Engine	80-hp Model O

Converted Specs

Equal span	31 ft. 0 in.
Engine model	90–100-hp OX

CURTISS 'H' MILITARY TRACTOR.
DR. BY RAY BOOTH. JAN. 1973.

specific; this is supplemented by the published record of army aeronautics for 1913 (*Aeronautics*, December 1913, page 201), which lists

among aircraft on hand at the end of the year "2 Curtiss H. 75 and 90 hp. resp." The 75-horsepower is believed to be the modified G described previously.

A close-up of the quadricycle landing gear on the Model H Tractor Scout, showing the shock absorber system and the hook-type brake at the rear of the center spreader beam.

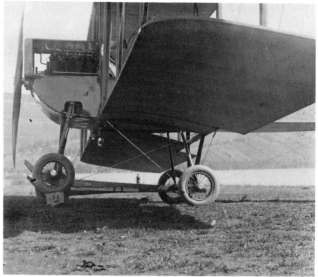

A close-up of the H Tractor Scout undercarriage.

The Model H ready for testing in its second configuration with the upper wing shortened and the ailerons mounted between the wings. Charles Niles and John Dale Cooper are in the cockpit.

The Beachey Special Looper, 1913

One of the most colorful and daring of the early exhibition pilots was Lincoln Beachey. In addition to the usual repertoire of turns, dives and low passes, Beachey established himself as the foremost practitioner of the art of looping. For this special maneuver, he had his Curtiss D Headless especially constructed and braced with additional interplane wires. In a letter to Capt. W. I. Chambers, dated October 18, 1913, H. C. Genung notes that "Beachey is with us at the present time and having a machine made to his order for the purpose of 'looping the loop.' He expects to accomplish this before Pegoud

reaches this country . . ." Adolphe Pegoud, a Frenchman, is credited as being the first pilot to accomplish this maneuver.

This special plane was reportedly built by James LaMont at the Curtiss factory. The engine was a standard 90–100 horsepower, probably an OX. It was wired with $^3/_{32}$-inch Roebling wire, doubled. The front and rear spars were doubly heavy, about 1½ by 3 inches. The wing span was 24 feet 3 inches overall, built in three sections. The tail outriggers were 2 feet shorter than the standard D, and the horizontal stabilizer was only 6 inches wide at the center, tapering to

Lincoln Beachey in his Special Model D Looper. The wings were shortened to 24 feet 3 inches. The spars were double thickness, 1¼ inches by 3 inches. Seatbelt and shoulder straps were installed. The whole machine was braced with $^3/_{32}$-inch Roebling wire, and double-braced wires were used in the vicinity of the engine bay. These extra precautions produced a heavier machine with increased drag.

Specifications

The Beachey Special Looper, 1913

Span   24 ft. 3 in.
Engine   8-cyl. V, Model OX, 90/100 hp

Reputedly, all of Beachey's performances were spectacular, but this was not part of the performance. This accident occurred in October 1913 at Hammondsport, where, for the first time, he was using a safety belt and shoulder harness, which probably saved his life.

Lincoln Beachey at the moment of crash, Hammondsport, October 1913. Beachey landed upside down, and he can just be seen hanging from his safety belt.

A later performance at Montreal in 1914 shows Beachey in fine form at low altitude, headed directly at camera. The plane was built by Beachey and James LaMont at the Curtiss factory in October 1913. *K. M. Molson Collection*

2 inches at the outboard ends. The elevators were increased in area.

The front wheel was 2 feet nearer the wings than on the D model and the pilot's feet were placed almost directly over this front wheel. The rear wheels were set slightly forward and the wings set closer to the ground than on the standard D, reducing the overall height to 7 feet. A safety belt was installed in addition to a shoulder strap to keep Beachey from falling out while inverted. The weight of this special machine was 901 pounds.

One of the most spectacular flights made by Lincoln Beachey with this special looper was a 300-foot flight inside the Machinery Hall at the San Francisco-Panama-Pacific Exposition.

In October of 1913, an unfortunate tragedy resulted from one of Beachey's exhibition performances. During one of his low-level passes over a tent, he misjudged his altitude and struck the tent, knocking two spectators off the tent ridge and killing one of them outright. He retained sufficient control to make a crash landing, demolishing his aircraft. The safety belts are credited with saving his life.

Beachey flying his Looper inside Machinery Hall, San Francisco. A 300-foot flight was possible within the walls of the hall.

The *Tadpole*, 1913-1914

The *Tadpole*, one of the Curtiss machines that appears to have no predecessor or successors, was assembled to establish empirically the proper relationship between the planing surface of the hull and the angle of incidence of the wings. The purpose was to make a smooth transition from the hydrodynamic lift produced by the hull to the aerodynamic lift of the wings. The *Tadpole* and its special tilting wing were short-lived in the evolution of Curtiss designs. The first successful flying boat used the standard Model E wing panels, but the rear spar had a drop of 5½ inches below the front spar. This increased the angle of incidence and no doubt aided in getting the boat out of the water quicker, but an angle of incidence of that magnitude undoubtedly imposed a substantial speed penalty once the flying boat was clear of the water.

In a letter from Curtiss to Henry A. Wise Wood dated January 15, 1913, Curtiss discussed the desirability of a device on the third machine, "which will improve the stability of the boat when subject to rough weather conditions when adrift without power." The ability to adjust the angle of incidence would make it possible to set the wings at a negative angle, as well as a positive angle, thereby killing any lift that might endanger the aircraft when at its moorings or adrift, making it less subject to the whims of the winds. The design of this tilting-wing flying boat is recorded in patent No. 1,287,249, in which the difficulty of getting a flying boat airborne is listed as the purpose of the patent.

Taking the design one more step, operating the wings differentially could provide lateral (roll) control, making ailerons unnecessary.

Another use for this unusual machine is recorded in *Aeronautics*, April 15, 1914, describing the beginnings of the new sport of air skiing. The description refers to the use of a flying boat

The *Tadpole* planing for takeoff. *Curtiss Photo Collection*

or hydro-aeroplane fitted with broad runners or skiis. A frozen lake and a snowstorm delayed an experiment and frustrated the experimenters, causing Curtiss to design the ski gear shown in the illustrations.

It is quite apparent that two configurations of the *Tadpole* existed. Type 2 is shown with skiis. Type 1 is shown with a rather unusual empennage incorporating a high-mounted stabilizer-elevator supported in part by a longitudinal strut attached to the propeller shaft of the aircraft. In the first case, the mechanism for tilting the wings and varying the angle of incidence is quite visible. In the second type of mechanism it is not visible, but ample clearance is provided between the rear spar and the deck of the hull to provide the desired movement for changing the angle of incidence. That they are both variations of the same machine is confirmed by the negative numbers in the Curtiss records. Precise dates for this development, other than those given in the above text, are not known.

The second (1914) version of the *Tadpole*, flying off snow-covered Lake Keuka. In addition to an angle of attack adjustment mechanism, there are also short skiis attached outside the hull, and the axle for wing rotation is clearly visible. The wings and empennage are standard 1913 F boat components.

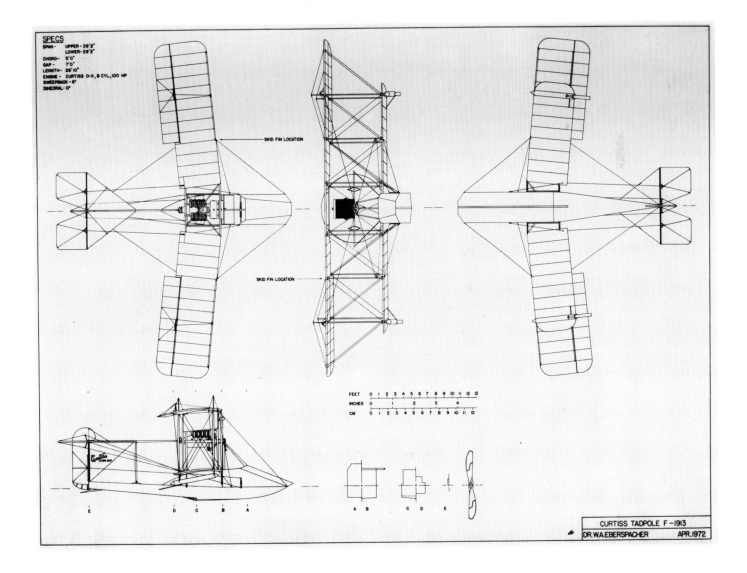

SPECS
SPAN - UPPER - 39'2"
        LOWER - 29'2"
CHORD - 5'0"
GAP - 7'0"
LENGTH - 28'10"
ENGINE - CURTISS O-X, 8 CYL, 100 HP
SWEEPBACK - 6°
DIHEDRAL - 0°

SKID FIN LOCATION

SKID FIN LOCATION

FEET
INCHES
CM

CURTISS TADPOLE F - 1913
DR. W.A. EBERSPACHER   APR. 1972

The U.S. Navy C-2 (AB-2) Flying Boat, 1913, Model F

The C-2, the second navy flying boat, accepted in October 1913, differed from the C-1 in several respects. It was powered by the 80-horsepower Curtiss O engine fitted with OX valve action. It had a decided **V**-bottom; the step was a deep **V**-notch, with the boat riding on the outboard tips of the **V** when at planing speed. Instead of the collapsible windshield used on previous boats, the sloping bow of the C-2 was strongly constructed and had a hinged panel in the center that folded forward to form a gangplank over the bow.

The hull had a maximum width of 50 inches and a depth of 46 inches. The total weight was 500 pounds. Fully loaded, the C-2 weighed approximately 2,400 pounds.

The wings were built-up, one-piece construction of very rugged structure with a 39-foot span upper wing and a 30-foot span lower wing. The chord was 66 inches and the gap 66 inches. The wings were covered with unbleached cotton coated with a new "dope" that made them practically transparent.

In a letter dated February 10, 1913, H. C. Genung, vice-president and general manager of the Curtiss Company, wrote Capt. W. I. Chambers:

We became interested in a transparent preparation for coating aeroplane fabric about a year ago, and have since made a number of practical tests, the results of which have been so satisfactory that we deemed it worthy of report to you.

We are sending you, under separate cover by mail, two small panels for the purpose of test. Panel No. 1 is covered with silk and has received four coats of the preparation. The silk has been employed as a covering solely for the purpose of showing the transparency of the liquid. Panel No. 2 is covered with a Sea Island cotton cloth (very desirable for aeroplane use) and has received five coats of the preparation. In

making tests on these panels, you will find the following points worthy of attention:

1. A broken rib or brace is easily seen.
2. Unaffected by the atmosphere. The cloth will retain its tautness indefinitely (a year's trial has proven this).
3. Any injured place can be patched and made as good as new. The patch will never come off (note patches on the panels).
4. Prevents the nails and tacks from rusting.
5. The preparation has a tendency to preserve the fabric. At the end of a year it will be found to be as strong as originally.
6. Unaffected by oil, gasoline or grease.
7. Almost non-inflammable. A lighted cigarette will burn a hole through it, but the fire will not spread. We have taken a panel coated with the preparation, and after smearing the surface with gasoline and oil, ignited it. In each instance, the grease was consumed and the fire went out without harming the coating in the least.
8. The preparation has a slight tendency to tighten any cloth on which it is applied. A very desirable feature.
9. Absolutely water-proof, causing the aeroplane surface to act as a float when in the water. Sixty hours of soaking has failed to show any presence of water in the panel.
10. The preparation can be colored without affecting its qualities.
11. A highly polished surface may be obtained.

In closing, we wish to say that we are prepared to furnish aeroplane surfaces coated with this preparation should they be desired. Any further information will be gladly given.

The boat was equipped with a 40-gallon fuel tank located behind the seat, in addition to the tanks adjacent to the engine. When delivered, the C-2 was fitted with a Sperry gyroscopic autopilot connected to the rudder and ailerons. The total cost was $6,800.

Instruments consisted of an airspeed indicator, a shaft-driven tachometer, a hull-angle indicator, a barometer (altimeter), an anemometer (airspeed indicator), gasoline gauge and a clock.

Tests completed on August 14 were observed by Capt. W. I. Chambers; Lt. H. C. Richardson, naval constructor, and Lt. P.N.L. Bellinger. Most tests were made by moonlight because the specifications demanded calm weather for certain trials. With a load of approximately 700 pounds, the average speed for ten flights, with and against the wind, was slightly less than 60 miles per hour. From an altitude of 400 feet, the aircraft glided 2,800 feet with the engine turned off.

The C-3 (AB-3), manufacturer's No. 231; the C-4 (AB-4), manufacturer's No. 232 and the C-5 (AB-5), manufacturer's No. 233 were sister ships, all delivered in November 1913 and all powered by the 90–100-horsepower Curtiss OX engine. Refinements in hull design and other details gave these three aircraft the configuration that was produced in quantity as the F boat of World War I. The unit cost of these three almost identical aircraft was $6,350, reflecting the economics possible with quantity purchasing. Accompanying these figures, in the papers of Capt. W. I. Chambers, is the notation that as of January 17, 1914, the C-3 was with the U.S.S. *Miami* at Culebra, as was the C-5. The C-4 was at Pensacola. The foredeck hood of these aircraft differed from that of the C-2. The hull bottom, as far back as the step, was the prescribed double-**V** similar to the Raymond V. Morris monoplane M boat. The bow was squared rather than pointed as in the M boat. Another distinctive feature of the C boats was the installation of two gasoline tanks mounted parallel to the engine bed and inboard of the center interplane struts. The tubular steel bracing for the engine and the tanks formed a rather complicated structure.

Specifications	
The U.S. Navy C-2 (AB-2) Flying Boat, 1913, Model F	
Span	39 ft. 0 in., upper
	30 ft. 0 in., lower
Length	26 ft. 0 in.
Chord	5 ft. 6 in.
Gap	5 ft. 6 in.
Engine	8-cyl. V, Model OX, 90/100 hp

The Langley Reconstruction, 1914

Because Dr. Samuel Pierpont Langley was the third secretary of the Smithsonian Institution and studied and promoted the study of aerodynamics, someone will undoubtedly accuse this writer of "promoting" the Langley machine by recording it here. The foregoing statement may seem peculiar and out of place here, but a photograph of the Langley Aerodrome in a popular aviation periodical, as part of a "photographic visit to the Smithsonian," brought forth several angry letters.

Let me quickly set the record straight. We are proud of the accomplishments of Dr. Langley

and his colleagues. Foremost among these accomplishments was giving aeronautics the cloak of respectability in an era when people who undertook to study this new science were considered at best fools, idiots or charlatans. The fact that Dr. Langley, an eminent scientist, undertook this study gave the field of aerodynamics respectability and encouraged others, among them the Wright brothers, to devote time, energy, money and frequently their lives to this new science.

The Langley Aerodrome, originally constructed in the Smithsonian shops, was built as a

Launching the Langley Aerodrome, which had been reequipped with a Curtiss OX engine and a two-blade propeller. A. V. "Fred" Verville and J. Lansing Callan are shown second and third from left in the photo. *Curtiss Photo Collection*

full-sized, man-carrying version of a successful model of a tandem monoplane that was built and flown in 1896. This model, which had proved the aerodynamics of this form of aircraft, was launched and successfully flown and retrieved over the Potomac River in the vicinity of Quantico, Virginia. On two occasions, October 7 and December 8, 1903, the aerodrome was launched from its houseboat catapult, but due to a number of circumstances was demolished in flight. The damaged components of the aerodrome were retrieved and returned to the Smithsonian. Shortly afterward, on December 17, 1903, the Wright brothers made their first successful powered manned flight at Kitty Hawk.

This brief note is added here to record that Curtiss in 1914, rightly or wrongly, reconstructed the Langley Aerodrome of 1903 and, with modifications, succeeded in flying the aerodrome from Lake Keuka. The effort was motivated, as in the case of several other unusual projects, by the constant maneuvering necessary to defend or challenge the Wrights and other patent holders. A number of changes were made from the original, among them replacing hollow ribs with laminated ribs and changing the wire bracing. These details are thoroughly recorded in two Smithsonian publications, both by Dr. Charles G. Abbot, then secretary of the Smithsonian Institution. They are *The Relations Between the Smithsonian Institution and the Wright Brothers*, publication 2977, Smithsonian Miscellaneous Collections, vol. 81, no. 5, September 29, 1928,

The Langley Aerodrome flies! Modified structurally, the aerodrome gets off the water of Lake Keuka. Note the deflection of the wings.

The 1903 Langley Aerodrome assembled for a test flight, May 28, 1914. *Curtiss Photo Collection*

which reviewed the background of the controversy, and *The 1914 Tests of the Langley "Aerodrome,"* publication 3699, Smithsonian Miscellaneous Collections, vol. 103, no. 8, October 24, 1942, which included Orville Wright's listing of the differences between the Langley Aerodrome of 1903 and the restoration of 1914. These publications are out of print, but for the serious historian, let me add that they were reprinted in *The Wright Brothers* by Fred Kelly, the biography authorized and approved by Orville Wright.

While the aerodrome was not regarded as successful, the Langley-Manly-Balzer engine, developed for the aerodrome, was a decided success. It was the first radial aircraft engine and produced 52.4 horsepower at 950 rpm for the then unheard of 30 hours, a total of three consecutive 10-hour runs.

Details of this engine may be found in the Smithsonian Annals of Flight publication, *Langley's Aero Engine of 1903* by my colleague, Robert B. Meyer, Jr., curator of Aero-Propulsion at the National Air and Space Museum.

Specifications
The Langley Reconstruction, 1914

Span	48 ft. 5 in.
Length	52 ft. 5 in.
Engine	Langley-Manly-Balzer radial, 52.4 hp @ 950 rpm
Weight gross	750 lb. w/pilot

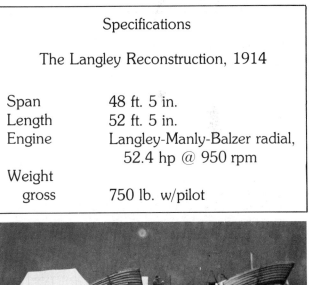

The Langley 1903 Aerodrome preparing for takeoff on Lake Keuka, October 25, 1914.

The Langley Aerodrome of 1903 restored with the original Manly-Balzer radial engine and modified Langley propellers. Charles Manly, in cockpit, was the pilot in 1903. Dr. Albert F. Zahm and Glenn H. Curtiss are seated on float. *Curtiss Photo Collection*

The M Boat, 1914

One of the most attractive flying boats built by Curtiss was the Model M, a designation that could also be construed to stand for monoplane or possibly even Morris. It was built for Raymond V. Morris and was completed and tested on Lake Keuka in early January 1914. Morris tested the machine under very trying circumstances. It was blizzard weather in early January with the temperature just above zero. Spray turned to ice immediately, and in a few minutes plane and pilot were coated. Morris made four flights the first day and several more later in the week. The monoplane flew well and fast.

The Model M certainly represented a high point in Curtiss design perfection for flying boats. Records indicate that it was so unique that "not a single stick matches up with anything previously turned out by the Curtiss plant." It had a double-fluted V bottom, similar to those pre-scribed for the C-3, 4 and 5 boats. The length of this machine was 22 feet; the beam 30 inches; the depth 36 inches. The engine was an OX (90 horsepower) and the finely shaped monoplane wing, with an area of 120 square feet, lifted the 1,200-pound aircraft. The pilot and passenger sat low in individual tandem cockpits cut into the cigar-shaped hull; only the upper part of their heads was visible. The overall span from the outboard tips of the swept tapered ailerons was 34 feet. The chord was 60 inches.

In form, the hull suggested a very long cigar: big at the forward, or cockpit, end, flat part of the way on the underside and tapered to a vertical knife edge at the rear end. The bow was pointed rather than square. On January 31, 1914, *Aero and Hydro* reported:

In construction the hull is unique. The frame is a basketwork of ash strips, the ribs carried completely around the longitudinal members. Around the frame was wound diagonally a first skin of $^3/_{32}$-inch mahogany planking. This was covered with heavy Sea Island cotton set in marine glue, and over this was secured another skin of $^3/_{32}$ mahogany plank, laid longitudinally. Not only did the partially completed hull look like a cigar, but it was wrapped like one. Two holes were cut in the tube to permit the entrance of the pilot, and possibly, of one passenger. The pilot's seat is low, both to give him every protection from the wind, and to place the shoulder yokes where the hull was widest, for freedom of movement.

The superstructure is novel. The wings are set about 40 inches above the hull, attached at the top to the welded steel structure supporting the engine bed, and braced

One of the "cleanest" aircraft designs of its day was the Model M Monoplane Flying Boat, shown on the shore of Lake Keuka, January 11, 1914.

below by struts extending to a cross beam which carries the balancing pontoons. Swept back at an angle of 7 degrees in an easy curve that finishes in the points forming the trailing edge ailerons they strongly suggest, at certain angles, the wings of a monster swallow. This illusion is fostered by the curve given the ribs and by the occasional uptilting of the ailerons on the high side of the machine. The rib curve is original though in some measure similar to that of the Bleriot XI bis.

Rudder, elevator and rear stabilizing surfaces follow the lines of those used in standard models of the Curtiss flying boats, modified as to size to fit this smaller machine.

The bracing system undoubtedly contributed considerable drag to this otherwise "clean" aircraft.

The Model M in flight purchased by Raymond V. Morris. The parabola-shaped spray shields are clearly shown.

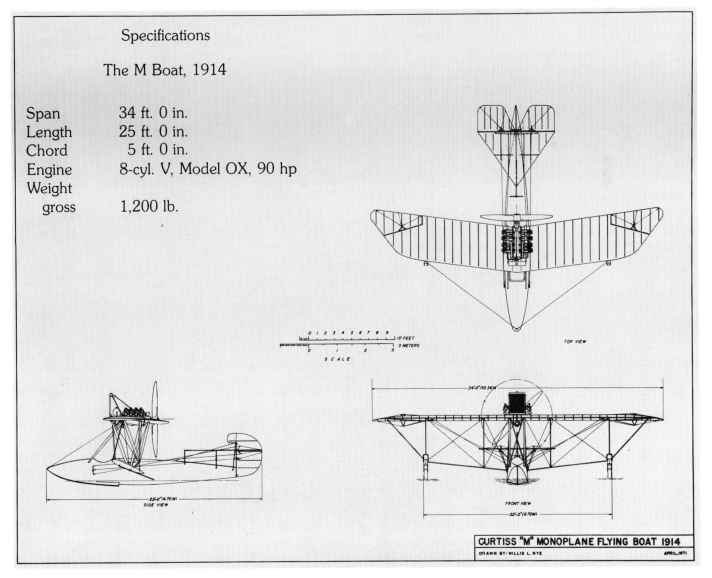

Specifications

The M Boat, 1914

Span	34 ft. 0 in.
Length	25 ft. 0 in.
Chord	5 ft. 0 in.
Engine	8-cyl. V, Model OX, 90 hp
Weight gross	1,200 lb.

SCALE

TOP VIEW

SIDE VIEW

FRONT VIEW

CURTISS "M" MONOPLANE FLYING BOAT 1914
DRAWN BY: WILLIS L. NYE   APRIL, 1971

The Italian F Boat, 1914

In 1913, the Italian Navy placed an order for three flying boats with specifications that differed from any previous hull design. The hull sides were to be straight instead of flared, as was then the custom. The flared hull was designed to accommodate the side-by-side seating and shoulder yoke control system still in use by Curtiss. The hulls of these Italian Navy boats were narrower, with the occupants seated in tandem. The slab-sided construction made it possible to plank the whole side with one sheet of three-ply mahogany rather than the strip planking then in common use.

An unusual and distinguishing feature was the hood for the occupants. The fabric hood was made up of bows, like a carriage hood, running longitudinally with transparent panels fitted in the cloth between bows and across the front. The opening was along the top center line, like an oyster shell, and the hood could be folded down inside of the elliptical-shaped cockpit.

The inboard wing panels were fitted with a transparent strip that made it possible for the rear occupant to look directly downward. The engine was braced against longitudinal movement by two bracing members that ran down at about a 45-degree angle from the engine bed to the forward deck. Bracing wires extended from the

Preparing the tandem-seat Italian F Boat for test flights from Lake Keuka in early 1914. The hull bottom is similar to the Model M Flying Boat and has a narrower beam than the standard Model F.

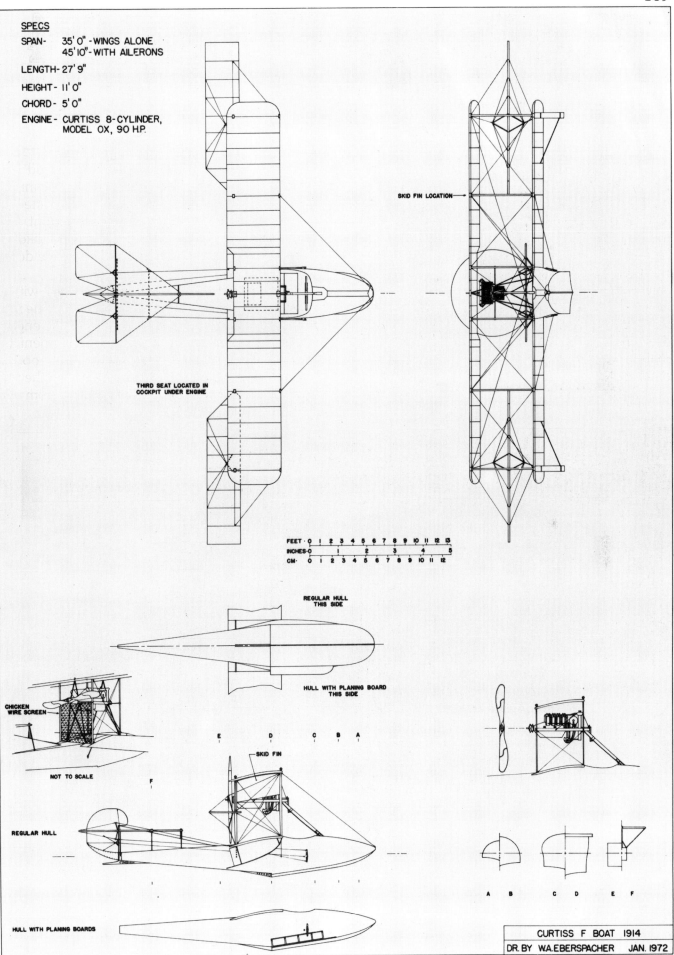

SPECS

SPAN- 35' 0" -WINGS ALONE
45' 10"- WITH AILERONS

LENGTH- 27' 9"

HEIGHT- 11' 0"

CHORD- 5' 0"

ENGINE- CURTISS 8-CYLINDER,
MODEL OX, 90 H.P.

SKID FIN LOCATION →

THIRD SEAT LOCATED IN
COCKPIT UNDER ENGINE

FEET· 0 1 2 3 4 5 6 7 8 9 10 11 12 13
INCHES-0 1 2 3 4 5
CM· 0 1 2 3 4 5 6 7 8 9 10 11 12

REGULAR HULL
THIS SIDE

HULL WITH PLANING BOARD
THIS SIDE

CHICKEN
WIRE SCREEN

NOT TO SCALE

E   D   C   B   A

SKID FIN

F

REGULAR HULL

HULL WITH PLANING BOARDS

A   B   C   D   E   F

CURTISS F BOAT 1914
DR. BY W.A. EBERSPACHER   JAN. 1972

upper bow to the middle interplane struts similar to the U.S. Navy C-3. The empty weight was approximately 1,440 pounds.

Aero and Hydro, February 7, 1914, reported:

CURTISS "CABIN" BOAT FLIES SUCCESSFULLY

Hammondsport, N.Y., January 31— Raymond V. Morris today made a series of flights here in a new flying boat built by the Curtiss Company for the Italian Navy. The machine differs from other Curtiss flying-boats in that it has an entirely enclosed cockpit or cabin, seats arranged in tandem, and an oddly shaped hull intended for work on large bodies of water.

Of the operators nothing is visible when the folding hatches are closed over the cockpit. They are provided with celluloid windows but are so well sheltered from the elements that waves washing entirely over the craft would not touch them nor could they swamp the boat.

Morris, accompanied by an official observer, put the boat through the usual series of altitude, speed, and weight carrying tests.

A close-up of the spray protection hood on the Italian Navy Model F Boat. Note the spar fitting at the midpoint of the hood and the manner of positioning the windshield. The pilot's view was very restricted during takeoff and landing when the spray canopy was in position.

U.S. Army Signal Corps S.C. No. 34 was a 1914 Model F Flying Boat. The caption on the back of this photo reads "has made . . . approximately 2,000 flights starting and alighting each time in salt water and staying in the air a total of 100 hours. There have been no repairs necessary to boat, planes or motor . . ." *Curtiss Photo Collection*

It left the water very quickly, climbing well and carried a useful load of approximately 800 pounds, but showed a mean flying speed only between 60 and 65 miles per hour.

A very noticeable feature of the craft is the crotch mahogany, showing all the grain of the wood, used in planking the entire hull. The boat is much longer and higher in the bow than previous models of Curtiss boats.

This is the tenth distinct type of flying boat produced within a year by the Curtiss factory, and from three to a dozen of each kind have been put into active service either in America or abroad. The machines have ranged from the little single passenger monoplane racer, through several styles of two and three passenger machines—including the over-water-and-land machines built for the navy—to cruiser types for four or more passengers.

Improvements were made to the standard, popular F boats. Like the Volkswagen of this era, the F represented a proven design that could be refined and improved. If any feature can properly delineate between the 1913 and 1914 models, it would be a refinement of the hull from an angular shape to a "well-rounded" profile. The wing floats were improved, from the canister type to a more aerodynamic and a more attractive wood configuration. Retrofitting of this new style float to earlier Fs probably caused some confusion as to which models were which, since

A 1914 Model F Flying Boat. The hull design has been refined aerodynamically and hydrodynamically. *Curtiss Photo Collection*

the float is one of the most noticeable structural components. Less apparent, but also improved, were the steel tube engine bearers. A 30-gallon tank was mounted under the rear seat. Fuel was pumped to a 3-gallon header tank behind the radiator, from whence it was gravity-fed to the engine, an OX of 90–100 horsepower.

Though the 1914 F wing panels were structurally the same as before, the upper panels were lengthened to accommodate increasing weight. The upper panels were joined at the center immediately above the engine. A drip pan was placed under the engine to protect the occupants. Side-by-side seating and dual controls were standard and the wing chord was reduced to 60 inches.

Additional structural improvements in the 1914 model were covered in patent No. 1,246,011, December 11, 1914, illustrations from which are included here.

The so-called "English" boat appears to be a hybrid 1913–1914 aircraft bearing the 1913 angular hull with wood floats. The ailerons were attached to the rear spar of the upper wing rather than having the characteristic interplane mounting that had always been a Curtiss trademark. Overhanging wings were achieved by mounting panels of equal length top and bottom; the upper panels were separated by a center spacer panel.

It is well to repeat here that the F designation applied to aircraft using wings constructed with continuous spars from root to tip as opposed to the D and Es, which were made up of easily packed short panels.

A late model 1914 F Boat. Note the change in the aileron position, and the antiskid fins located on top of the wing surface.

The Model F, 1915

If the term "standardization" can ever be applied to the F boats, 1915 would have to be a benchmark year, though only a few changes from the 1914 model were added. Foremost among these was the abandonment of the Curtiss shoulder yoke lateral, or roll, control in favor of the "Deperdussin" system, which used a wheel for lateral control and a rudder bar for directional control (yaw). Under accelerated construction for wartime training, a high degree of standardization became necessary. Orders from the U.S. Navy and the combatants in Europe made standardization mandatory. Records of Curtiss production for the period from August 1, 1914 to June 30, 1919 show that 105 F boats were built. Several other manufacturers also built this type. As late as 1920, the U.S. Navy was requesting bids for the sale of 181 surplus F boats.

The Curtiss catalog for 1915 was stressing the "sporting" aspects of the F, relating it to the thrills and exhilaration experienced in motor boating. By this time the Model F boats, the smallest of the Curtiss flying boats, had been flown over 500,000 miles without serious mishap. At a maximum speed of only 65 miles per hour this half-million miles represented a substantial number of hours aloft.

The hull design had been improved hydrodynamically, as well as aerodynamically. It was remarkably sturdy, considering its weight. The wing-tip floats were by this time improved also.

Wartime training necessitated the standardization of the airframe design and the controls of the F Boat in 1915. The refined hull lines are illustrated in this photo dated May 28, 1915. *Curtiss Photo Collection*

The result of these refinements was a rapid takeoff in 1,000 to 1,500 feet. The wing loading of 6 pounds per square foot and power loading of 29.7 pounds per horsepower resulted in a rate of climb of 1,500 feet/minute, though the top speed was a rather modest 65 miles per hour. All factors combined to make the F boat a front-running candidate as a trainer when the war clouds gathered.

The beginning of the standardization of controls came on August 1, 1915, as related in *Chirp*, December 1941. The U.S. Army Aviation Section of the signal corps, issued specification No. 1000 relating to training aircraft. Under clause 9, dealing with controls, it stated:

The line-up of Model F flying boats at the Naval Air Station, Pensacola, where they were used as the basic training machine for naval aviators.

Both the Curtiss (shoulder or chest yoke) and the Deperdussin types of controls shall be furnished ready for installation in both cockpits.

The control shall be dual for both types. By this is meant that two combinations are possible, i.e., dual Dep or dual Curtiss. Mechanical ease of operation is essential. The control to be installed will be indicated in the order.

In a report covering the operations of the First Aero Squadron with the punitive expedition for the period from March 15 to August 15, 1916, Maj. B. D. Foulois, commanding officer, wrote:

Foot bars had to be installed in all airplanes to enable the pilot to efficiently control the airplane in flight. The Curtiss shoulder control is not efficient in the control flight of large and heavy airplanes. The substitution of the French ''Deperdussin'' control has been recommended and it is understood that this latter type of control is to become the standard control of the Army.

Later, army seaplane specifications required that controls be of the standard ''Dep'' type, installed in the rear cockpit only and, finally, on advice from the American Expeditionary Force, the stick control became universal.

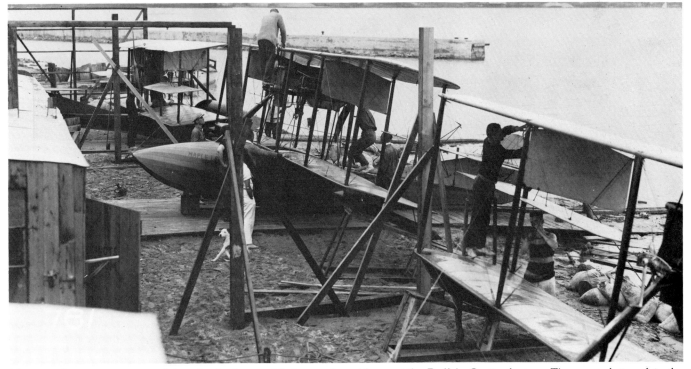

Mass production necessitated that the final assembly be made outdoors at the Buffalo Curtiss factory. The second aircraft in the line is the *Maple Leaf*, destined for Canadian use. *Curtiss Photo Collection*

The Model J, 1914

The Model G and H tractor biplanes were designed by Curtiss personnel largely by reassembling standard components in what was, for Curtiss, a radical tractor configuration. While they demonstrated their ability to fly, their performance, at best, was marginal.

During a trip to Europe in 1913, Curtiss visited the plant of the Sopwith Aviation Company at Kingston-on-Thames. One employee, too shy to talk, tagged along during Curtiss's half-day visit. That night, in London, B. Douglas Thomas, the shy employee, ducked into a shop to escape the rain. Another fellow, also taking shelter, was reading a paper. After a few minutes the two, Thomas and Curtiss, struck up a conversation. This conversation was to lead to the design of the first J.

Curtiss, en route to Paris, offered to pay Thomas's way if Thomas would accompany him. While in Paris, Curtiss suggested that Thomas resign his position with Sopwith and proceed with the design of a tractor biplane for Curtiss. During the winter of 1913, Thomas set up shop in a tent in his yard. He produced the design, a stress analysis and bill of materials, all of which he shipped to Curtiss at Hammondsport. Thomas received a terse cable in April 1914 to "come over." He arrived in New York in the spring of 1914 and proceeded to Hammondsport.

The J had been under construction during the winter months and was ready for testing on April 24, 1914. A detailed specification of the J and J-2 appeared in *Aeronautics* on September 15, 1914; however, the specifications appeared to be reversed. A drawing of the J, dated March 12, 1914, shows wings of equal 30-foot span. It also shows four ailerons fitted in the outboard trailing edge of each wing panel, which confirms what is shown in several photos of the first airplane. In an interview with Bruce C. Reynolds, copies of which were kindly furnished to me, Thomas stated that the "overhang" was added because of the weight of the pontoons. This also is confirmed by photos. A still later version supplied to the signal corps shows upper wings of

The Model J poses on the shore of Lake Keuka. Note the nose-over skids and the hydrofoil installed for water landing in case of engine failure. *Curtiss Photo Collection*

Fuselage construction details of the Model J.

greater span than the lower, and ailerons in the upper wing only.

It appears, therefore, that the first J, having equal-span 30-foot panels with four ailerons, was tested initially on floats. The second version, to better accommodate the weight of floats, had the upper wing extended to 40 feet, still using four ailerons, with the lower wing still using a 30-foot span. These could be designated the J and J Hydro (modified, for at least one photo shows the equal-span float version airborne, several feet above the surface of the lake).

The version furnished to the signal corps as No. 29 and No. 30 would fit the description of the production type J with an upper span of 40 feet 2 inches, a lower span of 30 feet, and only two 10-by-2-foot ailerons inset in the upper wing. No. 29, recorded as a J, was officially inspected at Hammondsport and delivered to San Diego on July 28, 1914. This machine undoubtedly was the one in which Lt. Lewis Goodier, Jr. established a record 1,000 feet/minute climb in September 1914. The second, No. 30, was not received at San Diego until October 13, 1914. No. 29 was destroyed on December 21, 1911, in an accident resulting in the death of Lt. Frederick J. Gerstner, and No. 30 was destroyed on October 11, 1915 in an accident in which Lt. Walter R. Taliaferro was killed.

An article in *Aeronautics*, September 15, 1914, states that a J-2 was also contemplated having 24-foot equal-span wings. It was described as a single-place "fast scout type."

Additional written or photographic evidence is not currently available to confirm the existence of this J-2 variant. If it was built, it would logically follow that the first army J, No. 29, could properly be designated as a J-3. It was not.

In September 1914, specifications for a contest were drafted for a military trainer aircraft. It was to be held at the Signal Corps Aviation School at San Diego, California, on or about October 15, 1914. With war under way in Europe, it was important to accelerate aircraft development. This contest was to be the first test held in the United States for the development of an airplane. The test board designated by order No. 16 consisted of Capt. Benjamin D. Foulois, Capt. Townsend F. Dodd, 1/Lt. Walter R. Taliaferro, 1/Lt. Thomas deW. Milling, 1/Lt. Joseph E. Carberry and Grover Loening.

The performance required was 70 miles per hour maximum, 40 miles per hour minimum; a useful load of 450 pounds; four hours of fuel and the ability to climb to 4,000 feet in ten minutes.

It was soon discovered, from flight tests conducted at Hammondsport, that the Model J was only the first step in producing an aircraft acceptable to the U.S. Army. Performance left something to be desired, especially the rate of climb. In anticipation of the announced military contest specifications, the design of a new model was begun. To expedite the project the fuselage of the Model J was used as the basis for the new aircraft, which was designated the Model N. A new set of wings was produced incorporating the midplane ailerons, a throwback to the earlier D and E models. The resulting aircraft did squeak past and was accepted for the army by a very optimistic review board, probably because none of the other aircraft tested came as close to the desired specifications.

The Model N was the third Curtiss aircraft designed by B. Douglas Thomas, following the Model J and the H-1 *America*.

A Model J with extended upper wing races past the photographer accompanied by a Model F Boat. *Wm. J. Hammer Collection*

A Curtiss Model J proves it can fly.

The Curtiss-Wanamaker Model H Boat, America, 1914

The largest flying boat of its day and the first two-engined flying boat was the Model H flying boat, more popularly known as the Curtiss-Wanamaker *America*. It was built for Rodman Wanamaker to attempt the first transatlantic crossing. The first reference to this is in a letter Curtiss wrote to Capt. W. I. Chambers, dated November 26, 1913, in which he stated: "The latest thing in aviation is a proposition for trans-Atlantic flight. I do not know as yet whether it will materialize, but it is assuming a very interesting aspect."

The flight was planned in response to the *London Daily Mail* prize of $50,000 for the first transatlantic crossing in a heavier-than-air machine. Responding to this prize offer, Rodman Wanamaker put up $25,000 for the construction of a flying boat capable of making this flight in commemoration of the 100th anniversary of peace between the United States and England. To carry out this theme the crew was to consist of one British and one U.S. crew member.

En route to Paris in 1913, Curtiss met B. Douglas Thomas and asked Thomas to accompany him to Paris to discuss the design of what was to be known as the Model J. While in Paris Curtiss was approached regarding the design of a transatlantic aircraft. On returning to the United States, Curtiss directed Thomas to join him in designing the J tractor and on completing this to come to the United States. In an interview with Bruce C. Reynolds, Thomas indicated that the *America* was designed and built immediately after the J.

Lt. John Cyril Porte, Royal Navy, poses beside the H-1 *America* hull during its construction. Porte was to have been the pilot for a planned transatlantic flight attempt. *Curtiss Photo Collection*

The British pilot was Lt. John Cyril Porte. The American pilot was George E. A. Hallett (later Maj. George E. A. Hallett, U.S. Army, Ret.). Hallett was basically an engine mechanic, who, in the course of his close association with Curtiss from the days of the first hydro of 1911, had been exposed to flying mostly as a passenger. The *America* project effected a change in this.

The firsthand story related by Major Hallett for this author on April 13, 1968, is as follows:

The original plan was to build a large single engined tractor type biplane, with a 160 H.P. Curtiss engine just being built, and to fly from Newfoundland to Ireland. I believe it was to drop its landing gear after take off to reduce drag and to land in Ireland on its belly. This plane was never built because the 160 H.P. engine (8 cyl. 5 × 7, later known as the "V-2") was demolished on the test stand early in its tests. I am told that some of the cast iron cylinders cracked and blew off.

Christening ceremony for the *America*, June 22, 1914. Left to right: Lt. John Cyril Porte, pilot; George E. A. Hallett (later major, United States Army), copilot, mechanic; G. H. Curtiss, builder; and Katherine Masson holding the reluctant champagne bottle that refused to break until Porte cracked it with a hammer. *Curtiss Photo Collection*

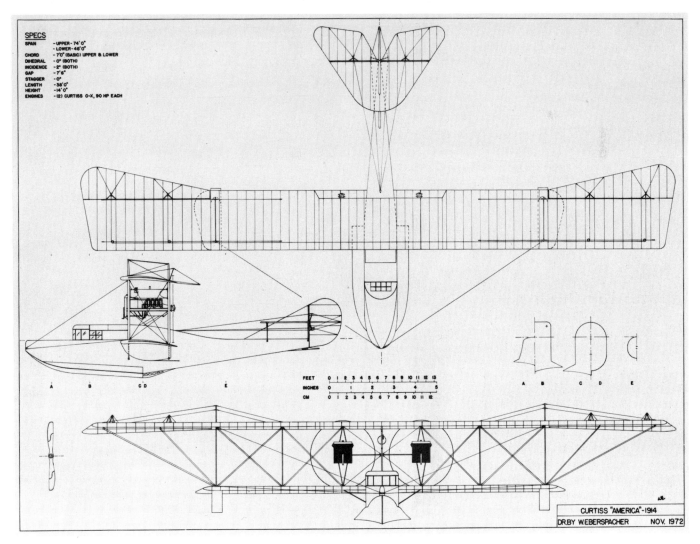

SPECS
SPAN — UPPER - 74' 0"
       — LOWER - 46' 0"
CHORD — 7' 0" (BASIC) UPPER & LOWER
DIHEDRAL — 0° (BOTH)
INCIDENCE — 2° (BOTH)
GAP — 7' 6"
STAGGER — 0°
LENGTH — 38' 0"
HEIGHT — 14' 0"
ENGINES — (2) CURTISS O-X, 90 HP EACH

CURTISS "AMERICA"-1914
DR. BY WEBERSPACHER   NOV. 1972

Plans for the plane and new engine were kept pretty "hush-hush" up to this point, but then I heard that the plan was changed to design a large flying boat with two 90 H.P. Curtiss "OX" engines, which were well developed and widely used for about 2 years. The flight with this plane was to start at Trepassey Bay, Newfoundland, and land in the Azore Islands at Funchal, I believe, and then to Lisbon and on to Plymouth, England.

At this point, the personnel problem came up. Lt. John H. Towers, U.S.N. was to have been the American pilot to fly with Lt. Porte, R.N., as English pilot and head of the project. Then the Hon. Josephus Daniels, then Sec. of Navy, said, "If an American Naval Officer goes, he will be in command."

On hearing about this impasse, and being an expert on the OX engine, I said to Mr. Curtiss, "What you need is a damn good engine man who can fly enough to 'take a trick at the wheel.'" When they considered that I had been an engine expert for 6 years and also an airplane mechanic for 4 years, they told me I had the job and must supervise the assembly and 30 hr. test of two OX engines, one right hand and the other left hand, each having counter-rotating propellers.

The plane, which was later christened *America*, was a twin-engined, "pusher" type flying boat, with biplane wings. The upper wing span was 76 feet, the lower wing much less. The wings and control surfaces were covered with dark red silk. The hull was planked with diagonal strips of very thin spruce, covered with linen, all on hard wood frame laid in Jeffries' Marine glue and painted to match the red silk on the wings. The hull had a step in the bottom like that of the Curtiss "F" boats of that year. This

The *America* is here fitted with a third OX-5 engine and a new style sponson hull to improve the takeoff of the aircraft under load. This hull design became a regular feature of Curtiss designs. In the end, the third engine was removed as being counterproductive, requiring additional fuel that would have started another round of redesign for takeoff because of the added weight. George E. A. Hallett, copilot and mechanic, is standing on the scaffold in front of the center engine. A. V. "Fred" Verville, later a well-known aircraft designer, is standing at the bow with his hand on a searchlight.

machine was designed by B. D. Thomas under Curtiss's direction. He came from the Sopwith Co. in England, and later headed the Thomas Morse Co. in the U.S. He also designed the Curtiss Model "J" and model "N" planes which became the "JN" or "Jennie" trainer of W.W.I fame.

The *America*'s instruments and controls were few and crude. They included a Craig Osborn compass (a well known English Marine compass), air speed indicator, and a curved level to show if the wings were level when we couldn't see them. This was very crude. Two ignition switches and two throttles were located between pilots. The tachometer was hand held and served both engines when we could see the propellers. It was a stroboscope made by the Sperry Gyro Co.

America's flying controls were unique. Because it obviously was impractical to handle the ailerons with the Curtiss "shoulder yoke," they were operated by a wide foot-bar, as rudders are handled now. Steering was done with a wheel on the control post and this was pulled backward and forward for longitudinal control.

America was assembled in the open, on the shore of Lake Keuka. It was formally christened, with champagne, by Katherine Masson and Lt. Porte.* Flight testing started immediately, mostly with Glenn Curtiss at the controls.

America flew beautifully at once, but it would not get off the water with 2200 lbs. of sand bags, which represented the estimated fuel load, so a summer of experiments and tests started.

A total of 28 changes, according to Dr. Zahm, were made in the *America*, mostly on the bottom of the hull and planing area. Hydrofoils were tried in two different locations. The hydrofoils were first placed on the sides of the hull extending out from the bottom for about 3 or 4 feet laterally. They helped a little. Then the foils were

relocated to a point under the step of the hull and about a foot below the bottom. The lift obtained with these foils was prodigious. As we left the beach they lifted the hull out of the water at about 15 miles per hour before we had any aileron control, so the plane would fall and because of beaching difficulties, we gave up the hydrofoils and went on with flotation and planing area experiments.

A third "OX" engine was added on the top wing with a tractor propeller, but it required too much weight in extra fuel and we were not able to get off the water. The aircraft was then converted back to the twin engine configuration.

Sponsons, integral with the hull, were added on each side and provided added flotation and planing area.† This was the final hull form, which was used on both sides of the Atlantic for some years on all large flying boats.

Finally Mr. Curtiss arranged to have Dr. Charles M. Olmstead of Buffalo, N.Y., make a pair of propellers of his special design for the *America*, and with them and the final hull changes, we got off the water with a little more weight than we needed. Charles Witmer and I had previously tested an Olmstead propeller on Harold McCormick's flying boat and had been able to get off the water with 4 people with one OX engine.

As mentioned previously, the *America* flew and handled beautifully from the start. Mr. Curtiss handled it perfectly, Porte handled it pretty well, but I found that I could get it off the water better than he could because I had a better "feel" of it in take-off. Having flown very little previously, the unique aileron control did not bother me at all because I had formed no habits with other controls. Porte was an exceptionally good navigator and an experienced seaplane pilot.

One day Mr. Curtiss and I were out in the *America* and he told me to fly straight down

---

*On June 22, 1914, at Hammondsport, amid due pageantry, the *America* was christened by Katherine Masson with a bottle of champagne from her father's wine cellar. The bottle proved to be too thick—so strong that after two throws by Miss Masson against the bow and two violent throws by Lieutenant Porte the bottle had to be broken by a hammer in order to complete the christening. The first flight was made the following day.

†As tests progressed and ballast was added to stimulate fuel load, it became apparent that the *America* would not rise from the water in its original form. She was too narrow, averaging only 4 feet in width, for effective planing under full load. The first modification consisted of sponsons shaped like horizontal **V**s, which contributed hydrodynamic and some aerodynamic lift.

the lake at about 200 ft. height. At first he had his hands on the controls, then began to play with the throttles, slowing down one engine at a time. Then he told me to land on the water and take off. He was no longer holding the controls! I took off and Curtiss slapped my knee and pointed to the throttles—we had taken off on one engine. Mr. Curtiss told me that was the first time he was ever a passenger.

Later, Mr. Curtiss did a lot of flying on one engine, finding how much weight he could take off with.

All that summer we had a dozen or more well known reporters there. Men like Harding from N.Y. and Joe Toye from Boston.

One day Mr. Curtiss and I started out with the full 2200 pounds of sand on board and soon found out that we could not get off yet, so, thinking to have a little fun with the reporters watching from the shore, Mr. Curtiss told me to slip 2 or 3 bags of sand overboard as he turned the plane around to make another try against the wind. The reporters could not see this, so after two or three such tries we got off and the watchers cheered. We told them why we got off when we got back to the beach.

After we could get off the water with the 2200 pounds of sand, we made a 44 mile flight to Penn Yan at the other end of the lake and back. We developed several slight water leaks on this trip. After making repairs the plane was disassembled, a new hull with the latest modifications was installed, and the machine was packed for shipment to Newfoundland.

At this time, England entered W.W.I. The Admiralty immediately recalled Lt. Porte to active duty, and our Navy could no longer place a destroyer every hundred miles along our route as planned to guide us and assist if necessary, and the flight was called off for these reasons and no other reasons.

At that time none of us believed we could not have made the flight successfully, but looking back on it, after some years and much experience, it seems to me that we could not have made it because, firstly, we had no way to give the carburetor hot air to avoid icing. I believe several of the early attempts to fly the Atlantic from 1916 to 1930 went into the sea because of carburetor icing. Secondly, there was too much

vibration in the engine installations, which would probably have caused broken water connections, etc. There also was a chance of icing on the wings, not to mention fatigue of the pilots. True, I had once worked in a machine shop for 72 hours straight, but that was under far less strain then I would have encountered in flight.

When the flight was cancelled, J. Lansing Callan, a good pilot who had been sent to the Azores and to Portugal to check landing conditions for us, was recalled. I believe he was to relieve either Porte or myself at the Azores if necessary.

Our preparations for in-flight maintenance may be of interest. I had a suit of "overalls" made with pockets about 18 inches deep, so nothing could blow out of them. In a pusher plane it is necessary to be very careful not to drop anything because it would certainly go into the propeller and possibly make serious trouble. Wearing a lineman's belt and having rings fastened in suitable places around the engines, I could hook on and have the use of both hands to work on anything within reach. One of the factory mechanics, at my request, made me a spring clip which I could push on to the end of an exhaust rocker arm to hold the exhaust valve off its seat to relieve compression in that cylinder so I could change a spark plug without stopping an engine. It was necessary to have a long socket wrench which fit quite tightly on the plug to hold it firmly until I could pull it loose and put it in my pocket. Of course I had to take some nasty shocks in disconnecting the spark plug wire and replacing it. It was easy to tell which cylinder was missing because there were no exhaust stacks or manifolds. I changed one plug in flight over Lake Keuka, to be sure that I could do so if necessary.

We were prepared to oil the rocker arms and fix small water leaks and had plenty of tire tape and safety wire and LePage's glue, which was good for fuel line joints. If I remember rightly, we were not able to carry a spare cylinder piston and connecting rod, which would have been desirable, because of the weight of these parts. Of course we carried plenty of spare spark plugs. In those days plugs often cracked, leaked or fouled with oil.

With the outbreak of World War I the *America* was sold to Britain, and shipped to Felixstowe, where continued development of the hull form was undertaken under Lieutenant Porte to adapt the airplane to Channel conditions. Hallett recalls that two aircraft were built under contract to Wanamaker. When the *America* was shipped, it was the second "unwaterlogged" hull that was shipped.

The *America* and twenty similar aircraft known as H-4s or *Small Americas* were ordered by Britain;* two were ordered by Spain. They were fitted with radial Anzani engines after arriving in England and after much modification they were used for coastal patrol work during the early stages of the war.

The structural details of the *America* are of interest. The fore part of the hull provided a crew compartment; the rear part was shaped like a whale, tapering to a vertical fin and horizontal stabilizer. The hull was formed of ribs and stringers to give it form. Over this frame, ¼-inch spruce was laid lengthwise and fastened with brass screws. On the **V** bottom, two layers of ¼-inch planking were laid at an angle to each other with fabric, soaked in marine glue, placed between the layers.

The hull interior, aft of the step, had four watertight bulkheads, 3 millimeters thick. Forward of the step was the fuel compartment, containing three fuel tanks with a combined total of 500 gallons. Fuel was pumped from these tanks to auxiliary tanks from which it ran, by gravity, to the engines. Forward of the main tanks was a mattress for one crew member at a time to recline. The bench-type seat was upholstered in corduroy to ensure reasonable comfort for the pilots.

The wingspan was 74 feet, the chord 7 feet, with a 6-inch camber. The spars were "I" beams placed about 18 inches back from the leading edge. The internal wing structure was trussed with piano wire for drag bracing. The spars of the lower wing passed through the hull.

The wings and tail surfaces were covered on both sides by Japanese silk and coated with "varnish" to ensure water and air tightness. Near the hull, extra ribs were installed in the wings and covered with plywood to support the weight of a man to enable servicing of the engines.

*Curtiss records show three H-2s, at a cost of $71,112 for Britain. These were undoubtedly lumped in with an additional fifty H-4s valued at $1,120,120. All of these were shipped by December 31, 1916.

Several trials were necessary to determine the correct placement for the floats and the correct size. These trials included the use of a sea sled design (see *Scientific American*, July 25, 1914), and in one instance the use of an additional engine, mounted on the center section of the upper wing. On July 23, the *America* made the first flight with these three engines installed. It was calculated that the aircraft could get off with an additional 1,500 pounds, 1,000 of which would have to be extra fuel. Tests indicated that the *America* could get off with almost 4,400 pounds on two engines and a full load with three engines operating. On the test flight, the total weight lifted was 6,203 pounds, substantially above the required gross. The empty weight in the three-engine configuration was 3,500 pounds. The two standard engines mounted on the *America* in parallel and in pusher configuration produced unequal thrust, which led to experiments with opposite rotation of the propellers, both rotating inward toward the hull.

As part of the preparations, the OX engines were tested extensively for durability and fuel consumption. On June 10, 1914, the following statement was released by the Curtiss Company:

At one o'clock this afternoon the two Curtiss engines to be used in the Rodman Wanamaker Trans-Atlantic flier completed a test run of thirty hours, having fulfilled every requirement in speed, power, durability and fuel consumption.

So far as was possible the expected flying conditions during the Trans-Atlantic flight were duplicated in every particular. The motors were started at seven o'clock Tuesday morning, mounted side by side, swinging duplicate propellers at the speed estimated as being required for raising the heavily loaded machine at the start of the big flight. For four hours the motors ran at an even speed of 1250 revolutions per minute. Estimating that after four hours enough fuel will have been consumed to permit a slower flying speed, the motors were then set back to twelve hundred revolutions per minute. At intervals of approximately four hours the speed was reduced during the day to a maximum of 1000 revolutions per minute, which was the slowest speed at which they were operated, though it is estimated the Wanamaker-Curtiss machine will fly with the propellers turning at 900 revolutions per minute.

A record of the performance of the engines was made every fifteen minutes, and during the entire thirty hours their respective speeds seldom varied more than five revolutions per minute. Temperature, water evaporation, oil and gasoline consumption were carefully checked every fifteen minutes day and night. At the end of the thirty hours run both engines were again speeded up to the maximum of 1250 rpm at which they started the long run. In the test room men kept constant watch during the entire run, in a roar that in a few minutes proved deafening to casual visitors but which seemed not to affect those on the job.

The total consumption of gasoline during the thirty hours of continuous running was 22½ gallons; the consumption of oil was 10⅝ quarts. As Lt. Porte expects to be in the air not more than twenty hours, he has at least a large margin of safety in carrying this weight of fuel and oil, though the big Wanamaker-Curtiss machine is designed to carry a load considerably in excess of that indicated by the test as being necessary.

As a test of the durability, reliability and economy of the 90–100-horsepower Model OX engine, four stock engines were subjected to a 30-hour running test. It was intended to reproduce as nearly as possible the conditions likely to prevail during the proposed transatlantic flight. For the first 4 hours the engines were run at full power, 1,250 rpm. After this initial period the rpm was reduced 25 rpm at the end of each hour until the engines' speed of 1,000 rpm was reached. During the test the engines were mounted in pairs and counterchecked for speed and fuel consumption every 15 minutes.

During the 30-hour test the average total fuel consumption was 142.5 gallons, and an average hourly consumption of 4.77 gallons was recorded. For comparison, 4-hour performance figures for two contemporary engines were selected, resulting in the following:

4-Hour Performance Test				
	weight (pounds)	gallons per hour	weight (engine and fuel)	weight (per horsepower)
100-hp Gnome	308.64	12.1675	686.4	8.07
70-hp Renault	462.966	9.26	709.0	9.946
90–100-hp Curtiss OX	430.0	8.0	638.0	7.505

The Model N, 1914

The announcement of an official signal corps trial board resulted in the production of the Model N, which, according to George E. A. Hallett and B. Douglas Thomas, was actually the original J reworked. The span had been increased to 38 feet 2½ inches, and the design reverted to the use of interplane ailerons. Though a very optimistic report on the N appeared in *Aerial Age Weekly*, March 29, 1915, stating that eight Model Ns were ordered, only one appears to have been delivered—accepted December 11, 1914, at a cost of $7,500. While it was declared to be one of the winners, it was only marginal in its performance, just "squeaking" by a very optimistic board. In order to meet the speed requirements, the wings had to be given an angle of incidence of zero degrees. The center of gravity had been placed too far to the rear, which resulted in a very unstable aircraft.

In the Model N, as in the Model J, the crew was

The Model N was a direct descendant from the original Model J. The fuselages were the same.

seated in tandem and equipped with controls in the rear seat only. The aircraft was powered by an OXX engine rated at 100 horsepower. Two plugs per cylinder and a ¼-inch larger bore were responsible for this increased power. The rudder dimensions were changed.

The wings were one-piece construction typical of the F type. They were internally braced by piano wire drag bracing. The rectangular cross section of the fuselage was 26 inches wide by 35 inches high at the cockpit and constructed of longerons that were 1¼ inches square in the area of the cockpit and tapered to 1 inch. Each side panel contained nine vertical struts, which were wire-braced in three directions, as in the J. The third and fourth vertical fuselage struts on each side were continued upward above the fuselage to form the cabane struts supporting the upper center section. All other details of cowl and fuselage were the same as in the original Model J. This same airframe was further modified to produce the JN to meet British government requirements.

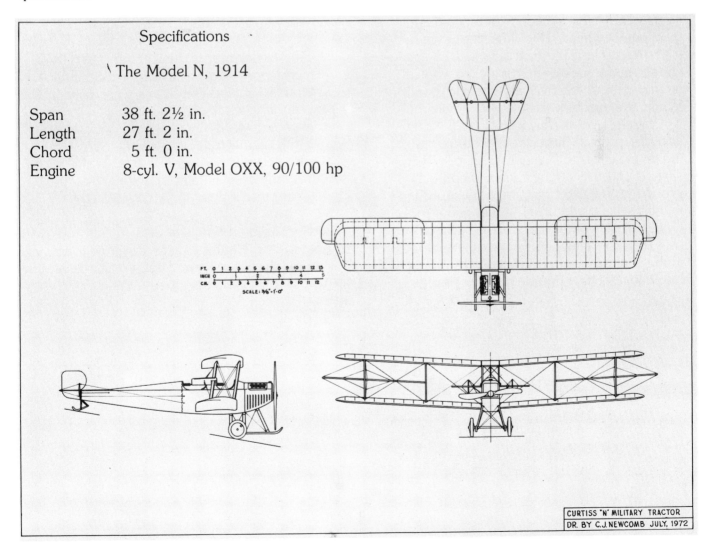

Specifications

The Model N, 1914

Span	38 ft. 2½ in.
Length	27 ft. 2 in.
Chord	5 ft. 0 in.
Engine	8-cyl. V, Model OXX, 90/100 hp

SCALE: ⅜"=1'-0"

CURTISS "N" MILITARY TRACTOR
DR. BY C.J. NEWCOMB JULY, 1972

The Sperry F Boat, 1915

The Sperry boat became one of the first, if not the first, flying boats to be adapted to amphibious operation by the installation of a retractable landing gear. The development of this landing gear is described in detail by Lawrence Sperry in *Aerial Age Weekly*, May 3, 1915, as follows:

The wheel gear used on Sperry's Curtiss flying boat can be attached by merely leaning over the edge, no one being obliged to get wet, as it is a simple operation requiring only a minute to put them on. The wheels are secured to the wings by two sockets, one situated at the front beam and the other at the rear beam just under the first pair of struts. The front socket is a tongue and groove joint whereby the wheel frame when it is hanging vertically from its sockets can be shoved in the socket and it is locked when it is turned and latched against the boat. When the machine is lowered down the runway the pilot merely leans over the side and raises a rod. Since the machine is resting on the water the wheels will turn in their sockets until the tongue comes opposite the groove and a slight backward push of the wheels releases the front socket and a forward pull brings them clear of the back socket. Floats are attached so the wheels float in the water and can be pulled in by a boat hook. In attaching the wheels the operation is similar. The pilot leans over the side of the machine, picks up the wheel and puts the rear end of the upper bar in the socket and pushes the other end of the bar forward into the front socket. The wheel is then pulled toward the hull and latched. Pieces of rubber are placed on the sides of the boat so the wheels do not scratch it in any way.

Development of the autopilot, or gyro stabilizer, for aircraft use began in the latter part of 1912 and was announced by Curtiss on October 14, 1912. By letter to Capt. W. I. Chambers, H. C. Genung, vice-president and general manager of the Curtiss Hammondsport factory, noted, regarding the Sperry controls:

The experiments made here at Hammondsport were, in a way, successful, although climatic conditions were very bad and there was a sort of hesitancy on the part of pilots toward trying out the controls when jointly connected. They operated so quickly when correcting a puff that even the pilot became confused and awkward maneuvering resulted.

The distinguishing features of this Sperry F boat were the bulbous bow designed to accommodate the autopilot and the retractable landing gear fitted under the wings.

The H-4 Small America, 1915

With the outbreak of World War I, the Curtiss-Wanamaker *America* found a ready market, for it was the only available flying boat of its size, although military development rapidly passed this design stage.

Lt. John Cyril Porte, who was to have piloted the *America* with George E. A. Hallet as co-pilot-engineer, rejoined the Royal Navy in August 1914. As a result of his experience with Curtiss, Porte had become a strong supporter of the flying boat. Back in service, Porte persuaded Cdr. Murray Sueter, director of supplies for air at the Admiralty, to purchase the *America* and a sister ship. The first arrived at the Felixstowe Naval Air Station, England, in 1915. The need to counter the German U-boats by aerial Channel patrols brought an additional order for four flying boats from Curtiss, one of which was a sister ship to the *America*, an H-1. The other three were H-2s. The four sold for $71,112. An additional eight flying boats were ordered from the Aircraft Manufacturing Co. in Britain, which was licensed by Curtiss to build them.

In an effort to increase the power to an acceptable level, the 90-horsepower OX engines, which were producing only about 85 horsepower in tests, were replaced by 110-horsepower Anzani radial engines. Five aircraft were converted initially.

A report in *Aerial Age Weekly*, June 28, 1915, indicates that an additional twelve H-4s were ordered from Curtiss according to a June 15 announcement in the House of Commons. The members of the British Military Flying Commission in the United States served as inspectors for these aircraft. In a letter to this writer on June 5, 1967, Capt. Frank T. Courtney recalls that the first group was sent to Felixstowe:

The type had undergone little testing, and when Porte went to work on it, all sorts of experimental changes were made and the results communicated to Curtiss. These changes were incorporated in a fairly large order, and these new craft were called the H-4. Porte experimented with the first few of these to incorporate features called for by the new increasing operational experience.

For purposes of your record it is important to remember that all these changes were strictly empirical, chop-and-change, by-guess-and-by-God. Hulls underwent all sorts of major and minor alterations, steps were added and subtracted or moved fore and aft, sponsons were added to increase the beam and their shapes variously modified, deadrise was varied to meet shock-absorbing or spray conditions. Curtiss would have been informed and consulted in the earlier changes, but as time went on the H-4 became less Curtiss and more Porte until it finally became the Felixstowe F-1. This boat, basically the H-4, had a good service record.

Meanwhile, on the basis of information which he had been receiving, Curtiss designed the H-12, of which several were ordered by Britain and Spain. To distinguish it from the H-4, it was called the "Big America." By a somewhat similar process of changes, this boat (the H-12) became the F-2 (on which, incidentally, I did a good deal of flying). This boat evolved into the F-3 and F-5.

The H-4 as it was modified on arrival in Britain. The Curtiss OX-5 engines were replaced by Anzani radial engines. Later the hull was much modified and strengthened to become the Felixstowe F-1. *J. M. Bruce, RAF Museum*

A total of sixty-two H-4s were built by Curtiss and an additional eight, already mentioned, were built in Britain.

The aerodynamic surfaces remained essentially as designed by B. Douglas Thomas. The H-4s did have unusual flight characteristics. They were nose-heavy when at cruise power and tail-heavy when in a power-off glide, a characteristic of a number of designs having a high thrust line (engines mounted high on the structure).

The H-4 was designed for weight-carrying and seaworthiness, as was its immediate predecessor, the *America*, or Model H-1. Compared to contemporary aircraft it was a large machine incorporating twin engines and a comfortable enclosed cabin.

The speed range was from 40 to 60 miles per hour, quite unspectacular. Normal endurance was 12 hours for a 720-mile range. At reduced power the endurance could be as much as 17 hours. Gross weight was 4,650 pounds, of which 1,400 pounds was useful load. Takeoff distance was 1,100 feet to 2,000 feet with a lift-off speed of about 50 miles per hour. Wing loading was 5.6 pounds per square foot.

Specifications

The H-4 *Small America*, 1915

Span overall, including ailerons	75 ft. 9¼ in.
Length overall	37 ft. ½ in.
Chord	7 ft. $^{21}/_{32}$ in.
Weight	
net	3,350 lb.
gross	4,750 lb.
Speed	
maximum	60 mph
minimum	40 mph
Power plant (original)	2 Curtiss OX— 180 hp total
Endurance, full throttle, full gross	12.3 hr.
Endurance, cruise, full gross	17.2 hr.
Fuel capacity	206.2 gal.

FLYING BOAT SECTION
CHURCHILL ST.

Production line for the H-4, known as the *Small America*.

The JN-2, 1915

An equal-span, tandem cockpit biplane was developed from the JN. It was used in small quantities by the Spanish government, as well as the U.S. Army Aviation Section of the signal corps.

The JN-2s were sent to take part in the punitive expedition under Brig. Gen. John J. Pershing. Thirteen of them arrived at Columbus, New Mexico, under command of Maj. Benjamin D. Foulois on March 15, 1916. The first reconnaissance into Mexico was flown on March 16. On March 19, eight JN-2s of the First Aero Squadron started from Columbus to Colonia Dublan. Four landed at Los Ascension because of darkness, one returned due to engine trouble and three landed at various points in Mexico. The JN-2s proved to be singularly unqualified for duty in this area, for they could not get over the mountains. This deficiency resulted in an immediate recommendation for the larger, more powerful R-2s.

Specifications	
The JN-2, 1915	
Span	36 ft. 0 in.
Length	26 ft. 0 in.
Chord	5 ft. 3 in.
Gap	5 ft. 3 in.
Engine	8-cyl. V, Model OXX, 119 hp
Weight	
gross	1,800 lb.

The JN-3, 1915

In early March 1916, Pancho Villa attacked the border town of Columbus, New Mexico. Immediately, Brig. Gen. John J. Pershing, who was later to become the commander of the American Expeditionary Force in World War I, was ordered to embark on a punitive expedition. Poor weather, the rugged terrain of northern Mexico and Villa's knowledge of the area made it necessary to call upon the First Aero Squadron for scouting duties. Shortly after the official reorganization of the First Aero Squadron at Fort Sill, Oklahoma, on July 1, 1915, they were assigned eight Curtiss JN-2s, which were modified in the field to the JN-3 specifications.

Upon receiving their orders on March 13, the First Aero Squadron flew their eight converted aircraft to Columbus, arriving on March 15, 1916.

In his *History of the First Aero Squadron*, Edgar S. Gorrell noted:

During the Mexican Campaign the duties consisted mainly of reconnaissance work. It was found that the type then in use, the Curtiss JN-3, possessed only limited military usefulness, it being impossible to fly across the Sierra Madre Mountains which have an altitude of 9,000 ft.

Therefore it was requested that two each of the following types should be tested under actual field conditions: Martin Model S; Curtiss R-2; Sturtevant; Thomas and Sloane. The only planes of which there is record were from the Curtiss Co., two type R-2 and N-8. These proved to be a great improvement over the old type.

In actuality, the JN-3s were grossly underpowered, and had been flown many hours prior to coming to New Mexico. By the end of March only two of the eight JN-3s were still in commission.

The report further indicates the type of assignment and the difficulties encountered by the First Aero Squadron during its assignment to the Mexican punitive expedition:

April 7, 1916, Aeroplane No. 42, Lt. Kilner, pilot, with mail and dispatches, from Geronimo to Colonia Dublan, distance 130 miles. Aeroplane No. 43, Lt. Dargue, pilot, Capt. Foulois, observer, from Geronimo to Chihuahua City, with dispatches for American Consul, distance, 105 miles.

April 14, 1916, Aeroplane No. 53, Lt. Dargue, pilot, Lt. Carroll, observer, on reconnaissance trip from Columbus, N.M. to Boca Grande, Pulpit Pass, Exaca Pass, Garretas, Janos, Ascension to Columbus, reconnaissance over the passes; record nonstop (AM) cross-country flight with passengers. Distance 315 miles. This reconnaissance trip was made for the purpose of locating a large body of Carrenzista troops, reported to be moving northeast towards our lines of communications. No troops were located within the area covered.

Aeroplane No. 45, Lt. Carberry, pilot, Capt. Foulois, observer, from Chihuahua City to Sateve with dispatches from American Consul to Gen. Pershing, distance 50 miles.

Aeroplane No. 52, Lt. Bader, pilot, Satevo to Ojito near Parral with dispatches from Col. Brown and Maj. Thomkins, distance 100 miles. From Ojito to Soquillo, distance 20 miles. On this later trip Lt. Bader located Maj. Howses' command. He was compelled to land near the column, on a very rough piece of ground, badly damaging his machine. Being in hostile country, 100 miles from his base, and unable to make the necessary repairs, the machine was abandoned. Lt. Bader proceeded with Maj. Howses' column.

Aeroplane No. 53, Lt. Chapman, pilot, with dispatches from San Andreas to San Antonio, distance 35 miles.

Capt. Foulois and fourteen men of the 1st Aero Squadron to Chihuahua City in squadron automobiles and trucks, with dispatches for American Consul. Lt. Willis and detachment to Parral in automobile with dispatches for Col. Brown, commanding troops near Parral.

Aeroplane No. 42 dismantled, condemned and destroyed. Lower wings of this machine were placed on Aeroplane No. 45, to replace wings that have been damaged in flight to Chihuahua on April 13th.

Total flights—5. Time—8 hrs. 3 mins.

April 19, 1916, Aeroplane No. 43, Lt. Dargue, pilot, Capt. Willis, observer, on reconnaissance trip from San Antonio to Chihuahua City, for the purpose of taking photographs and reconnoitering all roads and approaches to Chihuahua City. Left San Antonio at 5:25 A.M. Reconnoitered road, secured several photographs of same, then attempted to follow road leading west out of the city, through the foothills and mountains, in the direction of San Andreas. While reconnoitering, the motor began to vibrate badly and lose power. Efforts were made to turn around and retrace the course through more open country, but due to failure of the motor and terrific downward currents the pilot was unable to reach a good landing ground and was compelled to land on the side of a mountain having a slope of about 45 degrees. The machine was completely wrecked, turning over on both pilot and observer. Lt. Dargue escaped uninjured though badly shaken up. Capt. Willis was pinned down under the wreckage, both his feet being caught between the engine bed and the gasoline tank. He received a severe though not serious scalp wound and was considerably bruised about the legs and ankles. As the aeroplane was completely wrecked, it was burned on the spot. The two aviators, with their personal equipment, started at 9:35 A.M. this date to walk back to San Antonio, their nearest base, a distance of about 65 miles. They struggled continuously through mountains and valleys for two days and nights, suffering all this time for lack of food and water. They finally reached San Antonio on the morning of the 21st, completely exhausted, after almost 45 hours of continuous walking. Both aviators remained at San Antonio until April 23rd when they proceeded in an automobile to Narquita and turned in their reports to the division commander. Distance flown on this trip from San Antonio to Chihuahua City and vicinity, 100 miles.

In an interview much later, Foulois recalled that a major problem encountered with all planes was the separating of the laminated propeller sections due to the intense heat drying the wood and opening it along the glue lines.

Specifications	
The JN-3, 1915	
Length	26 ft. 9½ in.
Height	10 ft. 10 in.
Span	
upper	43 ft. 9 in.
lower	33 ft. 8½ in.
Chord	59½ in.
Gap	60 in.
Stagger	10 in.
Dihedral	1°
Incidence	1°
Airfoil	Eiffel No. 36
Area	212.25 sq. ft.
Propeller	8-ft. laminated wood

The Canadian JN-4 Cannuck

Kenneth M. Molson, in his *Notes on the Curtiss JN Aircraft Family*, states:

The designations of the various models comprising the JN family are fairly clear, however the Canadian JN-4 seems to have caused repeated difficulty. The aircraft was developed in Toronto directly from the JN-3 and independently of the Curtiss Company in the United States. It was known by Canadian Aeroplanes Ltd. simply as the JN-4 and no effort was made to tie in its designation with those used by the American firm. Later the prefix Canadian was added to distinguish it from the American relatives . . . the aircraft became known as the Canadian JN-4. Unfortunately it is often confused with the experimental model the JN-4C, even to the extent of assuming that the Canadian aircraft also employed the R.A.F. 6 wing section. A close study of photographs will show a number of details which will aid in the recognition of various models. An example of this is that if the aileron cable from the fuselage goes downwards to the lower wing then the aircraft is a Canadian JN-4.

Molson also notes that the JN-3 was supplied in quantity to the Royal Naval Air Service. Also used by the Curtiss Aviation School at Long Branch, Ontario, and by the Australians at Point Cook, Victoria. The Curtiss Company had set up production for JN-3s at Canadian Aeroplanes Ltd. at Toronto. Modifications were made to the JN-4 design when it was decided to use it in the Canadian Air Training Program. It was also decided that the aircraft used in this program should be manufactured in Canada. The type preferred was the De Havilland D.H. 6 because of previous familiarity with the machine and because it could use more than one type of engine. However, if the program was to get under way quickly it was more desirable to accept the JN-3 aircraft, which was already being produced in Toronto and for which tooling was available. This was accepted on the condition that certain modifications be made in the aircraft, under the direction of F. G. Ericson, former chief engineer of the Curtiss Aeroplane and Motors Ltd. of Toronto and at this time chief engineer of Canadian Aeroplanes Ltd. The modifications consisted of providing ailerons on each wing, interconnected with struts, changing the control system from the Deperdussin to stick control, and altering the rudder to bring it level with the bottom of the fuselage, making the Cannuck rudder almost semicircular in profile. The airplane otherwise remained almost identical to the American-designed JN-3.

Production figures for Canadian JN-4s have for years been subject to interpretation from logbooks and photographic evidence. Recently, a colleague, Alfred "Fred" J. Shortt, curator of the Aeronautical Department, Canadian Science Museum, delivered a paper that contained what is believed to be the most accurate record. The record was kept by an employee of Canadian Aeroplanes Ltd. who was in a position to accurately record the production figures.

In Shortt's paper, delivered at a meeting of curators in the spring of 1980, the figure given for the JN-4 Cannuck production was 1,288. To this should be added 1,631 sets of spares. How many of these sets were assembled as complete aircraft is unknown, but with these new figures the record is improved. It is known that about 120 aircraft were assembled from the spare sets after World War I by the Ericson Aircraft Company and J. V. Elliott Air Services.

Specifications	
The Canadian JN-4 Cannuck	
Span	
upper	43 ft. 7⁵/₁₆ in.
lower	34 ft. 8⁵/₁₆ in.
Length	27 ft. 2½ in.
Chord	4 ft. 11½ in.
Gap	5 ft. 2½ in.
Engine	8-cyl. V, Model OX-5, 90 hp
Weight	
gross	1,920 lb.

The Model K (KPB), 1915

The K boat was essentially an enlarged F boat, which resulted in increased speed and load-carrying capacity. While it was not so numerous as the F type, the K type was purchased in substantial numbers by Russia. In a note to the author, Roland Rohlfs, Curtiss test pilot, stated that he helped build fifty-four of these machines for Russia. Other production records set the figure at fifty-six, one of which, the "KLAVA," was tested and operated by Theodore C. McCaulay, Curtiss test pilot, at Toronto late in 1915. The total value of the Russian purchase was $1,010,700. In addition, twelve OX 90–100-horsepower engines and nineteen V model 160-horsepower engines were purchased at a combined total of $128,570.

While the bulk of the Ks were produced in 1915, at least one was tested by Walter E. Johnson as early as November 19, 1914, at Hammondsport.

For its time the K was the largest and fastest single-engine flying boat, with provision for three seats, one of which was in the bow of the hull, making it advantageous as an observer/gunner station.

A problem with the early models of the Model V engine caused postponement of the tests until 1915, at which time the testing was taken over by another Curtiss test pilot, Theodore C. McCaulay, at the Toronto plant of the Curtiss Company. The tests were witnessed by Lieutenant Petroskey of the Russian Purchasing Commission. During the tests McCaulay decided to make an attempt to win the Curtiss Marine Flying Trophy, which was conducted under the auspices of the Aero Club of America. On October 17, 1915, McCaulay, with two passengers, succeeded in establishing a record nonstop distance of 183 miles in 2 hours 27 minutes and an additional 122 miles with one passenger for a total of 427 miles in 5 hours 39 minutes flying time.

The Russian purchase contract for the K boats is one of the least known facets of their history. The problems encountered were later documented in transcripts prepared for possible court action following the war and after the Rus-

sian Revolution of 1917. The story is best told by quoting Walter E. Johnson, Curtiss test pilot:

I left this country for Russia, leaving New York about July 4th, 1915, arriving at Archangel, Russia, about July 14, from which point I went directly to Petrograd and met Mr. Ochs, the Curtiss agent, and Lieutenant Tschtofsky, and then went directly from Petrograd to Sebastopol, arriving there around the last of July. Mr. Witmer, Purinton and Bennett were in Sebastopol and had several "K" boats assembled ready for trial flights. I immediately prepared to make an official trial flight, with a view to having the machines accepted by the Russian authorities. Unfortunately, the motor stopped before I had made the necessary altitude, and I was forced to plane down from 2500 feet with a dead motor. The machine functioned perfectly; the balance was correct, and I had no difficulty in bringing the machine down and landing in very rough water without any injury to the machine. We were towed back to the harbor by a destroyer, and the waves were so high that when the destroyer went down in the trough of the waves we were unable to see any of the boat at all. This will give some idea of the height at which the waves were running when we had to make this forced landing.

We had considerable trouble with the oiling system. Oil would leak from the motor in such a quantity that it was impossible to make a long flight. Propeller bolts were continually breaking which made flying these machines hazardous. We did everything that we could to correct these two difficulties and advised the Curtiss company by cable what our troubles were, and what we thought needed to be done to make corrections. We were advised by the Curtiss company that the necessary parts were being shipped to us, which would do away with the oil and propeller troubles.

Model K Boat tests at Hammondsport, late 1914. Notice the bow cockpit for a military observer.

The Model K, which was larger than the Model F, was a big machine for its day, and production in the Curtiss plant was not easy, as is shown by "moving day" for the prototype Model K hull. *Curtiss Photo Collection*

Specifications

The Model K (KPB), 1915

Span overall	55 ft. 9 in.
lower wing	42 ft. 11 in.
Chord	6 ft. 2 in.
Dihedral	upper 0°, lower 3°
Area, including ailerons	590 sq. ft.
Sweep back	3°
Stagger	9½ in.
Overall length	31 ft. 5 in.
Weight	
net	2,700 lb.
gross	3,900 lb.
Useful load	1,120 lb.
Power plant	Curtiss VX 160 hp
Speed	
maximum	70 mph
minimum	50 mph
Endurance, cruise power	6.76 hr.

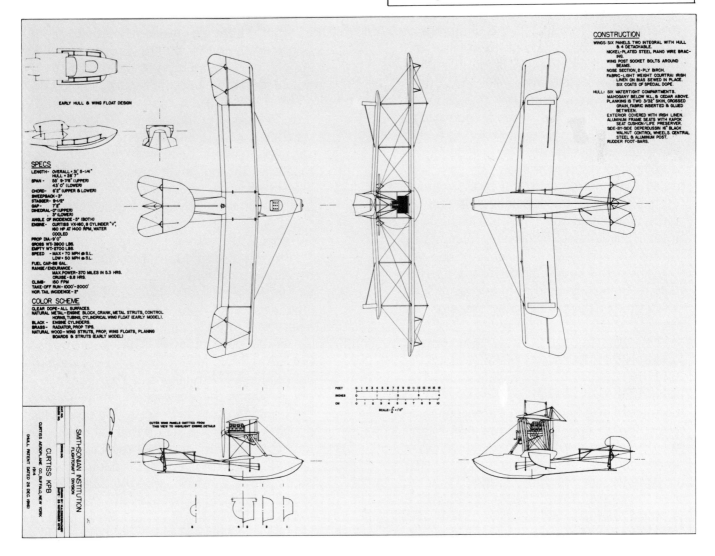

During this time we got practically no cooperation from the Russian authorities. This made it very difficult for us to go on and make any corrections, or to carry on the testing work. We were not allowed the freedom of the machine shop, and all of our work was practically done in a structure made out of old boat boxes and shipping crates.

The "K" boats were left out in the open with practically no protection against the weather, so that they deteriorated very rapidly. The hot sun would cause the surfaces to warp and the hulls to crack open. This was nothing that we could prevent because the authorities did not provide any shelter for the machines. We had no alternative but to set the machines up in such places as the commander designated. The metal parts on the first shipment of machines, which came by way of Vancouver and Vladivostok, were badly rusted, and many of the metal parts and wires had to be replaced, which took considerable time. As I understand it, this shipment of machines was piled under boxes of fish, and the brine which leaked through ruined many of the metal parts.

The Russian machine shop equipment was very meagre and totally inadequate to make repairs such as we needed to make. We could not get the use of any of their tools and had to rely entirely on our own very small equipment, so that it took us much longer to make the replacements and repairs, which were necessary in the course of ordinary test flying. We had to rely entirely upon our own tools, as it was impossible to buy any of this equipment in Russia, and the City of Sebastopol did not have a machine shop that was available to do any work for us.

The Russian officers at the station, whereas they had been friendly, gradually began to hold aloof from us and showed by their attitude that they were not willing to cooperate and help us get the machines in condition to fly. When Lieutenant Utgoff was in Sebastopol, he cooperated with us in every way possible, but after he left to come to America, we lost the one friend that we had. From that time on none of the officers showed us any courtesy or offered to help in any way that they could. We were left en-

tirely alone to work things out as best we could. The delay caused by waiting for new parts to come from the Curtiss company seemed to irritate the Russian flying officers, who thought that the machines should go together and be flown and accepted immediately.

A few days after I arrived in Sebastopol, Mr. Ochs came down from Petrograd to help us in getting the machines ready for the official tests. He had only been there two days when he suddenly disappeared, and it was about ten days later that we learned that he was in jail on a charge of being a spy, due to the fact that he had been in both Berlin and Vienna on business for the Curtiss company, as their agent, prior to the outbreak of the war. We had depended a great deal upon Mr. Ochs. As he spoke both English and Russian, he was of inestimable help to us. We were very much un-nerved by the whole affair and often wondered how long it would be before they put the rest of us in jail on some trumped-up charge or other. There was no American consul in Sebastopol, nor anyone to whom we could appeal, and the attitude of the officers was not such that we felt any security at all. We were working under these conditions and doing everything that we could to get the machines ready, so that when the new parts came there would be no delay in putting the machines through their tests.

According to my agreement with the Curtiss company, I was to leave Russia so that I would arrive home by the middle of October 1915. When I went to Lieutenant Tschtofsky and told him that, according to my agreement with the Curtiss company, it was time for me to start home, he refused to let me go until they had some assurance from the Curtiss company that another pilot would be sent over. They kept me in Sebastopol two weeks longer than I should have stayed. During this time I was forced to put in writing the reasons for failure to put the boats through their tests. My failure to do this would have meant that I should not have been given permission to leave the City of Sebastopol, so that I made a statement, giving, as my reasons that I had failed to put the machine through their tests, the trouble with the oiling system and the breaking of the propeller bolts. We had assurance from the Curtiss company that the new parts they were sending would correct these faults. I left Sebastopol about September 15, 1915, and I understood, at this time, that Mr. Jannus was coming over to fly the machine, and that the new parts necessary to repair the motors had already been shipped with one or more mechanics, who were to help install them.

The Curtiss company did everything that they could to expedite the shipment of new parts to us. They went to a great expense to send men with these spare parts to be sure that they would not be lost in transit, and made every effort to get the mechanics so that they would be acceptable to the Russian Government. It is my understanding, that when the new parts did arrive, and the motors had been fixed, ten or more machines completed their flying tests and were accepted by the Russian authorities. It was my opinion, when I left Russia, that the "K" boats would satisfactorily pass their flying tests if the oil trouble and the propeller trouble were remedied with new parts. From my knowledge of the new parts that were shipped, I have no doubt that these changes would correct all the trouble and that the boats would pass the tests satisfactorily.

On May 29, 1916, Official Washington awoke to find a K boat assembled during the night, parked directly across the street from the House of Representatives and in front of the offices of the National Aerial Coast Patrol Commission in the Coast and Geodetic Survey Building. By 10 o'clock over 200 members of the Lower House had crossed the street to see it. It was intended to be on exhibit for several weeks as a sample of the type of aircraft to be used at fifty or more stations along the 5,000 miles of our defenseless coastline from Eastport, Maine, to Cape Flattery, Washington. The plan would have been the first attempt at Airborne Early Warning patrols.

The K had a speed range from 50 to 70 miles per hour and a climb speed of 150 feet per minute. A cruising radius of 370 miles at full power was also good for its time, but the weight per square foot of wing area of 6.6 pounds and per horsepower of 22.9 pounds was considered high for aircraft in 1915. The hull was robust, permitting rough usage on the water.

The upper wing had an overhang of 6 feet 5 inches at each end, putting 59 percent of the wing area of 590 square feet in the upper wing. The wing consisted of six panels, two of which were integral with the hull. The hull was the V-bottom type with special consideration for lightness and strength and was 26 feet 7 inches long. It was divided into six watertight compartments by two-ply cedar of $3/32$-inch layers of mahogany with crossed grain. Between these was a layer of fabric set in high-grade marine glue. Planking above the waterline was cedar, with the entire exterior covered with high-grade Irish linen. Seating consisted of side-by-side seating forward of the wings for two pilots and a single-place seat forward in the bow of the hull.

Controls were Deperdussin dual, side-by-side. Two 16-inch black walnut control wheels were mounted on the aluminum control yoke. Rudder bars were reinforced with aluminum and mounted on a bronze pedestal. Rudder cables were doubled for security.

The engine was a Curtiss VX 160-horsepower model mounted between the wings. The fuel supply was contained in a 77-gallon tank located at the center of gravity of the hull with an additional 8-gallon tank located at the engine. Nine gallons of oil were carried.

The KPL, 1915-1916

At least fifty-four Ks were built for Russia. Following this, an interesting adaptation, or innovation, developed known as the KPL for K-Pusher-Land. Since I have been unsuccessful in obtaining confirmation from the Russian Embassy, I can only conjecture the following.

The well-recorded Russian winters probably reduced the operation of the K boats to something slightly below zero. It is reasonable to assume that either on speculation or in response to a Russian inquiry, Curtiss built a landplane fuselage that could use the aerodynamic components of the Model K during the long, cold winters. Photos of this interesting, if ungainly, fuselage show it to fit the K hull configuration. Construction photos indicate this fuselage to have been built around May 22, 1915.

Patents for this configuration were applied for on October 18, 1915, and granted November 6,

1917, under patent No. 1,246,015. Illustrations from this patent follow. One of the photos in the author's files states quite positively "Flying Coffin Built for Russia." James Wagner, who helped build at least one K, confirms that this one was built at Hammondsport.

The design lineage from the KPB is apparent in this construction photo of the KPL, a landplane variant of the KPB. *Curtiss Photo Collection*

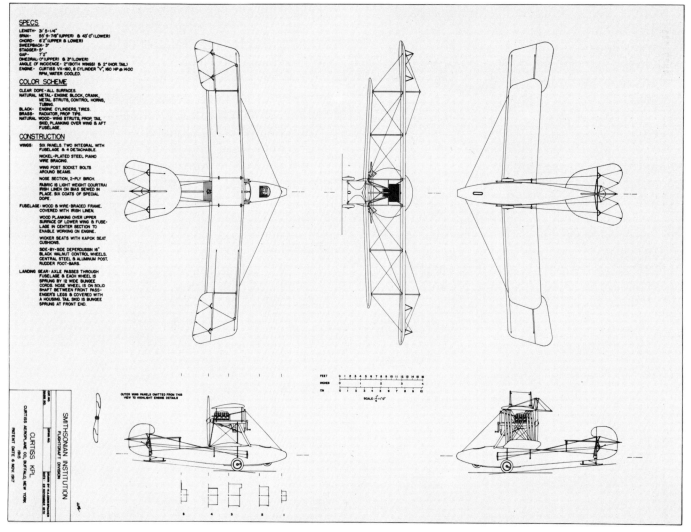

The N-6 Hydro, 1915

One of the most elusive Curtiss aircraft models has to be the N-6 Hydro. The N-6 was a development of the basic hydro, the Navy AH-8.

Three N-6s were ordered by the U.S. Navy and designated numbers A-63, A-64 and A-65, though to the best of our knowledge only one was delivered.

The N-6s were ordered during the latter part of 1915, but were condemned shortly after delivery of the first aircraft. Like the army, the navy condemned this type of aircraft in favor of the now conventional fuselage-type aircraft.

The N-6 was designed as a naval training machine and for possible use by sportsmen. Two seats were installed forward of the wings and could be protected by a spray shield. Performance was adequate for use as a trainer but little else, because of a speed range of only 45 to 65 miles per hour. The rate of climb was about 300 feet per minute. It had an endurance of 1⅓ hours or about 90 miles. Additional larger tanks could be easily fitted if required. It was fitted with a single 16-foot main float, in typical Curtiss configuration, with wing-tip floats for balance on the water.

The wings consisted of six panels with a combined area of 380 square feet. The upper wing had an overhang of 4 feet 10 inches at each end.

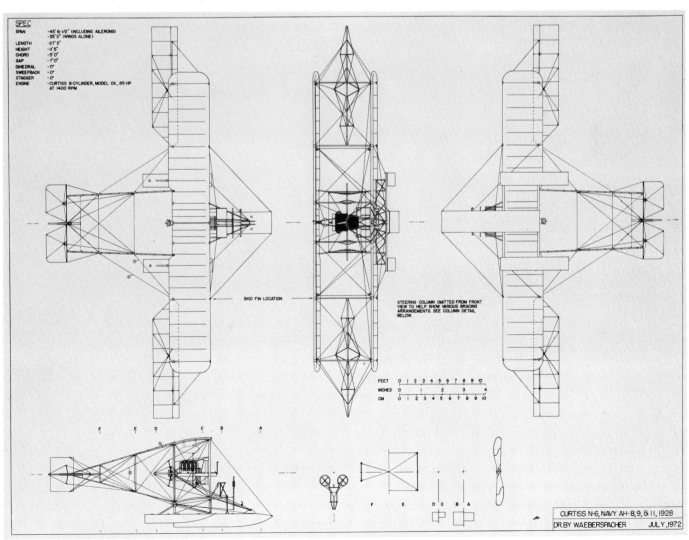

SPEC

SPAN	-45' 6-½" (INCLUDING AILERONS) -35' 0" (WINGS ALONE)
LENGTH	-27' 5"
HEIGHT	-11' 5"
CHORD	-5' 0"
GAP	-7' 0"
DIHEDRAL	-0°
SWEEPBACK	-0°
STAGGER	-0°
ENGINE	-CURTISS 8-CYLINDER, MODEL OX, 85 HP AT 1400 RPM

SKID FIN LOCATION

STEERING COLUMN OMITTED FROM FRONT VIEW TO HELP SHOW VARIOUS BRACING ARRANGEMENTS. SEE COLUMN DETAIL BELOW.

CURTISS N-6, NAVY AH-8, 9, & 11, 1928
DR. BY WAEBERSPACHER   JULY, 1972

Unlike its predecessor, hydros of this type used "I" beam spars similar to contemporary F-type flying boats. The crude protective nacelle was built of four spruce longerons with struts and steel wire bracing. It extended 5½ feet ahead of the wings and was attached to the single float by two streamlined struts. The float was the V-bottom type, 16 feet long, 18 inches high and 30 inches wide. It was divided by bulkheads into four waterproof compartments. It was sheathed with ³/₁₆-inch mahogany covered by "doped" fabric. The bottom was two layers of ⁵/₃₂-inch mahogany with cotton fabric embedded in marine glue. Wing-tip floats were of similar construction including a V bottom. Controls were dual, side by side, of the Deperdussin type. An ash control bridge of an inverted U shape was mounted to clear the pilot's knees. On this bridge were mounted two 16-inch black walnut control wheels.

Tail surfaces similar to the earlier D and E hydros were carried on bamboo outriggers rigidly braced with steel wires. Nonskid planes were located above and below the upper wing on each side to improve stability.

Unlike its predecessors, the D and E hydros, this model had an instrument panel. This elementary panel had mounted on it a tachometer and oil pressure gauge plus the necessary electrical and ignition switches.

Specifications	
The N-6 Hydro, 1915	
Span overall	45 ft. 6½ in.
Chord	5 ft.
Area	383 sq. ft.
Length overall	27 ft. 5 in.
Weight	
net	1,100 lb.
gross	1,800 lb.
Useful load	700 lb.
Power plant	Curtiss OX, 85–90 hp
Fuel capacity	36 gal.
Endurance at full throttle	4.3 hr.
Endurance at cruise throttle	6.0 hr.

The Model N-8

The N-8 was a development of the N, which passed the army evaluation tests of November 1914 by the skin of its teeth. It was not ordered into production, but the best features of the J and the N were blended to produce the JN, which was developed into the ubiquitous "Jenny," or JN-4D. The N-8 retained the Curtiss shoulder yoke aileron control, whereas the JN-4D used the stick control system for military aircraft.

The N-8 saw very limited use with the U.S. Army Signal Corps' Aviation Section in pursuing Mexican bandits along the border. Four aircraft, S.C. Nos. 60–63, were dispatched to Columbus, New Mexico, in April 1916. Tests conducted with the N-8s between April 23 and 29 confirmed that they were little better than the JN-3s. Lt. Byron Q. Jones, a member of the Technical Aero Advisory and Inspection Board, stated that the engine in the N-8 was better than those in the JN-3s but that the purchase of any plane must be considered as an experiment until tested. A furor developed after derogatory articles appeared in the *New York Times* and the *El Paso Herald*. Though the pilots were not happy with the N-8s they denied charges that they gave information to the reporters. The authors of the articles stoutly maintained that their articles were based entirely on personal observations. On May 9, 1916, a board of officers at Columbus, New Mexico, recommended condemnation of the

The N-8 was a continuation of the N series and was not highly regarded by pilots of the Pershing expedition in Mexico. The planes were not ordered under the N-8 designation, but as JN-4s. For practical purposes it was a stretched-wing JN-3.

N-8s, declaring that they lacked proper controls, were very slow-climbing, had weak landing gear, were too slow and inadequately powered. With this many strikes against them, the N-8s were removed from frontline service and shipped to North Island, San Diego, California, to be used as trainers.

The N-8s were difficult to distinguish from the JN-4Bs, differing externally only by the addition of a longer wing center section amounting to an additional 10 feet of span. Additional area was obtained by tapering the ailerons slightly with an increased chord at the outboard tip.

Most of the N-8 airframe was carried forward to become the basis of the N-9 and N-10. The N-9 was powered by a 150-horsepower Hispano-Suiza engine and was often referred to as a seagoing "Jenny"; it was mounted on a single central float with wing-tip balance floats. It was used by the U.S. Navy in the same manner as the army used the JN-4Ds to train pilots in basic flight, gunnery, bombing, etc.

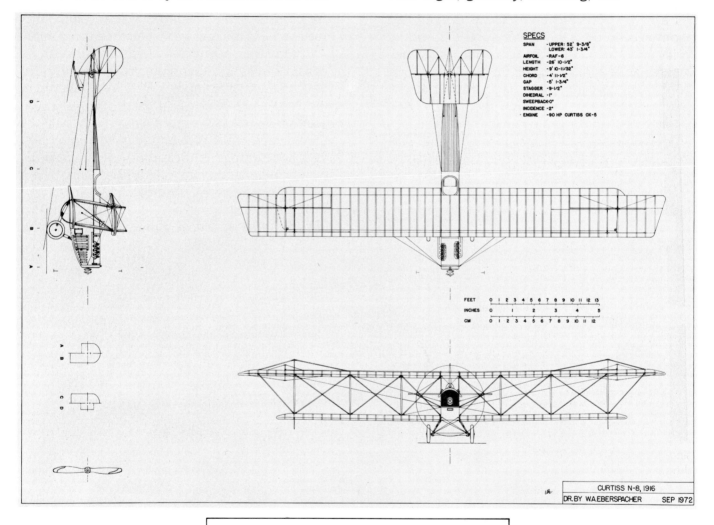

CURTISS N-8, 1916
DR. BY W.A. EBERSPACHER   SEP 1972

Specifications	
The Model N-8	
Span	52 ft. 9⅜ in., upper
	43 ft. 1¾ in., lower
Length	26 ft. 10½ in.
Chord	4 ft. 11½ in.
Gap	5 ft. 1¾ in.
Engine	8-cyl. V, Model OX-5, 90 hp

The Model O

Little, if any, record of this model exists, giving a fair indication of its merits. The best and simplest way to describe it would be to say that it was a Model N with the fuselage widened to accommodate the crew in side-by-side seating. In view of the instability of the Model N, due to a rearward center of gravity location, it would not be surprising if the Model O were constructed specifically to place both crew members in the same longitudinal location and at a more favorable position in relation to the center of gravity.

Using components from the Model N, this experimental Model O was assembled. During tests the Model N was reported to be tail-heavy. The Model O moved the rear pilot forward, making it similar in arrangement to contemporary flying boats.

The JN, 1914

Some doubt exists regarding the existence of an aircraft that can be, or was, labeled JN. The JN designation probably was a generic term applied to the aircraft—with the JN-2 being the real beginning of the series.

In the Curtiss catalog titled *Curtiss Military Tractor Aeroplanes 1915*, the JN is described in detail; however, the illustrations are of the J. The variations from those of the J are so slight as to create doubts. Since these variations are so minimal, it is difficult, if not impossible, to identify or differentiate between two such similar machines solely from photographs.

The Model R, 1914-1915

The first of the R series made its debut on December 6, 1914, but the major development of the R took place in 1915 as a result of the punitive expedition in Mexico. The high altitude of the Mexican terrain and the poor climatic conditions quickly sidelined the JN-2 aircraft. The R was in the early stage of its development and was pressed into service.

Though the original specifications called for interchangeable OX (90 horsepower), OXX (110 horsepower) and V (160 horsepower) model engines, the primary installation was the 160-horsepower Model V.

The equal-span, 38-foot wings were modified quickly, replacing the interplane ailerons with the inset ailerons in the outboard trailing edge of the upper wing panels. In this regard the R followed the same evolution as the Model J.

The R could be fitted with either the Curtiss shoulder yoke and control wheel or the Deperdussin control system. The pilot and observer were seated in tandem in an elongated 7-foot open cockpit that distinguishes the first R from the succeeding variants.

Probably the simplest and most appropriate description of the R type was made by a Curtiss employee of that era who described it as a scaled-up JN, 50 percent larger in power and in

After assuring themselves that the prototype Model R was manageable and the takeoff run was within prediction, the Curtiss people refitted it as a landplane and flew it off the ice of Lake Keuka. Note the oversized cockpit and the convertible landing gear.

area. In its original form the R was an ungainly looking machine, complete with nose-over skids protruding forward from the main gear of the tripod landing gear. The cockpit, a gaping expanse in the upper center fuselage, was of bathtub proportions and appeared to have been designed for three, possibly four persons, rather than the two crew members that the plane was capable of lifting.

First tests were made on Lake Keuka on December 9, 1914. The limited level land area at Hammondsport dictated that the R be tested on the waters of Lake Keuka in the same manner that the J had been tested. A single crude float was fitted and was supplemented by the usual outrigger wing-tip floats. With the "stiffening" of the waters of Lake Keuka, further tests were conducted on January 9, 1915, in the landplane configuration from the frozen surface of the lake.

Like the J, the R was to be developed through a number of variants, some of which gave a good account of themselves.

Specifications

The Model R, 1914–1915

Span	
upper	38 ft. 0 in.
lower	38 ft. 0 in.
Chord	72 in.
Area	450 sq. ft.
Length overall	28 ft. 0 in.
Rudder area	16 sq. ft.
Elevators	16 sq. ft.
Crew	2
Speed range	55–85 mph
Endurance	5 hr.
Climb	4,000 ft. in 10 min.
Engine	Curtiss V, 160 hp
Price	$15,000
Hydro equipment	$500

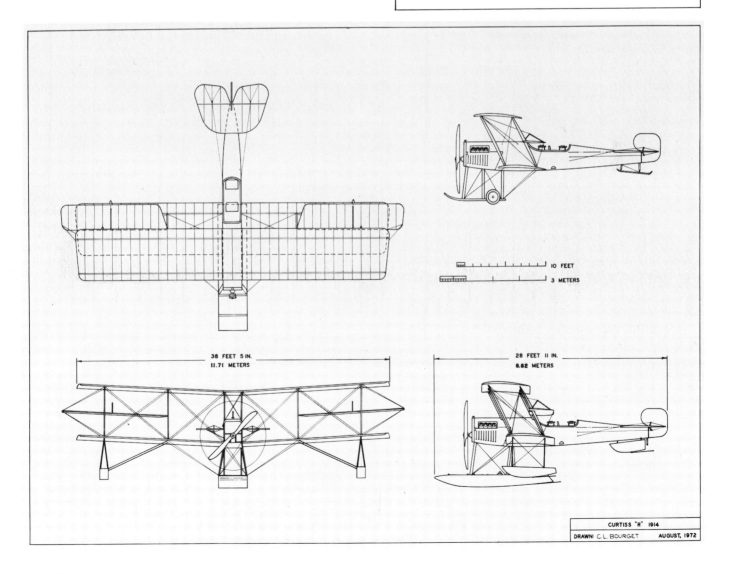

CURTISS "R" 1914
DRAWN: C. L. BOURGET   AUGUST, 1972

The R-2

The R-2 used the RAF No. 6 airfoil, which was the best available at the time and gave the best combination for speed and lift. The use of three-ply wood for ribs and "I" beams for spars were standard construction practices. Also, two-ply plywood was used to sheath the leading edge of the wings to maintain the profile and prevent sagging between ribs, thereby increasing efficiency. Courtral Irish linen was used for covering, with six coats of dope.

The fuselage was rectangular in cross section with four longerons of ash. Aluminum cowls were used for the forward fuselage and engine. Seats were in tandem and windshields were provided for both cockpits. Controls were the now standard Deperdussin type with the 16-inch control wheel mounted on an inverted **U**-shaped control bridge to clear the pilot's knees. A mahogany dashboard was standard and mounted an elementary group of instruments consisting of a tachometer and an oil pressure gauge, plus switches and a gasoline valve.

The engine was the Curtiss VX of 160 horsepower, which required a takeoff run of about 300 feet and produced a maximum speed of 90 miles per hour.

A development of the basic R tractor biplane, the R-2s received their baptism of fire in a literal sense, being detailed to the First Aero Squadron with Pershing's punitive expedition. Twelve R-2s were delivered to Columbus, New Mexico, for operation with Pershing's forces.

The punitive expedition turned out to be a testing ground for several types of aircraft then in current production. The N-8s had been tried and found to be deficient in several respects, particularly in altitude performance. The R-2 then in production was selected as an immediate substitute even though Glen Curtiss chose not to recommend them for this duty.

In spite of a recommendation by Lt. Byron Q. Jones, a member of the Technical Aero Advisory and Inspection Board, to purchase Sturtevant (a competition of Curtiss) planes, the board considered the R-2s to be the most satisfactory and purchased them for the First Aero Squadron in place of the Sturtevants.

The R-2s' performance in other circumstances was quite impressive. On April 1, 1916, Steven (Stephenson) MacGordon flew an R-2 with a passenger from Newport News, Virginia, to Washington, D.C., and returned in 4 hours and 45 minutes. On April 19, Victor Carlstrom, flying an R-2, established a three-man American altitude record of 11,180 feet at Newport News, Virginia.

On April 22, four new R-2s were received at Columbus, New Mexico, as replacements for the JN-2s, following the destruction of seven of the eight remaining JN-2s. The R-2s were tested and found unsuitable for Mexican service. On May 1, two additional R-2s were received at Columbus and by May 25, all twelve had been received. May, June and July brought constant troubles. According to Foulois, interviewed many years later, defective propellers and defective construction of the aircraft and engine parts all contributed to the problems. In spite of these problems, 540 flights were made by the First Aero Squadron, totaling 345 hours and 43 minutes.

During this Mexican service, pilots were "constantly exposed to personal risk and suffering due to the inadequacy of the planes. Pilots often were forced to land in the desert and hostile country. In almost every case the planes were destroyed or abandoned."

In addition to those purchased for the U.S. Army, the Royal Naval Air Service purchased 100 of the R-2s for reconnaissance. Not more than half a dozen were operated, though at least one was used for radio experiments. A single aircraft was fitted experimentally with the 200-horsepower Sunbeam engine.

The R-2A was a variant of the basic R-2, developed for the Air Mail Service. The only difference between the two aircraft appears to be the elimination of the forward cockpit, thereby creating a mail bin with a hatch contoured to the fuselage at that point.

Specifications

The R-2

Span		
overall, including ailerons	48 ft.	0 in.
lower wing	38 ft.	10 in.
Chord	6 ft.	3 in.
Gap	6 ft.	3 in.
Stagger	7° and 9½°	
Area, including ailerons	504.9 sq. ft.	
Length overall	28 ft. 5 in.	
Weight		
net	1,800 lb.	
gross	2,800 lb.	
Engine	Curtiss VX	
	160 hp	
Speed		
maximum	90 mph	
minimum	50 mph	
Range	5.1 hr.	

An experimental R-2 on the ground.

The R-3, 1915

The R-3 was basically a hydro version of the R-2 with an increased wing area to support the addition of the float gear. This was probably the first instance of Curtiss changing from his preferred single-float hydro gear to the twin-float configuration. No record of tests has been found that would explain the reason for this departure from his normal design philosophy. Furthermore, no record of use of this design has been found by this writer. As in the case of the R-2, the RAF No. 6 airfoil was used. The span of the upper wing was increased, the fuselage was lengthened about 11 feet, and the ailerons were inset in the upper wing, replacing the interplane ailerons of the R-2. The increase in span of the upper wing was accomplished by the addition of a large center wing panel in the upper wing. Top speed was only marginally greater than the 90 miles per hour of the R-2. Construction details were the same as for the R-2.

The Model R-3 was a further refined Model R incorporating twin floats, which was a departure from the usual Curtiss single float preference. Afloat, the R-3 rides tail-low. The controls are similar to contemporary hydros using the shoulder yoke and control wheel.

Specifications

The R-3, 1915

Span	
overall top wing	50 ft. 3 in.
lower wing	35 ft. 4 in.
Chord	6 ft. 3⁵/₆₄ in.
Gap	6 ft. 3 in.
Stagger	12½°
Length overall	39 ft. 4⅛ in.
Weight	
net	2,650 lb.
gross	3,300 lb.
Engine	Curtiss VX
	160 hp
Maximum speed	90–95 mph
Endurance, cruise power	3 hr.

The R-3 on the ice at Hammondsport, New York.

The Curtiss C Canada

With the outbreak of war on the European continent, the demand for aircraft became acute. The Curtiss Aeroplane and Motor Corp., endeavoring to sell aircraft to the Canadian government and the British government, decided to establish a training school and manufacturing plant in Canada.

A manufacturing plant at 20 Strachan Avenue, Toronto, was leased. The managing director of the plant was J.A.D. McCurdy, who made the first airplane flight in Canada, piloting the Aerial Experiment Association *Silver Dart*. The largest manufacturing venture was to be the *Canada*, a large twin-engine bomber. Derived from the Curtiss H-1 *America*, the *Canada* was, in fact, a landplane version of the *America*. The wings and tail surfaces were copies of the *America* geometry with the upper wing having 1-foot 10-inch greater span, the same as the H-4s. The initial test flight of the *Canada* was made using the same OX-5-type engines as used in the *America*. The larger 160-horsepower Curtiss VX engines were not delivered in time for the test flight, making the engine substitution necessary. The flight was made from the Long Branch, Toronto, aerodrome at about the end of July 1915 with Anthony Jannus as test pilot. Shortly after this, Jannus left for Russia to continue the acceptance test flights on the Model K flying boats and others. During one of these test flights Jannus was killed.

It is interesting to note the parallel between the *Canada*, which was a landplane version of the H-4, and the KPL, similarly a landplane version of the K flying boat. In each case, the landplane configuration left much to be desired appearancewise. Like the H-4, the *Canada* was of unequal span. The tail surfaces, which looked right on the flying boat, looked like an afterthought when attached to the engine nacelles and the truncated fuselage by three booms and a generous number of wires. The landing gear was also a bit unusual, consisting of tandem wheels fitted to each main gear and a tail skid attached to the lower tail boom just forward of the rudder post.

The *Canada* passed its acceptance test on September 7, 1915, witnessed by Cdr. John C. Porte, Royal Navy, who was to have been the pilot of the *America* for the intended transatlantic flight and who later became well known as the designer of the Felixstowe series of flying boats. At the time of the acceptance tests of the *Canada*, wartime secrecy prevailed, requiring Porte to operate in North America under the

The C-1 *Canada* is posed for the photographer. The test flights had to be made with Curtiss OX-5 engines because the more powerful Model V engines were not ready. *Shell Company Foundation Collection*

assumed name of J. B. Scott.

The *Canada* was significant for several reasons, including the installation of a Sperry-designed auto stabilizer and bombsight. It was also the first twin-engine aircraft to be built in Canada, the first aircraft of Canadian design to go into production, the first Canadian design intended for military service and the first bomber of Canadian design. Interestingly, a flying boat version of the *Canada* was contemplated as indicated by patent No. 1,228,382. The design concept had made a full circle.

The crew consisted of three: a pilot in a cockpit located at the rear of the fuselage, and an observer and bomb aimer in two positions in the nose of the nacelle. Orders were placed for an additional eleven improved *Canada* aircraft designated as Model C-1. Ten were for the British War Office and one, No. 3700, was for the Admiralty.

It is known that the prototype *Canada* was test-flown at Farnborough, but no record of the shipment or use of the C-1s has been located.

The *Canada* takes off at Farnborough. Its parentage is evident from the wing and rudder. The wing was the same as the *America*.

Specifications	
The Curtiss C *Canada*	
Span	75 ft. 10 in., upper
	48 ft. 0 in., lower
Length	33 ft. 5 in.
Chord	7 ft. 0 in.
Engine (2)	8-cyl. V, Model VX, 180 hp @
	1,400 rpm
Weight	
net	4,700 lb.
gross	6,300 lb.

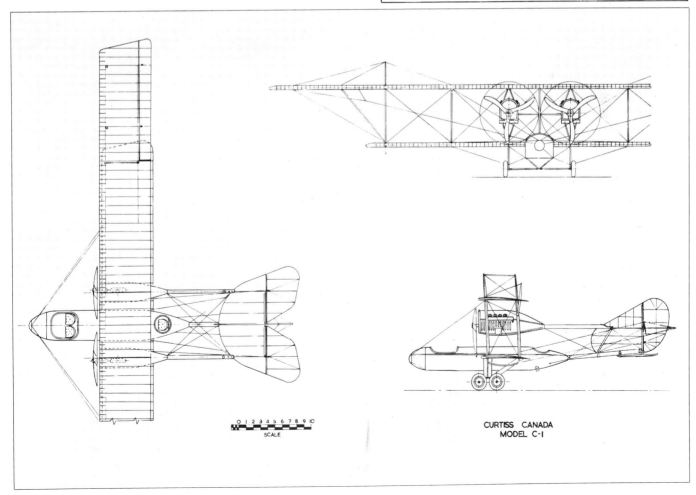

SCALE

CURTISS CANADA
MODEL C-1

The Curtiss H-7 TB Super America

The H-7 *Super America,* also known as the *Transatlantic H-7,* had a short history, possibly due to the fact that it was not acquired by a United States government agency and, of the completed airframes, two were shipped to Russia to become part of the ill-fated K boat fiasco. The H-7 probably would not have fared better on its own, for it was also burdened with the early undeveloped Curtiss V-type engine. Some of the trials and tribulations of the Curtiss group in Russia are related in the section on the K boat. The same shipping faults, failures and bungling befell the H-7s.

By July 1915, orders for two H-7s had been received from Russia. These were built in Buffalo at the Churchill Street plant and, after the flight tests were completed on these two aircraft, additional orders were confidently expected.

The first testing of the H-7s started at Toronto on October 13, 1915, but it was not until October 19 that the first successful test flight took place. This first flight, with Theodore C. McCaulay flying solo, was quite spectacular. As he lifted off the lake surface, the plane climbed at an alarming angle. McCaulay, in an effort to prevent a stall, pushed the controls all the way forward, but to no avail. He figured that his only chance to avoid disaster was to cut the power and to catch it before it hit the water. He almost succeeded, but damaged the overhanging panel of the top wing, but not the hull.

McCaulay concluded the test flights on December 13 after having made sixteen flights. Fourteen flights were made with the first hull, and two flights were made with a second hull. On December 18, 1915, the aircraft was loaded aboard freight cars for shipment back to Buffalo. During all of these tests, Lt. Victor Utgoff of the Imperial Russian Navy either observed the tests or participated in the flights personally. Several records were established during the course of the tests. One record was set on November 10, 1915, when a useful load of 2,100 pounds was carried.

The H-7 was tail-heavy in the extreme, re-quiring eighteen 100-pound bags of sand to be placed in the forward gunner's cockpit before the plane would fly level. Subsequently, the H-7 was rerigged, moving engines and other fixed equipment forward. After a number of flights it was concluded that a change in hull design was necessary, and while the tests were in progress, a second hull was constructed that was used for the final flights conducted at Newport News, Virginia.

These were to be long overwater flights with full loads and passengers. Furthermore, they were under the auspices of the Federation Aeronautique Internationale observers. The first of these flights, on May 4, 1916, was with pilot and five passengers. Its duration was 2 hours and 23 minutes. The second flight, on May 6, 1916, lasted for 3 hours and 1 minute with pilot and four passengers. The Russians were impressed, as was the U.S. Coast Guard, which at this time was trying to establish an aviation service. As a noble gesture, Glenn H. Curtiss made a personal gift of an H-7 to the U.S. Coast Guard. Record after record was established and observed by congressional committees. It was a most exciting time.

At the conclusion of the demonstration McCaulay was asked to return to Buffalo by way of Washington, D.C., to enable naval constructor H. C. Richardson to examine the hull with a view to redesigning the hull of the NC-1, which was just in the design stage. After a three-day stopover in Washington, McCaulay took off with seven persons on board and headed south over the Potomac River. When in the vicinity of Mount Vernon, Virginia, at 100 feet altitude, one propeller shattered, throwing a fragment into the second propeller while the H-7 was still in a climbing attitude. The plane slipped and flipped upside down, crashing in the Potomac and instantly killing two crew members, Louis Crants of Hammondsport, New York, and Charles A. Goode of Elyria, Ohio, who were in the forward gunner's cockpit. Four others were seriously injured. McCaulay was thrown clear but struck a rigging wire, which caused him to be hospitalized. He was scheduled to depart for Russia two weeks after this crash to assist in the acceptance flight tests of the K-type flying boats. However, Anthony Jannus made the trip in his place and during a test flight of one of the Russian planes off Sebastopol he was killed.

With the two H-7s that Curtiss sent to Russia, a full set of extra wings was also sent, as was a full set of tail surfaces, a full set of struts and masts and an extra set of wing-tip floats. Minor items such as strut sockets, cables, turnbuckles, nonskid panels and the usual nuts and bolts were also included.

The two H-7s for Russia were shipped to Vladivostok and via the Trans-Siberian Railway to Sebastopol. This was a difficult journey even in the best of times, but necessary in view of prevailing wartime conditions.

Records indicate that in addition to the test aircraft built and tested in late 1915, two were built in April and four in June of 1916, a total of seven H-7s. Disposition of these later H-7s is not known positively; however, there is a possibility that some components were used in the construction of the H-8 that followed.

The problems encountered with the K boats and probably the H-7s were mainly attributable to the propellers. Shipment in the ship's extremely hot hold, followed by exposure to the high humidity of the Russian seacoast combined to warp the propellers. When installed for flight testing, the resulting vibration of the propellers broke the crankshafts of the then developmental Model V engines. The same climatic conditions and the lack of experience in handling and launching the aircraft by the Russian sailors resulted in the bottoms of the boat hulls dropping out when the aircraft rose from the water, or caving in when alighting on the surface.

Specifications	
The Curtiss H-7 TB	
Super America	
Span	77 ft. 0 in., upper
	49 ft. 2 in., lower
Length	39 ft. 2 in.
Chord	7 ft. $^{21}/_{32}$ in.
Gap	7 ft. 5½ in.
Engine	8-cyl. V, Model VX, 160 hp
Weight	
net	4,500 lb.
gross	6,600 lb.

The Curtiss H-7, one of the transitional designs built in small quantity.

The Curtiss H-8 PB/TB, 1915

The last of the 1915 crop of aircraft produced at the Churchill Street plant of the Curtiss Aeroplane and Motor Company at Buffalo, New York, was the H-8 Flying Boat. One would have expected great things from this design, for the design team included such well-known engineers as Dr. Albert F. Zahm and Chance M. Vought, in addition to the regulars of the Curtiss design group. Such was not the case, however, for only a single H-8 was built, in December 1915.

The first version of the H-8 represented a turnabout in the design progression, reverting back to a pusher configuration for propulsion. This design made it necessary to change from the twin-boom configuration of the H-7 to a single boom connecting the engine section of the center bay of the wings to the intersection of the vertical fin and the horizontal stabilizer. As part of this arrangement, the horizontal stabilizer was fitted to the top of the vertical fin and was directly

in line with the line of thrust of the two pusher propellers.

Apparently the pusher configuration left much to be desired, for, before it was sold to the British government for the sum of $15,085, the engine-propeller arrangement was changed to a tractor configuration. The resulting aircraft carried serial No. 8650 when it was delivered to Felixstowe, in England, for tests sometime before May 1916. The propeller problem still persisted as it had with the H-7s and the K boats sent to Russia, and the Model Rs along the Mexican border. Lt. H. A. Ward of the RAF states that the H-8 had a nasty habit of shedding its propellers, in part due to the high rpm of the 160-horsepower Curtiss VX engines, which were not fitted with a reduction gear.

A rather interesting event illustrates the situation. In passing the H-8, Ward asked, in a jocular way, where the safest position for a crew member would be in case of propeller trouble.

The H-8 was originally a pusher design. This was changed before its delivery to Felixstowe Air Station. *Curtiss Photo Collection*

The engineer who was then test-running the engines made two pencil marks on the inside of the fuselage, denoting the danger zone. Before the H-8 left the slipway for a flight test, a piece of propeller was thrown through the fuselage exactly between the two pencil marks. After that episode, the engines were replaced by two Rolls-Royce Mark I engines of 250 horsepower, and the first test flight at Felixstowe was made successfully.

The conditions prevailing as a result of wartime operation quickly demonstrated the inherent weakness of the H-8 and also of the first of the later H-12 hulls. The principal structural troubles centered on the hull bottoms. Again, this was the same problem that was experienced with the H-7s in Russia. Hulls that had proven to be quite adequate for lake and river testing in the United States and Canada proved to be inadequate for service on the open sea of the English Channel and the seas surrounding Britain. Problems encountered with this hull as well as with the H-4s and the H-12s prompted the design by Cdr. John C. Porte of the F-1, which was completed in November 1916. This was the first of the Felixstowe flying boat series. The F-1 hull was fitted with wings from the H-4 *Small America* and a pair of 100-horsepower Anzani engines.

The H-8 was to have additional mileage, for, in keeping with the Curtiss practice, the usable portions showed up later. The wing structure showed up again on the H-12.

The H-8 was a large aircraft, the largest built by the Curtiss Company to this date, with an upper wingspan of 92 feet 10 inches and a lower wingspan of 66 feet 11 inches. For comparison, the H-7's upper and lower wingspans were 77 feet and 49 feet 2 inches. Its gross weight of 6,850 pounds gave a wing loading of a modest 6.2 pounds per square foot of wing area, as calculated by Chance M. Vought. These figures were for the second version, the tractor configuration tested in England.

A bow view of the H-8 showing the planing bottom of the hull.

Appendices

Appendix 1

Accounting for Aircraft Built by Curtiss During the Years 1909–1910 (from testimony prepared by Curtiss's lawyer for Herring-Curtiss litigation)

No. 1.   Aeronautic Society

This is the machine ordered before the H. C. Co. was organized. It was finally delivered late in July 1909 and Willard took it and flew it for the Society that fall. He had it at the Cincinnati meet on November 12–14, 1909, and flew it in competition with Curtiss.

Willard still had this machine at the Los Angeles meet, January 10 to 20, 1910, and entered it for the Aeronautic Society. Later this machine was sold to one Charles J. Strobel, and late in January Willard leased a machine from Curtiss. *Aeronautics*, March 1910, reports:

> The Curtiss aeroplane belonging to the Aeronautic Society having been disposed of, Willard has secured another Curtiss machine for exhibition work.

The same periodical in April 1910, states that Strobel took the machine from Los Angeles to Tampa, Florida, in charge of Sam Tickell, who had been assistant to Willard. Tickell tried to fly it, but smashed it up badly, and it went back to Toledo where Strobel lived, and, at the time the article was written, was being overhauled.

No. 2.   The Rheims Machine

This machine can be easily traced. After return from Europe it was exhibited in Wanamakers and in Boston and then went to the Los Angeles meet, January 10–20, 1910. It was used by Curtiss in his flights. After the meet it was taken by Hamilton to San Diego and on January 24 and 25, 1910, was used by Hamilton in making a flight into Mexico and back.

Hamilton still had the machine after Curtiss returned from Los Angeles to the east, for the AEA resolution of February 12, 1910, authoriz-ing Curtiss to sell three machines, mentions them as "the Rheims machine and the two machines now at Los Angeles."

Hamilton seems to have taken this machine with him on an extended trip, until Curtiss met him at Los Angeles, and on April 22, 1910, it was included in the bill of sale from Hamilton to Curtiss, and on April 25, Hamilton gave Curtiss a receipt for this one machine, so it seems Hamilton kept and continued to fly with it. Notice that this machine seems to have been in Hamilton's possession *all the time* after the Los Angeles meet in January, until and including after the San Antonio meet in April.

No. 3.
The Warner Machine

This has always been called No. 3 and I believe this is correct. In *Aeronautics* for August 1909, there is an item dated June 22 that says that Wyckoff, Church and Partridge had just been appointed selling agents and that within 24 hours Wurster sold a machine to A. P. Warner, delivery to be made within 50 days. The contract for sale of this machine has not been found. The machine order is No. 575, and states that order was received July 6, 1909, and that is was shipped September 25, 1909. In *Aeronautics* for October 1909, there is an item headed "Third Curtiss Plane Ready," referring to the Warner machine.

This machine apparently was not shipped at first to Beloit, Wisconsin, but was on display at Madison Square Garden at the show held there from September 25 to October 2.

Just where this machine went at first after this show is not clear. Warner certainly got it sometime in October, because he made an affidavit at Los Angeles for Curtiss, dated January 15, 1910, in which he swore that he made many flights with it at Beloit *in October 1909* without using the rudder to preserve balance.

I find no further mention of this machine during the fall or winter. It is not mentioned among the machines at Los Angeles. In *Aeronautics*, March 1910, page 110, is an item as follows:

The Warner aeroplane, which has been on exhibition at the Philadelphia Automobile Show, coming there from the recent Corn Show at Des Moines, goes next to the Buffalo Automobile Show, February 14–19, thence to Cleveland, Feb. 21–27, Pittsburgh, March 26 to April 2, returning to the Warner factory at Beloit for further flights.

If this program was carried out, it accounts for this machine and precludes the possibility of Curtiss having had it up to April 2, 1910, at least.

In *Aeronautics* for June 1910, page 197, there is an item stating that the Warner machine had been sold to Joseph Seymour, an auto race driver, for exhibitions. The item is not dated.

No. 4.
The Plew Machine

This is nowhere called No. 4, but I think it must be this number from several circumstances. It is the next sale, in order of time. This contract of sale was drawn by Herring and is dated September 23, 1909, and was mailed by him to Hammondsport. It is Ex. 481. The contract price was $5,000. The machine order is No. 641 and states order received September 23, and that the machine was shipped November 30, 1909, and price in the order is $4,000. The letters among our papers show that Plew objected to taking it unless the price was reduced and objected to signing a restricted contract, but finally did sign it and took the machine. It also seems from the correspondence that he had a man named Brodie employed to fly it and that in November Brodie was at Hammondsport learning to fly. It also appears that Curtiss gave him some instructions at the Cincinnati meet, or at least planned to do so, as appears from Curtiss's letter to Herring on November 10, where he says: "I am going to Cincinnati to instruct Plew's man and make some flights."

After Plew took his machine on November 30, I can find no further reference to what he did with it, except an item in *Aeronautics* for April 1910, which says:

Otto Brodie was in Dallas, Tex., March 4, 5, and 6. Brodie is demonstrating for James E. Plew of Chicago.

No. 5.
The Arnold Machine

This is the machine that Herring sold to Mrs. Arnold, in the absence of Curtiss, and paid Ray Hall $300 on account and deposited the balance in the Chemical National Bank. I call this No. 5 because Curtiss, in his letter of December 1, 1909, to Mrs. Arnold, sent her a regular contract form to sign (which she did not do), and said in his letter, "We cannot hold aeroplane No. 5 for you after Saturday, December 4, 1909."

In December, Hamilton went on his first flying tour, taking in St. Joseph and Kansas City. From there he went to Los Angeles. I conclude that the machine must have been this Arnold machine, and that it was one of the three machines later sold to Hamilton. Hassett claimed in the bankruptcy proceedings a lien on this machine on the grounds that Mrs. Arnold had paid for it and that it belonged to her, but this claim was disallowed or withdrawn and he was allowed to file a claim simply for the money which had been paid and received as a dividend on it.

No. 6.
DeRiemsdyk Machine

The contract for the sale of this machine is dated December 18, 1909, and describes the machine as *No. 6*. This would seem to identify the machine. The machine order is No. 719 and was received on November 21, 1909. The machine was shipped December 18, 1909. This machine was shipped abroad and certainly could not enter into any subsequent accounting for machines used by Curtiss. It will be noticed that the machine order is dated ahead of the contract. What seems to have been the case is that DeRiemsdyk placed the order and then made trials of the machine and finally signed the contract when he took it. I find in *Aeronautics* for January 1910, a mention of this sale as well as an item dated December 12, 1909, stating that DeRiemsdyk was then at Hammondsport making trial flights.

No. 7

There is no mention anywhere of a machine called No. 7, but I think there must have been such a number for the reason that the machine sold first to Harmon and later to Johnson is called No. 8. This will appear more fully below.

No. 8

The records show some mix-up about the sale of this machine. It seems that Clifford Harmon entered an order for a machine and this is order No. 716 dated November 23, 1909, with a deposit that day of $1,000. Across the face of this order is written the following:

> This machine delivered to Frank H. Johnson Merc. Co., on order 732. Payment on $3000 check stopped, leaving Harmon with deposit of $1000 to apply on new motor.

Turning now to the Frank H. Johnson account, we find that on December 21, 1909, he took an agency contract in California and agreed to take eight machines, and eight orders were entered, numbered from 732 to 739. On December 24, 1909, he made a deposit of $206.25 on each of the orders, or $1,650 in all. Order No. 732, which is one of the orders for a complete airplane, had written across the face of it the following:

> This machine is the one shipped to Harmon, transferred from C. B. Harmon, 716. Total $4125, deposit December 24, $206.25. Balance January 27, $3870.

The plaintiff has also put in evidence the regular sales contract that Johnson signed for the machine, dated January 22, 1910, in which the machine is described as *No. 8*.

The result of the transaction as it finally worked out was that Harmon stopped payment on his check for the balance on his machine and Johnson took the machine and paid for it but did not take his other seven machines. This left Harmon with a deposit to his credit of $1,000, which was later credited to a new order. Johnson did not take the other seven machines.

Situation at the Time of the Los Angeles Meet

As we have so far traced the history of the machines, the situation at the opening of the Los Angeles meet was that No. 1, the Aeronautic Society machine, was sold and delivered and being operated by Willard; No. 2, the Rheims machine, was unsold and on hand; No. 3, the Warner machine, was sold and delivered; No. 4,
the Plew machine, was sold and delivered; No. 5, the Arnold machine, was unsold and was being used by Hamilton; No. 6, the DeRiemsdyk machine was sold and delivered; No. 7 is not accounted for; No. 8 was shipped to Los Angeles for Harmon but was not finally taken by him.

In *Aeronautics* for February 1910 is a short account of the results of the Los Angeles meet, written while the meet was in progress. In the article is the following statement:

> Glenn H. Curtiss has his eight cyl. Rheims machine here, Charles K. Hamilton and Charles F. Willard have the stock type four cyl. Curtiss machine.

In *Aeronautics* for March 1910 is an article by Professor Twining giving a complete account of the meet, covering each day's events. In this article is the following:

> Paulhan had two Farmans and two Bleriots; Curtiss brought the 8-cylinder Rheims and two regular types, one for Clifford B. Harmon and one for Frank Johnson, the California agent for Curtiss machines; Charles K. Hamilton had a Curtiss and Charles F. Willard had the Aeronautic Society's machine, the first one built by Curtiss.

Here we have five Curtiss machines mentioned as being at Los Angeles. Leaving out the Aeronautic Society machine, it is stated that four Curtiss machines were there, three of them brought by Curtiss and one by Hamilton. The machine brought by Hamilton must have been No. 5, the Arnold machine. The three machines brought by Curtiss are stated to have been the Rheims machine and two 4-cylinder machines, one intended for Harmon and one for Johnson. The machine intended for Harmon must have been No. 8, which, as shown above, was finally taken by Johnson. This leaves one machine to account for, and I cannot account for it unless it was No. 7.

At the close of the meet, therefore, and after Johnson had taken No. 8, the machines left must have been No. 2 (Rheims), No. 5 (Arnold) and a third machine which I cannot account for unless it was No. 7.

Curtiss came home from Los Angeles and apparently left these three machines there.

Contract with Willard

In the latter part of January, the machine of the Aeronautic Society having been sold to Strobel, Willard made a contract to fly with a machine leased from Curtiss. No copy of this contract has been found but it seems to be clear from all the papers that it was about this date.

The account of the Aeronautic Society machine given above says that after it was sold, Willard secured a Curtiss airplane for exhibition work. This must have been one of the 4-cylinder machines left at Los Angeles, for Hamilton continued to fly the Rheims machine.

Sale to E. Henry Wemme

One more complete machine was sold and that sale was to E. Henry Wemme of Portland, Oregon, who took the dealership there. There is nothing to identify this machine. No copy of the sales contract has been found. The order is dated January 3, 1910, and states that it was shipped January 7, 1910, but does not state where it went. If it went to Portland, Oregon, it could not have been one of the machines that Curtiss left at Los Angeles when he returned from the meet in January. Then what machine was it? We have accounted for eight machines, five sold and delivered to purchasers (Nos. 1, 3, 4, 6, 8) and three left at Los Angeles (2, 5, 7) for use in exhibition work. If Wemme took delivery at Portland, this makes nine machines built up to February 1, 1910.

In *Aeronautics* for March 1910 is an item reading as follows:

E. Henry Wemme, of Portland, Ore., has taken the Oregon agency for the Curtiss machine and engaged George W. Kleiser as demonstrator.

In the April issue is the following:

Otto Brodie was in Dallas, Tex., March 4, 5, and 6; Brodie is demonstrator for James E. Plew, of Chicago. Hamilton in Portland, March 5, 6, 7 together with E. H. Wemme the Portland Curtiss agent. Frank H. Johnson, Curtiss California representative, flew at Stockton, Cal., March 5 and 6.

In the June issue, page 197, giving an account of the San Antonio meet, is the following:

Eugene Ely, who bought the Curtiss aeroplane owned by E. Henry Wemme, the Curtiss Portland (Ore.) agent, made his first flight at Portland on April 27.

This is all the information I can gather. It looks, therefore, as if Wemme took delivery of another machine, aside from the three machines left at Los Angeles, and kept it until he finally sold it to Ely. The books of the Herring-Curtiss Co. show that this machine was sold for $5,000, of which $500 was paid January 22, 1910, and the balance of $4,500 was paid January 27, 1910. The machine order is No. 740.

Sale of Three Airplanes to Hamilton

Hamilton and Willard, as shown in various articles in *Aeronautics*, were on a tour in February and March flying in various places and apparently had the three machines left at Los Angeles. In the resolution of February 12, 1910, Curtiss was authorized to sell the Rheims machine and the two machines left at Los Angeles. It would appear, therefore, that these three machines were still on hand and unsold and Willard must have been using one of them. I can not account for the Wemme machine by saying that it was one of these three machines, for the dates would conflict—the shipment to Wemme and the payment by him occurring before the sale of the three machines to Hamilton.

Sale to Whipple Hall

Hamilton sold one of these three machines to Whipple Hall. That seems to be agreed to by everybody. It looks as though Hall continued to fly with this machine and that it did not come back to Curtiss. In *Aeronautics* for June 1910, is the following:

Whipple Hall, in a Curtiss machine, made some flights at Fresno, Cal., under the auspices of the Driving Club and also the Union High School League. Hall's machine has had the surface increased.

Sale to Harmon

In the account of No. 8 machine we have noted the fact that Harmon finally refused it and that it left him with a deposit of $1,000 to his credit. There appears in the file another order,

No. 925, dated March 24, 1910, from Harmon for an airplane *without engine*. He made a deposit on March 28 of $250, and his deposit from the previous order of $1,000 made $1,250 paid toward this machine. Apparently he returned this machine, for he is credited on April 6, 1910, by "Frame, Returned." This left the machine consisting of a complete airplane without engine on hand when the receiver took possession, and the receiver included such a machine in his inventory and apparently continued to have it on hand for some time. At least the inventory was not completed until May and this airplane appears in it, or at least one complete airplane so appears.

Appendix 2

Curtiss's Letter to Henry Wood Documenting Curtiss's Early Interest in a Hydro-aeroplane.

Coronado, Calif.
January 15th, 1913.

Mr. Henry A. Wise Wood,
New York, N.Y.

Dear Mr. Wood:

Answering the questions in your letter of January 9th, I do not recall when I first thought of combining the hull and the fuselage for water flying.

We built the first one in the fall of 1911, at Hammondsport, N.Y., and shipped it to San Diego to try. This was equipped with two chain driven tractor screws, but owing to repeated accidents to the transmission this machine was never taken in the air. We did, however, give it several runs on the water.

This type of machine was first flown at Hammondsport in the spring of 1912. The second machine being constructed immediately on my return from California. The form of this second hull was changed many times before it would leave the water readily.

A third machine was built embodying the improvements suggested and after some alterations this was adopted as standard and is the one after which the machines sold to the Army and Navy and those shipped abroad were modeled.

The rough water problem was taken up with the third machine. I sent it to Ontario Beach, on Lake Ontario, and made two trips to try it out in rough weather. It was here for the first time that I tried the movable wings, for stability on the water.

This device was very successful and it seems to me it will be an absolute necessity on future flying water craft.

Other important improvements resulted from these Ontario trials.

As you may not be familiar with this device, I am enclosing a rough sketch, as we use it. Any part or all of the surfaces of a biplane or monoplane may be utilized to accomplish the same purpose.

Many water machines have upset as a result of encountering a side wind, when adrift without power. A slight tilt of the planes gives the wind a chance at the surfaces and if the lee surface once gets under water, the wind and side drift are bound to turn the machine over. You can see from the sketch that with the surfaces tilted the action of the wind is to depress the windward wing and lift the wing, thereby assuring positive stability on the water.

Head or stern winds have no tendency to upset the machine.

If any further information is desired I will be glad to furnish it.

Yours truly,
Glenn H. Curtiss

Dict. G.H.C.

Appendix 3

Price List, Curtiss Aeroplanes and Hydro-aeroplanes

All prices quoted are F.O.B. Hammondsport, N.Y., and the terms are ten per cent (10%) cash with the order, and balance on delivery.

If instruction is desired while awaiting the delivery of an aeroplane, twenty per cent (20%) of the purchase price must accompany the order, instruction being included in the price of each machine.

MODEL D.
Standard Curtiss Aeroplane. Equipped with four-cylinder 40 h.p. water cooled Curtiss motor. An excellent machine for exhibition work.
Price . . . .$4,500.

MODEL E.

Weight Carrying Curtiss Aeroplane. Has more extensive surface than the standard machine. Equipped with four-cylinder 40 h.p. water cooled Curtiss motor. An excellent machine for altitude and cross-country flights.

Price .... $4,500.

MODEL D-60.

Standard Curtiss Aeroplane. Regular exhibition type of speed machine. Equipped with eight-cylinder 60 h.p. water cooled Curtiss motor. Entire outfit identical with that used by the famous aviators of the Curtiss Exhibition Co.

Price .... $5,000.

MODEL E-60.

Curtiss Cross-Country, Military Type Aeroplane. Equipped with eight-cylinder 60 h.p. water cooled Curtiss motor. Especially adaptable to passenger carrying, cross-country and military requirements.

Price .... $5,000.

MODEL D-75.

Same as Model D, but equipped with eight cylinder 75 h.p. water cooled Curtiss motor. Capable of developing a speed of over 60 miles an hour.

Price .... $5,500.

MODEL E-75.

Same as Model E, but equipped with 75 h.p. water cooled Curtiss motor.

Price .... $5,500.

HYDRO ATTACHMENT.

Curtiss Hydroaeroplane Attachment. Interchangeable with Wheel Running Gear on all machines. For rising from and alighting on the water. (Sold to owners of Curtiss Aeroplanes only.)

Price .... $500.

Appendix 4

Curtiss's Instructions, Inspection of Aeroplanes after Assembling

1. See that all belts are placed as follows: On lower planes bolt head underneath, and on upper planes bolt head above planes. After nuts are set up tight on bolts, drill holes underneath and put in cotter pins.

2. The turnbuckle is stronger than the wire but may come loose. In wiring up the machine place turnbuckle nearest the propeller, then in case they do come loose, the wire will not get in the propeller.

3. Tape all small bolts likely to come loose.

4. Tape all tires to rims of wheels.

5. See tape on center position of steering wheel.

6. See carburetor and radiator braced to prevent vibration.

7. See water pipes braced.

8. See that the tail bamboos in wake of the propeller are covered with tin—in case the propeller breaks and strikes the bamboos the tin will prevent the bamboos from collapsing.

9. Place safety wires on all rocker arms.

10. Safety wire all snap hooks:

Snap hooks at the top and the bottom of rear control king pin posts.

Snap hooks at the top and bottom of each aileron.

Snap hooks on both upper and lower aileron wires where they make fast to the control seat.

Snap hooks on the 4 leads to the rear control from the control post.

Snap hooks on the two leads from the control post to the rudder.

11. Safety wire front control to bamboos.

12. Safety wire tail planes and rear control to tail bamboos.

13. Safety wire front control and tail bamboos to main planes.

14. Safety wire all wire or other braces likely to get in the propeller in case they should come loose.

A safety wire is simply an additional safeguard, to hold the vital parts of the machine, in case the bolts or turnbuckles placed for that purpose should come loose.

Tests and Precautions before Making Flights

1. First lift aeroplane by two outboard forward ends of lower planes and see that all wires are taut. Then do same with two outboard after ends of lower plane.

2. Before starting the engine, inspect the gasoline tank, oil tank, and the radiator, to make certain that there is sufficient quantity of gasoline, oil and water.

3. Set up caps on gasoline tank, oil tank, and radiator with pliers to make sure that they are set up tight.

4. Before starting the engine, put a pint of oil in the forward end of the crank case to insure proper lubrication.

5. Test out engine. Open cock on gasoline line and tape same to prevent it closing. See all switches closed, then open throttle and crank the engine, to take in a charge. Open all switches and start engine. If engine fails to start the first time that the propeller is turned, make sure that the propeller has stopped, as accidents have occurred due to propeller starting when the propeller had apparently stopped. Have men holding the aeroplane and run engine for five minutes, adjusting the mixture until the best results are obtained, and test out engine at all speeds.

6. While the engine is running, try switches and break cut out, to see that they short circuit the magneto and stop the engine.

7. Before getting in aeroplane, test steering wheel, making sure that when the wheel is turned to the right the vertical rudder turns the same way, and test the controls and the ailerons. After getting in the machine, make the same tests.

8. When starting on a flight, have men holding the machine by the tail, and open up the throttle gradually, until full speed is attained. When ready give signal, and men start the machine by shoving it, which will ensure a quick getaway.

Appendix 5

A Typical Month in the Naval Aviation World of 1911

(Extracts from a report dated March 31, 1911, from Lt. T. G. Ellyson to Capt. Washington I. Chambers, USN, Chief Naval Aviation)

1. This report is made in detail in an attempt to bring out all the points of the instruction and training here. Attention is invited to the fact that there were six pupils under instruction, namely, Lieutenants Beck, Kelly, and Walker, U.S. Army, Witmer and ST Henry, civilians and myself, and each pupil received practically the same amount of instruction. Again the weather conditions were such that we were not allowed to practice be-tween the hours of 11:00 A.M. and 5:00 P.M., as the wind was generally too strong for beginners, though Mr. Curtiss and some of his aviators made flights at all times during the day, and our practice seldom began earlier than 8:00 A.M.

2. March 1st. Practice aeroplane, standard four cylinder machine, single surfaces*, model 1909, fitted with 30 H.P. engine, 1200 r.p.m.; cylinders 4″ × 4″. Fitted new crank shaft and new propeller, diameter propeller 6′, pitch 4′ 6″. On test obtained engine thrust of 210 lbs., at 980 r.p.m. This was the first time that sufficient thrust had been obtained to make the machine fly. Made four flights over half mile course, average length of flights 400 feet, average height 6 feet. Found that the machine could be balanced to a greater or less degree by the use of the rudder.

March 2nd. Mr. Curtiss experimented with his triad (aeroplane rigged to rise from or land on either the land or water), and found that with the extra weight of the wheel lifting gear the pontoon, 14′ × 2′ × 1′, did not afford sufficient flotation to enable the aeroplane to rise from the water.

Mr. Curtiss carried passengers in his hydro-triplane. This machine was a standard biplane with third surface added, and fitted with a 60 H.P. engine, at 1400 R.P.M., cylinders 4″ × 4½″. The passenger's seat was on the pontoon almost immediately under the operator. The aeroplane rose from the water easily and handled well in the air, but the passenger was wet through by spray from the pontoon before the aeroplane rose. Only those under instruction were carried, the idea being for them to become accustomed to the feel of the machine in the air. While Witmer was being carried as a passenger, the engine was throttled when the aeroplane was at a height of about thirty feet, and a gliding landing was made. The extra weight caused a mistake in judgement and the pontoon, which was made of ³/₁₆″ spruce, struck the water with too great force, and split, causing the pontoon to sink. The water was shallow and no further damage was done.

March 4th. Made four flights over the half mile course. A 10″ extension was fitted to the crank shaft, between the shaft and the propeller, affording an additional bearing, which reduced the vibration, which it is thought will prevent the crystallization of the crank shaft and subsequent

---

*Fabric cover on upper surfaces only.

breaking. All crank shafts which have been broken, broke at the web nearest to the propeller and the metal was found to have become crystallized. In order to fit this extension the engine was moved forward, and then to prevent changing the balance, the radiator was moved back as far as it would go.

March 5th. A new course, a mile and half long and fifty feet wide, was completed this date and all subsequent flights were made over this course. Made eight runs over course, average length of flights one mile, average height 15 feet. On one flight the wind got under the front control and lifted the forward part of the machine so quickly, that the machine was almost stopped. The front control was pushed forward and a safe landing made.

March 6th. Made six flights over long course, length of flight, one mile, height twenty feet. Lost compression on #3 cylinder. Examined piston and rings, ground in exhaust and intake valves, trouble not removed. Further examination showed that the screw on the rocker arm was loose, which prevented the intake valve from closing properly. Removed tail, which consisted of stabilizing planes only, and fitted tail belonging to a standard eight cylinder machine.* The object of this was to become accustomed to the use of the rear controls as fitted to all later models, and to cause the aeroplane to fly more strongly. This tail was heavier than the one formerly used, and the machine was heavy by the tail without noticeably increasing the lifting power.

March 7th. Made six trips over the long course. Found that the aeroplane was out of balance, due to the use of the heavier tail.

March 8th. Replaced the box front control with single surface front control, the same as fitted to all the later make standard machines. This control was much lighter and two feet shorter than the control formerly used, and upon trial it was found that the tail was too heavy and that the machine would not fly. The stabilizing planes of the tail were raised one inch and the rear controls given a droop of three inches, in order to give the tail more lift, but still the machine would not fly. The radiator was then shifted forward 5 inches, but the machine was still heavy by the tail and would not fly. Made six runs over the long course but was unable to get the machine off the ground.

March 11th. An eight cylinder machine was made up from one of the machines which had been used for water experiments. A stop was placed under the throttle so that it could only be opened to about half power, and I made two trips over the long course. I had been warned that the machine would be very sensitive and that the speed would be so great that landing would be difficult. Having successfully flown the four cylinder machine, which was slow and sluggish in movement, I did not realize the sensitiveness of the eight cylinder machine, even after repeated warnings. The machine rose easily, but was so sensitive to the control that I did the "dutch roll" for the entire course. In attempting to land I found difficulty in keeping the machine on the ground, and only landed after having made a succession of bumps. This experience strengthens my belief, that a four cylinder aeroplane is absolutely necessary for the initial instruction work.

March 13th. Made eight runs over the long course in the eight cylinder machine, with the throttle stopped at half power. Lieutenant Beck, Witmer and myself, used the eight cylinder machine and the other three pupils the four, which gave us more opportunity for practice.

March 14th. Added third panel† over the engine section with the idea of slowing down the machine, so that we could practice making turns. In trying out the machine, Lieutenant Beck made a bad landing and broke one of the lower wing panels on each wing of the machine.

March 15th. Made fourteen flights over the long course, using the full power of the machine, the machine rigged with third panel over the engine section. The machine handled well and the addition of the extra surface did not materially lessen the speed of the machine. Added two additional panels over the sections adjacent to the engine section, to further reduce the speed. Up to this time a four cylinder radiator had been used, but this failed to keep the engine cool, so it was removed and an eight cylinder radiator installed in its place. This was placed as near the engine as possible and a passenger seat was rigged between the radiator and the operator's seat.

March 16th. Made two flights over the long course. Made two flights with Mr. Curtiss, in order to get the feel of the machine in turning

*The 1909/1910 machines had fixed rear stabilizers; the elevator was in front of the aircraft.

†The triplane was a "D" configuration with this panel added for experiments described here.

before attempting to turn myself.

March 17th. Mr. Curtiss made flights in his hydro-aeroplane in a twenty mile breeze and choppy sea, the first time that it had been tried in anything except smooth water. The machine rode easily and very little spray was thrown into the propeller.

March 18th. Made two trips over the mile and a half straightaway course, and three trips over a circular course of approximately five miles. This was the first time that I had been allowed to make a turn. The flights were made at an average height of from 75 to a 100 feet, and the aeroplane was allowed to bank only a very little on the turns, and the turns were as large as they could be made, approximately a half mile in diameter. On my last trip the radiator boiled and the water which overflowed grounded the magneto and the engine cut out. At this time I was at a height of about fifty feet and over a level spot, so was able to land safely and without damage to the machine. This brought out a point which had been constantly drilled into us, which is always to keep over the open ground, in case a landing should become necessary. Removed the third surface from the practice machine, which left the machine a standard eight cylinder machine.

March 20th. Made twelve flights over the five mile circular course in a standard eight cylinder machine, average altitude 200 feet, highest altitude 400 feet. When the first flights were made the air was absolutely calm, but when the last flights were made there was a strong breeze, twelve miles an hour, and the sun shining on the different kinds of ground made the air uneven. Mr. Curtiss expressed the opinion that we were flying in rougher air than many aviators would fly in even at exhibition meets.

Made two flights as a passenger with Mr. Curtiss. The aileron wires were rigidly connected to the control seat. The flight was made to determine whether or not the use of the ailerons caused the aeroplane to deviate from a straight course. The ailerons were used vigorously and did not cause the machine to swerve, nor was the rudder used to counteract any tendency to swerve. The passenger seat was immediately in the rear of the operator's seat, and all of the movements of the operator were closely observed.

March 22nd. Made six flights over the mile and a half straightaway course and four over the five mile circular course. Glides were made at the end of each of these flights. The first glides were made from a height of 30 feet. The machine was pointed downward and the power shut off. On the first glide I brought the machine up too quickly, lost headway, and the machine settled straight down from a height of six feet and bumped hard. The machine should be inclined at a sufficient angle to keep control, and it should always be started at a sharp angle to keep sufficient headway for control of the machine. The speed of a glide can always be lessened, but if the machine were not started at a sharp enough angle, and should start to settle, it would be almost impossible to regain control of it. The last glides were made from heights of 150 to 200 feet, when the wind was gusty and the flying rough. Made both right and left handed turns, with the rudder hard over and the machine banked well up.

March 23rd. Made four flights, practicing sharp turns and high glides at the end of each flight. While Witmer was banked well up on a turn and at a height of about a hundred feet, the crank shaft broke, also breaking the crank casing. He righted the machine and made a safe landing without injury to the machine, which shows that the glides must be practiced before any heights are obtained. When the engine stops on a turn the operator is in a dangerous position, and only a cool head and much practice at gliding will enable him to land safely. This is the first crank shaft that has ever broken in an eight cylinder Curtiss engine, and the cause of its breaking is explained by the fact that this engine was built to be used with a push propeller, and hence only one thrust bearing was fitted, but it was used for a long time with a pull propeller, on one of the first hydro-aeroplanes, and there being no thrust bearing to take up the thrust, the crank shaft was worn and crystallized, causing the break.

Mr. Curtiss made a flight using only one aileron, in order to demonstrate the fact that in case one aileron should carry away the machine could still be easily controlled. One aileron was disconnected and allowed to swing loose. There was an eight mile wind blow-across the course when the experiment was made, the flight being made over a straight course to show that the machine was not being balanced by the use of the rudder. When in flight the loose aileron assumed a neutral position and the machine was easily controlled by the use of the other.

There being no machine available for practice, and little chance of obtaining a new crank shaft inside of a week, Mr. Curtiss suggested that Witmer and myself accompany Aviator Robinson to San Bernadino in order to get the experience of unpacking and setting up a machine in the least possible time, and of dismantling and packing up the same. This was the first exhibition that Robinson had given, the aeroplane was not properly packed, and there were repairs to be made, which would not be found in the average machine. Taking time from the moment that we started to open the boxes, we set up the machine and had it ready for operation in a little less than four hours. The machine was taken apart and packed up in one hour and twenty minutes. Only three men were working on the machine. With the machine rigged as at present and a trained crew of six men, four to do the actual setting up and two as assistants, the machine can be set up in an hour and a half and taken down in one hour. With a few minor changes this time can be reduced.

(Signed) T. G. Ellyson

Appendix 6

First Known Airplane
Flight Manual

Instructions issued with the 1911
Glenn Curtiss "Pusher"

Rules Governing the Use of
Aeronautical Apparatus

1. The aeronaut should seat himself in the apparatus, and secure himself firmly to the chair by means of the strap provided. On the attendant crying "Contact" the aeronaut should close the switch which supplies electrical current to the motor, thus enabling the attendant to set the same in motion.

2. Opening the control valve of the motor, the aeronaut should at the same time firmly grasp the vertical stick or control pole which is to be found directly before the chair. The power from the motor will cause the device to roll gently forward and the aeronaut should govern its direction of motion by use of the rudder bars.

3. When the mechanism is facing into the wind, the aeronaut should open the control valve of the motor to its fullest extent, at the same time pulling the control pole gently toward his (the aeronaut's) middle anatomy.

4. When sufficient speed has been attained the device will leave the ground and assume the position of aeronautical ascent.

5. Should the aeronaut decide to return to terra firma, he should close the control valve of the motor. This will cause the apparatus to assume what is known as the "gliding position," except in the case of those flying machines which are inherently unstable. These latter will assume the position known as "involuntary spin" and will return to earth without further action on the part of the aeronaut.

6. On approaching closely to the chosen field or terrain, the aeronaut should move the control pole gently toward himself, thus causing the mechanism to alight more or less gently on terra firma.

Index

The Pfitzner monoplane.